This book is available in quantity at special discounts for your group or organization. For further information, contact:

Triumph Books
814 North Franklin Street
Chicago, Illinois 60610
Phone: (312) 337-0747
Fax: (312) 280-5470
www.triumphbooks.com

Printed in U.S.A.

ISBN: 978-1-60078-979-3
Design by Meghan Grammer

Photos courtesy of the author unless otherwise indicated

To the memory of my parents:

Thank you for your unconditional love and support.
Not a day goes by without me thinking of you.
Your light continues to guide me.

CONTENTS

FOREWORD

When I reflect back on my 13-year NFL career and the realization comes that I was able to play with John Unitas for 12 years, my immediate thought is that no receiver in NFL history had a better deal. He was a combination of the physical, the mental, and the heart. I've seen no greater competitor in all my years in football. He could not be intimidated. In one game, an opponent hit him in the face, busted his nose, and blood poured out. He reached down, got some dirt, stuffed it in his nose, got back in the huddle, called a pass play, and threw a touchdown pass! That was Unitas. He was single-minded in purpose—win games. Praise, publicity, acclaim, and attention rolled off him. He took it in stride with his usual smile.

Weeb Ewbank, our head coach, had instinct and sense enough to hand over the play-calling job to John; brilliant move. John was a natural for this responsibility. The defense couldn't figure him out. He was unpredictable—run when a pass was expected, pass when a run was expected. He used all his weapons—split end, flanker, tight end, halfback, and fullback. None of us gave a flip. We just did our jobs when he called our play. Confidence was one of his strongest assets. I believe it was a God-given natural gift. As a matter of fact, when I think of it, I believe God designed John Unitas to be the quarterback he was, and I don't think God left anything out!

I haven't even mentioned his physical gifts yet: his arm strength and accuracy, his durable body that could shake off hits, his quick feet. His college coaches at Louisville, Frank Camp and Frank Gitschier, had trained John well in how to take the snap, drop back, step, and deliver. His fundamentals were flawless. His throwing delivery would be adopted by perceptive quarterback coaches at all levels of football.

John was popular with us players. He never got full of himself. Having a beer with the guys was one of his pleasures. He laughed easily and had a great sense of humor. John was real in every sense of the word. He wasn't just my QB, my teammate; he was my friend. It's still hard for me to believe I was able to play with arguably the greatest quarterback of all time.

Raymond Berry
Baltimore Colts wide receiver (1955–67)
Pro Football Hall of Fame (1973)
February 3, 2014

INTRODUCTION
TREE SHADOWS

I'm now 58 years old. I've always been John Unitas, the emphasis on Unitas. While most people, men in particular, have carried a name with them their entire lives, I've always understood that this name means something different, usually important and almost god-like, to many people, fans who have their own ideas, right or wrong, of what it means to be John Unitas. The difference between me and my father is that he didn't have to live all of his life in the shadow of fame and expectations. I have.

It would be easy to say this has simply been a burden, but that wouldn't be fair. While some shadows are dark and scary, like the shadow of someone sneaking up on you at night, others, like the shadow of a tree on a hot July Baltimore afternoon, can be soothing. I think of my father's shadow as like that of a tree with deep roots and bearing fruit, a solid figure that stands tall for a long time and withstands the vagaries of nature, its shadow gentle. Being John Unitas has been a blessing. It has opened doors. I've been able to see places and meet people because of my father that the ordinary football fan would never see or meet. But for every door it has opened, it's also led to misconceptions about me and my family.

Why I've been blessed has less to do with my father's name and more with his character. Dad just happened to be an NFL quarterback. People have put him on a quarterbacking pedestal, and as a football player, he deserves to be there.

But his life wasn't easy, as he struggled with a failed marriage and bad financial investments. I have had the typical struggles of adulthood but have also lived vicariously through my father's public struggles and mistakes. He wasn't perfect off the field; then again, no father is. He cared about his children. He carpooled us to school, spanked us with his hair brush, and came to my games when he could. After football, he and I worked together. And through all of this, we ended up best friends. He will always be my father, but as adults we became so much more.

****

I grew up in Baltimore although I was born in Pittsburgh, just like Dad. I was raised in Baltimore while he came of age here. It was here that he went from being a cut Pittsburgh Steelers draftee to a record-setting championship-winning quarterback. It was also here that his name became as synonymous with Baltimore as crab cakes, Natty Boh beer, the Inner Harbor, Brooks Robinson, and the Star Spangled Banner.

It has been in the suburban neighborhoods of Baltimore County that I moved from toddler to teenager to college student and finally to a married man with two children. I was fairly typical growing up in the 1960s with a father who had a crew cut and a mother who stayed at home and took care of the kids. If we hadn't lived less than 15 miles from the Baltimore harbor, we just as easily could have been living in Middle America. I roamed the neighborhood with my friends, sneaking into swimming clubs after hours and smoking cigarettes in the woods behind our house. The big oak tree in the neighbor's yard served as home plate in softball games and home base in games of kick the can.

It was a carefree time when parents let their children go up to the local elementary school to play without supervision or skateboard to the 7-Eleven for candy and a Coke. It also seemed like the country was tearing at its seams: Vietnam, school desegregation, the AFL and Al Davis, and long-haired hippies. I lived in that gap, and I didn't always understand my dad, but today I realize I couldn't have done it without his help and role-modeling. He was an old-school guy surviving in a new-school age.

Dad had an inner strength and moral toughness, the same strength he revealed on the football field, but it wasn't football that made him. Instead, he made football, not in a grand sense, not in today's sense of entitled athletes who feel they are bigger than the game. He brought his greatness to the game. If he hadn't played football, he would have had the same indomitable character. The only difference is that he wouldn't have been famous, and knowing my father, he wouldn't have minded that. But he dealt with fame as best he could.

It has been 56 years since the greatest game ever and 45 since the New York Jets upset my father's team, the Baltimore Colts, in Super Bowl III in maybe the most important NFL game ever. While those two events may mark his life as a football player, it was the first anniversary of the terrorists' attacks, September 11, 2002, that mark the most important date for me with my father. It was the day he died suddenly, unexpectedly, a day that I still get misty-eyed over. And why shouldn't I? I lost a man who influenced my life for 45 years.

Lots of people lose parents. I lost both of mine within six months of each other. Dealing with the death of a parent, particularly both parents, is hard. My feelings are no different. I'm not special in my grief. As a matter of fact, my grief is pretty typical, but it still hurts, throbbing like a crushed knuckle that occasionally slaps a rushing on-coming lineman.

What happened soon after my father's death is what has made his death that much harder—the grabbing for control of his legacy between family members, myself included. What happened is not a shining example of grace or class. Events both in mine and my father's lives have lacked grace or class. He was human. He wasn't perfect. I know that.

What I haven't had since he died is the chance to mourn, to grieve, to reflect about his life, to make sense of what he means to me. By understanding what he means to me, maybe I can understand what he means to the world outside me and my family, why his name and image still resonate though few of his records remain and pro football has become a different game.

Our relationship wasn't simple or easy. Because my father always gave his best, he expected everyone around him to do the same. As his namesake, I do the same. I take his legacy seriously. As his son, I take loving him more seriously.

There are life-size statues of him on pedestals in Baltimore and Louisville. They are well-deserved. While he wasn't a perfect father, he was good enough, and I put him on a pedestal in my mind. I've built his pedestal after careful consideration. His place in my life isn't based on legends or myth, an outsider's fleeting glance, and in that glance thinking that he knows the "real" Johnny Unitas. Dad raised me and I lived with him; we became business partners. I watched him as a grandfather loving his grandchildren. I've seen more than a glance and know that whatever the simple legends of Johnny U are, the reality is complicated.

I know the "real" Johnny U. It's time everyone else does, too.

CHAPTER 1

Fallen Granite

September 8, 2002
Carolina Panthers 10, Baltimore Ravens 7

It was the opening weekend of NFL season, and the Baltimore Ravens were on the road against a downtrodden Carolina Panthers team. While every season—in every sport—begins with all teams undefeated and full of optimism, these two teams seemed to be headed in opposite directions. In 2001, the Ravens had made the playoffs and Carolina had ended its season with a 15-game losing streak. Baltimore had lost to the Steelers—there's my dad's hometown again—in the divisional playoff game. In early September they were less than two years removed from winning the first football championship for Baltimore since Super Bowl V 30 years earlier, a game my dad started and the Colts won.

The Panthers, like the Ravens, were an expansion team, beginning in the NFL in 1995. Their owner, Jerry Richardson, was a former NFL player. He wasn't just any player—he was Dad's teammate during the 1959 season, catching a touchdown pass from him in the Championship Game against the New York Giants. Richardson also played in 1960 and caught eight passes. Legend has it he retired from the NFL because he and the Colts' office couldn't agree on a contract amount, arguing over a $500 difference.

Today's game didn't feature Richardson or my dad, although my dad had an interest in the game. For the Panthers, it was the debut of their new coach, John Fox, and for the Ravens, it was the debut of their starting

1

quarterback, Chris Redman. Obviously, Fox did a nice job as a new coach, winning the game.

Redman was drafted in the third round in 2000 and played in two games that year, completing two passes for 19 yards. He didn't play in any games the following year. Today, he was starting, and statistically, he played a solid game. He was 20-for-34 for 218 yards and threw a touchdown in the first quarter. He wasn't outplayed by the Panthers' starting quarterback, Rodney Peete, who was 12-for-19 for 136 yards. Peete did enough to win, an attribute my father saw as far more important than yards passed or awards won.

ESPN reported that the game focused "on a blue-collar game plan." It was the kind of game my father was used to seeing when he played although he didn't necessarily play "blue-collar" football. He was born blue-collar, but as a quarterback, he understood the need for a sophisticated offense. Today, however, both teams ran the ball a fair amount. The Panthers used the game to jump-start a 7–9 season, a vast improvement over the previous year, while the Ravens slogged their way to the same 7–9 season, a huge disappointment after making the playoffs in 2001.

The game is historically insignificant to the NFL, but it isn't when thought about in connection with my dad. Both starting quarterbacks that day were winners of the award my father started, the Johnny Unitas/Golden Arm Award, given to the top senior college quarterback in the country. Peete won the award in 1988, the second year of its existence. Unlike my father, he had played at a football powerhouse, USC, but like my father, Peete lasted a long time in the NFL. Redman won the award in 1999. He is the only winner to have played at Louisville, my father's alma mater. While at Louisville, Redman broke most of my father's passing records, many of them by a mile. Unlike my father, who would go on to an 18-year career in the NFL and be voted the greatest quarterback of the first 50 years of the league, Redman would play about 10 years in the league, starting on and off, and sometimes not playing for entire seasons.

Little did either player know on that Sunday, while Redman's life stretched out in front of him with the great possibilities of the unknown, that my father's life was almost over.

FALLEN GRANITE

Wednesday, September 11, 2002, rang uncertainty in most everyone's heart. It did mine. The terrorist attacks on New York, Washington D.C., and Pennsylvania were a year past, and memories of that tragic day still smoldered. There had been threats that more could happen on the anniversary of the four plane crashes, so my anxiety wasn't without reason. My father and I had never really discussed 9/11 except for him to comment that, "Those people were fucking crazy." I agreed, but part of his interpretation may have been clouded by his disdain for foreigners.

Three days earlier, the Ravens had lost their opening game of the season. The two days prior had felt more like summer with temperatures in the low 90s, but today felt more like fall with temperatures in the low 80s. It was also a typical day for Dad. He went to his office he shared with Richard Sammis, an old friend who sold cars. Sammis was known as Mr. Nobody because that was the moniker he used on his television ads; he was also a big Colts and Ravens fan. His love of football went beyond simply following the home team. He had been one of the main advertisers for every Baltimore pro football team since the 1960s. He'd befriended my dad and eventually given him office space at his dealership. I don't know what Dad was doing that day at the office—probably futzing around, keeping himself busy until it was time for lunch and then his daily workout. That's what he did—went to his office, had lunch, and worked out.

He ate lunch at his go-to restaurant, Michael's, getting his favorite dish: liver and onions. He wasn't supposed to eat liver and onions—he wasn't supposed to eat a lot of things since having open-heart surgery nine years earlier—but he kept himself in good shape for a 69-year-old. He wasn't his playing weight in his prime, but he wasn't far from it. He still walked with those slumped shoulders and bow-legged gait as if he'd just gotten off a horse. His hair was longer now, not the shorter, iconic crew cut. His face, always somewhat chiseled and etched, had deepened, almost as if his face was granite.

He left his office, saying good-bye to Richard, who he called Tricky, and telling him over his shoulder as he walked up the stairs that he would bring the coffee tomorrow because it was his turn. After eating lunch, he met Bill Neill, the longtime physical therapist for the Colts and Ravens, to work out. Neill, like Sammis, was more than a functionary in Dad's life. He'd started out taking physical care of him since his early days as a Colt, but Neill was now a friend, a man my father confided in and respected, a man who understood my father foremost as a person, not simply someone who was a great retired quarterback. My father knew lots of people, but he got close to few. Neill was one of the few.

I was having a typical day, too. I was futzing at my desk on the second floor of my office when I heard a scream from downstairs and then the pounding of footsteps. Sheila Harvey, the receptionist of the construction company that I rented space from, was yelling, "Did you hear? Did you hear? Your dad's dead. He's dead. I just got a call from my sister." Sheila wasn't just someone who I walked past every morning and evening as I came and went from my office. She was a childhood friend of mine. Her family and mine grew up in the same neighborhood about three houses apart. She is like a sister to me. She knew my father beyond the field. She'd seen him many times in the yard or in our kitchen. While none of my friends knew him well, she knew him.

"What are you talking about?" I asked, my stomach now roiling. My mom had died just three months earlier, unexpectedly, and my insides knew what hearing tragic news meant.

"It's on the radio, on WBAL," she said. Her face was ashen. Whether he was dead or not, she wasn't joking. She wasn't here to tell me that the media had it wrong. There was something in her voice and the way she sagged in my office doorway that said I needed to be prepared. It's one thing to know it, but it's another to grasp.

My phone rang, breaking the silence between Sheila and me. It was Sandy, my stepmother, a woman I didn't really like but got along with, at least on the surface. Over the next month, little did I know as I heard her screaming voice that day, repeatedly saying, "He's gone, he's gone" that many of my reasons to

4

dislike her would be confirmed. Sheila was right.

"Sandy, where is he?" She was difficult to understand, her words slurred, everything running together. He was at St. Joe's Hospital, but first I needed to pick up Paige, my half-sister, the youngest of my dad's second family. I headed there. I was thinking what most people think in circumstances like this. *This can't be true. There's a mistake. Let me have just one more moment with my dad.*

His granite face was ashen, his eyes lifeless. He looked so small on the gurney, a sheet pulled up to his chin. He sort of looked like my father but not the father I'd known. Sandy wailed in a room off to the side. I had called Christine, my wife, and she was dealing with our children, J.C., a freshman in high school, and Jillian, still in elementary school.

My dad was dead.

****

Dad had called me earlier that morning. He wanted to confirm the time of J.C's football game the next day. When my father made a plan, he stuck to it. It was part of his unspoken code, a code that my dad lived by. It manifested itself in his actions, many of them on the football field, an image that the public came to see as my dad. He was more complicated than that. Everyone is, and just because my father is the greatest quarterback ever doesn't lessen his complexities or solve the mystery of being human.

The irony of Dad's death is that J.C. was to play his first football game ever. Not only was it going to be his first game, but he might play some quarterback. That was J.C.'s dream—for his grandfather to see him play football.

****

While we're all going to die, I wasn't prepared for my dad's death, although maybe I should have been. He'd had open-heart surgery nine years earlier and almost died then. Throughout August 2002, he was not himself. I didn't notice, but Christine did as only a woman and daughter-in-law can. My father had been traveling to Florida often that summer, playing a lot of golf, and thinking about the upcoming wedding of Joey, his oldest child with Sandy. It was exhausting for him. He was keeping up with that younger group of married couples who were Sandy's friends. They were more active. Dad liked golf, but if it was 90 and humid, he was willing to skip playing that day. Instead, Dad preferred sitting on the patio, drinking a Michelob, watching television, listening to the kids talk. That was more his thing than socializing with "friends."

Although Dad and I spent a lot of time together, we were probably more like typical fathers and sons; we talked about practical matters and avoided emotions and feelings. I also missed the signs that maybe not all was right with him. Christine didn't. She mentioned more than once that my father didn't seem himself. I waved a hand at her as if I was shooing away a fly. He was Johnny Unitas. He didn't feel stress; he didn't get tired. Maybe I'd bought into the myth he wasn't mortal.

After his passing she'd told me about a day in late August when he returned some tiki torches he'd borrowed for a wedding shower for Joey. She said it was hard to engage him. He was distant, like he was listening to something far away, something only he heard, and it was distracting him. She could see it in his eyes. He wouldn't look at her, like he usually did. My wife and father got along well, so well that she called him Dad, and he treated her like a daughter. She felt that Sandy had been talking to him and putting certain notions in his head. He'd had a lot to think about, and I don't know, he just wasn't himself that late summer.

Christine saw my father as laid back but in good spirits and mood; few things got him wound up. He always had wonderful things to say, always loved having company, but she could tell that he'd reached his max. I wish I could say I'd seen the same things. He had been short with me a couple of times—about what I can't remember—so I backed off, which was how I handled situations like that. That's the kind of relationship I had with Dad.

****

Fallen Granite

The funeral was held on Tuesday, September 17, at The Cathedral of Mary Our Queen with Cardinal William Keeler, the Catholic archbishop, officiating. The Cathedral is large, holding about 2,000 people, and every seat was taken. I don't remember much once we pulled up to the entrance. We—my brothers and I—carried my dad up the five granite steps. I spoke at the funeral as did Raymond Berry, my dad's favorite receiver, and his brother, Leonard. I'm told John Mackey—a tight end and Hall of Famer who played 10 years with Dad and now beset with Alzheimer's, got up from his seat and wandered the aisle, unsure where he was. I'm glad I didn't see it because Mackey was the player, with my father throwing to him, who revolutionized the tight end position. He was never lost on the field; it was the one place where he was most at home.

But he wasn't the only lost person. I was, too. So were my siblings and my children and my half-siblings. So were Dad's teammates. So were his fans. While the era of my father and his teammates had long passed, his funeral simply confirmed that there was no chance of reclaiming those rollicking years where Memorial Stadium was called the World's Largest Outdoor Insane Asylum. That stadium was gone, replaced with a new stadium—clean and full of luxury boxes and loge levels with full bars and TV monitors—that represented the new era of football, a game that was sanitized even though the violence on the field probably hadn't changed. The Colts had moved from Baltimore in 1984 to become the Indianapolis Colts. When something familiar disappears, people can feel lost. I did.

I was already thinking about our business that my dad and I had set up, Unitas Management Corporation (UMC), that focused mainly on personal appearances and card shows but also had a website that sold Unitas paraphernalia, signed balls, and jerseys. I was also worried about holding the family together, particularly the First Family—my three brothers and sister from my dad's marriage to Dorothy. She had died less than three months earlier, and losing two parents that close together, particularly from a relationship that dissolved while we were still either children or teenagers, was rough. I was worried what would happen to the extended family—my four siblings and I and our three half-siblings, products of the marriage between Dad and Sandy.

I had every reason to worry. Sandy didn't get along with me, but she also didn't get along with any of my siblings. Dad, the family's figurative quarterback, made us behave like a team. He didn't keep us together as much as he didn't allow us to disintegrate.

Prior to the funeral, Sandy, younger than my dad but now looking older, pale, and saggy faced, as we approached the limos, took me aside. "I'm going over to the funeral home to make sure they've done everything right with your father." I wasn't sure why she was telling me. That seemed like something a wife would do before the funeral of her husband. I nodded. "But don't tell any of your siblings." This was weird. I'm still not sure why I couldn't tell my brothers and sister. I still don't know why she needed to go.

Two events can expose the soft underbelly of a family: weddings and funerals. My father's funeral was no different. I guess the real issue when he died, an issue we're still figuring out and probably always will be, is who has control over my father's legacy. While all families that divorce and end up with two sets of siblings are complicated, ours might be more complicated. Fame is a curveball that most people don't understand, and few realize its power.

Sandy didn't want to follow my father's wishes as outlined in his will. She didn't want him cremated, and that's what he wanted. He had been adamant about this. Sandy had her own ideas. Luckily, Joey, my father's oldest from the second family, argued in favor of following Dad's wishes, convincing his mother that it was the right thing to do. That's what my father represented: doing the right thing. I couldn't talk to Sandy, nor could my siblings. We couldn't talk about issues that mattered—my father split himself between the two families as best he could, it seemed.

The funeral posed a problem. My father was a hero to many in the public, particularly here in Baltimore, yet at the same time, he was our father. We'd shared him a lot already. How to share our father with the public—not an easy concept as we'd figured out while Dad was alive—wasn't a problem that was going to be solved with the stress of a death and impending funeral. Sandy wanted a spectacle. I was worried about a three-ring circus. I wasn't the only one; my siblings didn't want that, either. The kids didn't get their way. Again.

I remember snapshots of that day: my brothers and I carrying the casket up the steps of the Cathedral; Raymond giving his eulogy; a full church; Baltimore's Cardinal Keeler officiating; Uncle Leonard speaking about his brother and crying at the end of his eulogy; Jillian yelping while being the altar girl, worried that she was embarrassing herself. She later told me that as she was sobbing, Cardinal Keeler laid his hands on her head and said, "Just don't worry. He's in a better place." That calmed her.

The funeral was both spectacle and solemn. It didn't turn out to be the spectacle that I thought it might—no fans standing along Charles Street wearing football gear—but it was large and sensory overload. The Colts marching band played. As we left the Cathedral, attendees formed a tunnel to the hearse. People I'd never met before grabbed me and my siblings, my children, anyone close and connected to my father, and whispered nice platitudes: "He was a beautiful person. He was a beautiful man." Everyone was saddened yet celebrating the life of my father, a life that took him to the heights of pro football but affected many people, particularly here in Baltimore, in profound ways. I can't go out today without someone telling me a "Johnny U" story, a personal interaction between my dad and them. The funeral was the culmination of that. Just like the 1958 game was his coming-out party, his funeral was his farewell.

After the funeral and on the way to the burial, J.C. sat next to me in the limo. He was a pale, cried-out little kid in a black suit. Sandy said, "I hope my husband's behind us." She said it with such arrogance, as if, "I'm Mrs. Johnny Unitas, and you're not." *No, I'm not,* I thought, *But I am his son.*

I pondered what Sandy meant and what the future held. High above the cathedral flew a small plane dragging a banner behind it, like one over M&T Stadium on a football Sunday. What the banner said was both moving and ironic: "Unitas We Stand." It would be years before I understood the irony. Fluttering above our limo, my father in a casket behind us, were three simple words that would ultimately prove not to be true.

CHAPTER 2

Leaving Lithuania Behind

September 20, 1933
New York Giants 23, Pittsburgh Pirates 2

Nineteen thirty-three was the 14th year of the National Football League and arguably the first year of the NFL as we know it. In 1932, the league played a Championship Game only because there was a tie, not because it was planned. The next year, however, the league was split into two divisions with a Championship Game to determine the league's winner.

Even with an accidental Championship Game and one planned for 1933, the league was struggling in the most obvious way: the Depression. Its eight teams were the fewest since the league's inception in 1920. This would be the first year of a Pittsburgh team, bought by Art Rooney for $2,500. The problem with having a team in Pittsburgh hadn't been interest; rather it was college football and Major League Baseball. Pittsburgh was the kind of town that warranted a team; it was industrial, tough, and blue collar, the foundations of the NFL. College football was a place for the intellectuals, the thinkers, the schemers of Xs and Os to show off their physical moxie. Michigan finished the year ranked No. 1 while Princeton was the only college that was undefeated and untied. The Ivy League as we know it today didn't exist.

The second problem with the NFL was its image. The Eastern media considered it a bunch of beer-drinking, rough-housing, ne'er do wells, with the ownership of the teams oftentimes connected to gambling. The Pittsburgh franchise was no different. Rooney paid for the franchise with money won on the horses. Furthermore, the team wasn't called the Steelers yet. They were called the Pirates, attaching themselves to the baseball version mainly for marketing and recognition. A couple other NFL teams were doing the same.

In the Pirates' first game, played on a Wednesday evening because of Prohibition and "blue" laws, the Pirates lost to the New York Giants 23–2 at Forbes Field. Approximately 25,000 fans showed up for the game. The Giants scored first and led 7–0 at halftime. The Pirates' only two points came on a safety in the third quarter. As the *Pittsburgh Post-Gazette* reported, the Giants proved to be too much for the hometown Pirates, pulling away in the fourth quarter. The league was so new and unknown that the paper referred to it as the National Professional League.

However, this wasn't the football that I am used to watching. The helmets were leather and without face masks. The Giants threw the ball 14 times, completing seven, while Pittsburgh only threw it seven times for one completion. It was a game of possession and field position. As Art Rooney said, football in Western Pennsylvania bore little resemblance to the game played in the Ivy League schools. Football around Pittsburgh was tough and hard-hitting, a reflection of the industrial and mining interests of the area. It wasn't pretty, and it wasn't meant to be.

That same year John Constantine Unitas, my father, was born less than five miles away from where the Pittsburgh Pirates played. By the time the Pirates, later to be the Steelers and an interesting part of my dad's life, lost to the Giants—the same team he would face in the NFL Championship Game in 1958—he was a little more than three months old. My mother, Dorothy Hoelle, also from Pittsburgh, was yet to be born. That would happen on July 23, 1934. Thus introduced to the world, quietly, were three major influences on my life: Dad, Mom, and the NFL.

LEAVING LITHUANIA BEHIND

Dad was born on May 7, 1933, at the height of the Depression in Pittsburgh, a city that felt the Depression every day. That day, President Franklin Roosevelt gave a fireside chat about the banking crisis facing the

American people. Money was tight. There were no easy answers, he said. That would be a theme of my father's life: money and what to do about it. His birth and Roosevelt's radio speech happened on a Sunday, another theme. It would be on Sunday afternoons, at 2:00 PM, in Baltimore that Dad would rise to his greatest fame. His fame on the football field would create the opportunities for money. But in May 1933, Dad was seemingly light years from either money or fame.

Here are some important facts about my father's childhood. He was quiet and grew up working class but not poor as has been made into myth. His rags-to-riches storyline is one most biographers take. He was active in sports and loved them. He got shot by a stray bullet when my Uncle Leonard was playing around with a gun in the backyard. He was expected home by dinner, which his sister prepped and then his mother cooked shortly after she got home from work. He lived a pretty typical childhood. (Unlike mine. I had almost everything I could ever want: dirt bikes, fishing rods, a swimming pool in the backyard, and Little League–like experiences in football and basketball.) My father wore hand-me-downs from his older brother and neighbors, played pick-up sports with schoolmates and neighborhood kids his own age, and created activities and games to stay busy. His friends and neighborhood were his world.

Two important events Dad experienced weren't typical. First, he is the son of two Lithuanian parents, both of whom were born in Europe and came with their parents to the United States to have a chance at a better life. In terms of the American Dream, my father lived it. His life materialistically was far better than that of his parents. The second event was his dad, my granddad, dying when Dad was five years old. This made life hard, but not unbearable; it made life different, but not unlivable. Both his father dying young and growing up in an ethnic household had far greater influence, particularly psychologically, than my dad ever imagined or talked about.

****

Pittsburgh in 1933 was a different place than it is today. Steel was king and so were soot, smokestacks, and unemployment. The Steelers were not king, and pro football was considered a sideshow, controlled violence, and an opportunity to bet. Not long after my father was born, pro football was also born in Pittsburgh. They had to play their games on Wednesdays as local law didn't allow baseball games, much less football, to be played on the Sabbath. Then, less than seven weeks after the Pittsburgh Pirates (the forerunners to the Steelers) played their first NFL game, Pittsburgh repealed its "blue laws," allowing baseball and other sports to be played on Sundays. College football had Saturdays locked up, and the NFL on Wednesdays probably wasn't going to make it over the long haul. Prohibition also ended when my father was little more than six months old. On December 5, the idea of football on Sunday with a beer became a reality. While the Steelers would take 40 years to become more than a second-division team in the NFL, except during World War II, their existence was at least secure but not legendary like it is today.

My father's start is just as complicated. Not his birth or the early years of his life or even the death of his dad. He is the third child of four with an older brother, Leonard, an older sister, Millicent, and a younger sister, Shirley. His parents lived a working-class existence.

The story of how his parents arrived in Pittsburgh and eventually became Dad's parents wasn't an easy journey and was probably typical of how immigrants actually made it here, unlike the idealistic and mythologized versions we like to hear. Little is known about how the Unitas side of the family got to America, where they came from, or why they even left Lithuania. Much more is known about my dad's mom's side of the family.

My grandmother's maiden name is Rudzawich. It appears Eve Rudzawich came to America when she was young, probably around 10 years old. She came with her sister, two years younger, and her brother, Connie, to Ellis Island. Connie almost kept Eve from getting into the country because he had a medical skin issue and the authorities didn't let him off the boat until a doctor saw him. That's when the first piece of luck of the Unitas story happened. Her brother only had a rash so he didn't need to be sent back to Lithuania. Eve needed to get to West Virginia where her mother's older brother, my dad's great uncle, lived, having come to America a few years before.

As was typical of immigrants getting off the boat, no one spoke English, and the authorities didn't understand Lithuanian. As they were looking for someone who at least spoke Polish, a gentleman standing nearby understood them and said he happened to be heading in the direction of West Virginia close to where they wanted to go: Century. That was the next piece of luck. He also had a truck, another piece of luck. So my dad's mother, her parents, and two siblings piled into the back of the truck, along with their luggage, for the journey from New York City to Century, West Virginia. The man let them out a few miles from Century, and my grandmother's family walked the last few miles.

Once in town, they asked about Eve's uncle and were directed to his house. It wasn't hard to find. Century was a mining town where everyone knew everyone else. There was a bigger problem, however: when Eve and her parents showed up at the uncle's house, he wasn't expecting them. The letter Eve's mom sent to her brother had never arrived, but doing what family often-times does for family, Eve and her family moved in with her uncle and his wife, and everyone went to work in the mines. The idea of making do would be a repeated theme for much of Dad's life.

My dad's father's story, the Superfisky story, is even more arduous. My grandfather's mother died when he was young, similar to my father's dad dying young. In this case, the father couldn't take care of my grandfather and his siblings so he put them in an orphanage. Once my grandfather's older brother reached 16 years of age, he left the orphanage, and my grandfather, two years younger, did the same thing when he turned 16. He also had a set of twin younger brothers who stayed in the orphanage longer and both later died, one while hopping a train. There were also two sisters, who will appear briefly in my father's life.

Somehow my grandfather worked his way to Century where he met my grandmother. Eventually, they moved to Pittsburgh where my grandfather started a coal delivery business, and then he died suddenly at 38 years of age when Dad was only five. At the time of his death, the family lived in the Brookline neighborhood, the same neighborhood where my mother was born and grew up. But about three years after my grandfather died, my dad and his siblings and mom were forced to move to the Mt. Washington section of Pittsburgh because my grandmother, Helen, couldn't afford the house in Brookline.

As has been mythologized, Mt. Washington was a step down in terms of prestige and socio-economic class, but my father's family wasn't poor. They weren't rich, either. A lot has been made of both the move and the fact that the street running in front of Dad's house was not paved. It was crushed stone, but most streets in the neighborhood were paved, just not theirs. Furthermore, Dad's family owned a truck that was used to deliver coal, but no car. Running directly above their street was one of the four funiculars that transported commuters up and down the hill that Mt. Washington sat on overlooking downtown Pittsburgh and the confluence of the Allegheny and Monongahela rivers that joined to form the Ohio River.

****

Dad grew up basically without a father. His mother worked and worked hard, or she was back in school improving herself. Dad and his siblings were expected to do what was right, and in a lot of ways, they raised themselves. It was a different time, and kids were expected to be on their own. In his household, it wasn't Leonard who raised Dad, as has been offered in other biographies; instead, it was his older sister, Millie, who is three years older. She came home from St. Justin's school each day and prepared the kitchen for dinner. If Dad and his younger sister, Shirley, had homework, she supervised. According to Millie, Dad wasn't a difficult child. He did what was asked. Usually, after school he and Shirley went outside and played with their friends. Millie also got them up in the morning and fixed their lunches. The high school part of St. Justin's, at least when she was there, was 10 blocks farther west than the elementary school. She left before they did, so she'd wake them up and threaten them, telling them that if they were late for school, they'd get in trouble. They never did.

As with anyone's childhood, my father's wasn't as simple or idyllic or difficult or logical as it's often portrayed. Millie remembers being in charge, but Uncle Tony, the man at whose house in Century Dad's mom arrived unannounced, came to live with Dad's family on Williams St. because of the Depression. He had a long handlebar mustache, and he always wore an apron as if he were a butcher or chef, doubled up and tied. He wasn't the only relative to do so, but later when the others got their finances straightened out and moved out, Uncle Tony stayed. He wasn't a commanding presence in the house, but he was always there, keeping an eye on the kids.

Dad had vivid memories of his father. Although he worked hard and for long hours delivering coal, he was a presence. On Saturdays during the summer he would scrub out the back of coal-delivering truck and invite all the kids in the neighborhood to pile in the back of the truck to go to South Park where a public pool was located. They'd leave right after lunch and stay until the smaller pool closed around 5:00 pm. On the way home they stopped at Isley's, a convenience store that sold ice cream and candy. Everyone was allowed one sweet—most of the kids got ice cream cones—and after finishing their treats, it was home, possibly for another treat.

While Dad's father was alive, his mother worked at a bakery on Saturdays. At closing she was allowed to take what wasn't sold. The kids would have had their weekly baths—if they hadn't been to the pool—and would be on the living room floor with the Sunday paper, part of it delivered that afternoon, spread on the floor, reading the funnies and waiting. When she got home, everyone got a bakery treat from her bag and glass of milk. Always a glass of milk.

These special occasions ended when my grandfather died. Life got difficult, but not so difficult that it was harsh or unbearable. There were no more treats out of a bag, and eventually a move from a cul-de-sac—Fortuna Avenue—in Brookline. Their house in Brookline was bought by a family from Buffalo who had to be rich because only rich people lived in New York, or so the Unitas kids thought. Now, it was life in Mt. Washington on William St., which they shared with men who were masons, factory workers, detectives, and a civilian employee of the police department. Nearby was a small black section and everyone, regardless of color, played together.

****

Dad was always quiet. He didn't take after his mother who was outgoing or Shirley, his younger sister who talks, not excessively, but wasn't generally quiet. Dad was quiet and had been as long as anyone could remember. Millie isn't sure where his quietness came from, but she knows that he was that way as a boy and remained that way throughout his life.

My father didn't just one day appear as an NFL quarterback, or the quarterback that he's known as being: a tough, quiet leader who didn't seem to mind pressure and particularly loved the last two or three minutes of a game. Much of what the public knows of my father was part of who he was from birth. I know that's hard to imagine, but my dad, like most people, didn't develop in a vacuum or suddenly become what we know. It was a long process.

Millie talks of never really knowing where her brother was. Not literally. Figuratively. He was often in the room physically, but he was so quiet, everyone forgot he was there. One afternoon, before their mother got home from work, Millie heard a knock at the door. When she opened the door, it was a couple of Dad's friends. Given the customs of the time, although Millie wasn't yet out of high school, his friends still called her ma'am. She asked what was the matter.

One of the boys said, with Dad standing slightly behind him, his hand on top of his head, "We were throwing rocks into the air and one came down and hit John on the head." She looked and there was a small cut and a little bleeding, but nothing too serious. She asked if it hurt.

"No," Dad said. She asked if he was sure and if he was hurting anywhere else. Again he said, "No." She offered to put some Mercurochrome, and she got the standard response, "No." With the third and final no, the boys turned around and headed back out to play.

****

Only saying what he needed to say, that was my father. One of the reasons so much has been said about his childhood is that he never really spoke up about it. As his older brother, Leonard, has said, much of what's been written and said about Dad's growing up is fiction. We've created a story to meet our needs. I'm as guilty of it as anyone. What he didn't tell me about his childhood, and it was a lot, I've had to fill in.

That doesn't mean he didn't have his moments. There was the time he got shot. Yes, my dad got shot when he was about eight. The family had recently relocated to Mt. Washington, and my grandmother was at work. Leonard, about 12 or so at the time, had saved his money and bought a bb gun. As luck would have it, he'd found a .38 slug like the police used to wear on their belts. Leonard, wanting to mess around with his new gun, put the slug in a piece of telephone pole, ordering Dad to go around the house so that he didn't get hurt. Leonard crouched behind a wall and shot his bb gun at the slug. On his third shot, he hit it. Little did Leonard know, but Dad hadn't stayed where he told him. Instead, he had snuck up behind on the wall. The slug's casing shot back and hit Dad in the leg. Leonard called the police—he had some explaining to do that was complicated but eventually understood—and they took Dad to the hospital where he had surgery to remove the casing. They couldn't get one small piece out, so he had a little bit of a bullet from Pittsburgh with him for the rest of his life.

Helen, Dad's mom, was tough, and obviously she had to be.

When she got home that evening and learned what had happened, she was hopping mad. She did what any single mom trying to raise four kids basically by herself would do: she took that gun away from Leonard and broke it into pieces.

CHAPTER 3

The Unknown from St. Justin's

October 5, 1948
Cleveland Browns 14, Baltimore Colts 10

It was raining, hard at times, and had been for about 24 hours. The field was slop, and while that was bad, there was more bad news on the way. The Cleveland Browns were coming to town, and they had never lost to an Eastern Division team since the beginning of the All-American Football Conference. That was worse. Yet, there was more. The game was being played on a Tuesday night, the first night game in Colts and Baltimore history. And that wasn't the last of it: the game was on a Tuesday night because it had to be postponed from the Sunday two days earlier because Navy had played a game there on Saturday. Navy's contract stipulated that no game could be played 24 hours before or after their game. College football, especially Naval Academy football, pushed pro football to the back burner. The only thing that could make the situation worse for the Colts was the outcome of the game. And it did.

My dad never mentioned this game or the AAFL, but before my father, most football historians consider Otto Graham as the greatest professional quarterback. He did something that will probably never be matched again: he led the Browns to 10 consecutive Championship Games. The first four were in the AAFL, a league that most people at that time considered inferior.

Maybe it was, but what the Browns did after entering the NFL proved otherwise. After the 1949 season, the NFL accepted three AAFL teams: the Browns, 49ers, and Colts. While the Colts struggled in their initial NFL seasons, Cleveland and Graham went to six more NFL Championship Games, winning three of them. But the Browns were more than Graham. They were

Paul Brown's team, and Graham happened to be his quarterback. Whether that's accurate or not, that's the perception, even today.

Nonetheless, the Browns were coming to Baltimore with a chip on their shoulder. While they had never lost to an Eastern Conference team in the regular season, they had recently lost to the Colts in the final preseason game, a game that ruffled Cleveland's feathers as the team accused the Colts of playing dirty. Cleveland sportswriters went so far as to call the Colts "monsters" because both Graham and Marion Motley, the Browns' great running back, were injured.

Even with the rain a good crowd showed up—more than 22,000 fans witnessed the contest, although team officials expected no more than 10,000. The game got off to a good start. After two short dives into the Browns' defensive line for little gain, Y.A. Tittle threw a 78-yard touchdown pass as the receiver tip-toed down the sideline. Less than 90 seconds in, and the Colts led. The lead wouldn't hold up, however, as Graham threw a short TD pass late in the third quarter for the 14–10 victory. Paul Brown called it the best game his team had played up to that point in the AAFL.

The Colts would go on to tie for the Eastern Division lead with a 7–7 record. The Browns would win the Western Division, finishing the season undefeated and easily winning the Championship Game, defeating the Buffalo Bills 49–7, the same team that defeated the Colts 28–17 in a championship play-in game.

It would be the Browns' only undefeated season among their seven championships won between 1946 and 1955, the years when my father was coming of age, moving from high school to the University of Louisville. It was also more years of growing pains for pro football. The NFL was still struggling to find itself. The AAFL had the same teams in 1948 as 1947, but only barely. Pro football was still a minor-league sport, playing second fiddle to college football. Although the Browns were a dynasty, the NFL was still looking for a legend, someone to put the league on his shoulders and guide it out of minor-league status. That man, my father, was only 15 when Graham visited Baltimore. Graham retired the year before my dad came into the league.

The final insult to the Colts/Browns game: Navy lost to Cornell 13–7, and the Midshipmen would finish their season 0–8–1, losing eight straight before tying Army.

THE UNKNOWN FROM ST. JUSTIN'S

My dad lived the typical life of a teenager—albeit a quiet one. He had friends who he goofed around with; he played football but he also played other sports; and he went to school, but it seemed more likely that he attended so he could play football and hang out with his classmates rather than to study and get good grades. A lot has been written about his childhood and high school years, but much of it is myth. Once Dad became famous, it seems the fans needed an explanation that did justice to his greatness. Yes, he was a great football player, but it wasn't because he threw thousands of passes through a swinging tire in the backyard. He wasn't Roy Hobbs of *The Natural*, an unknown with prodigious talents. He was an unknown, and much about how he became the greatest quarterback in the history of the NFL is unknown mainly, I think, for one reason: my father didn't talk much about his childhood. He didn't talk much about his past at all. He was never one who would reminisce about throwing the winning touchdown pass to beat the arch-rival his senior year in high school. My mother didn't talk about Dad's past or her past, either. Part of my dad's character—and it served him well—was his knack for always looking forward. He seemed to do the same thing with his high school years.

While we occasionally went to Pittsburgh to visit relatives, the Pittsburgh past is something it seems my father put behind him. It isn't that he left Pittsburgh in his rearview mirror because he thought he was better than the place or people or because there were traumatic events that needed to be forgotten. Rather, he found his place in Baltimore and that was where his future was.

Dad attended St. Justin's High School in the Mt. Washington section of Pittsburgh. It was a small Catholic school that fielded a football team in the

B-class of Pittsburgh high schools. In many ways—not that this was how my dad and his teammates saw it—St. Justin's was a blip on the football radar of the talent-rich Pittsburgh and Western Pennsylvania area. It wasn't part of the Western Pennsylvania Public School Association, and that organization's schools dominated the *Pittsburgh Post-Gazette* regional rankings. It wasn't even in the A-class of the local Catholic schools. Unlike schools such as Central Catholic in Pittsburgh, Aliquippa, and Donora, football-crazed communities in the greater Pittsburgh area, for example, St. Justin's didn't have a storied football past. Those other schools regularly drew anywhere from 2,000 to 15,000 fans on a Friday night. St. Justin's was so small that it didn't even own a football field or have a field for its home games. Almost no one from St. Justin's went on to play college, much less pro. Scouts weren't beating the door down to convince high school seniors to come to their college. About ten years later, Bryant, the famous head coach at the University of Alabama, made special trips to Beaver Falls to see Joe Namath play and to visit with Namath's parents. That didn't happen with my father.

Simply because he wasn't well known or highly recruited by college scouts didn't mean he wasn't known and appreciated locally. Although St. Justin's didn't play a powerhouse schedule, according to some of his teammates, their games were well attended (for St. Justin's), mostly by fans interested in seeing Dad. Even playing for a small Catholic high school, Dad managed to make somewhat of a name for himself. While most teams they played had more than 100 kids, some even more, St. Justin's didn't have more than 150 boys in the high school.

****

Everyone who knew Dad as a teenager always comments on how quiet he was. That might have been part of the problem: Dad's quietness while playing for a small school in a smaller conference kept him out of the limelight. I don't think his greatness magically appeared; it simply took time for others to discover it. If his high school coach, Max Carey, hadn't done some leg work for him, Dad might not have gone to college. Maybe today a player can be very good and be discovered and have websites and ESPN touting his greatness, but in the late 1940s, generally it was a world of who you knew. Tooting your own horn didn't hurt, but that wasn't Dad's style. It wasn't then and never would be.

****

One night, Millie had a date and after dinner. She asked Dad to finish washing the dishes, saying that she would be home late. Dad said yes. Later that evening, when Millie returned home, everyone was asleep. She walked into the kitchen only to discover that while the dishes were cleaned, they weren't dried. The sink was full of unwashed pots and pans.

In the morning, she asked, "John, why didn't you wash the dishes like I asked?"

He said, "I did."

Millie pointed to the sink full of pots and the stack of dishes on the counter. "But what about those?"

Dad chuckled. "You didn't ask me to dry them or wash the pots and pans." Millie also chuckled.

While Dad didn't necessarily say a lot, he did have a sense of humor, friends, and interests in teenage distractions beyond football and basketball. Nonetheless, football dominated his life. He was a good basketball player, solid and steady, but he didn't love it. He played baseball, not for the school but in the open fields around his house. He also had a boxing speed bag in his basement that he and his friends messed around with on quiet afternoons and weekends. Once school got out for the day, Dad was outside playing, running around the neighborhood, until dinner time. While his teenage years weren't always easy, they seemed almost Huck Finn-ish in their languid pace and seeming lack of stress. Maybe this is mythologizing Dad in a different way, and if it's not myth, it's at least romanticizing him.

He had a quiet style on the field. He didn't say much, but when he did, his teammates listened. Dad, I've come to find out, always had an interesting relationship with his center, the teammate he had to interact with on every play. At St. Justin's, James Liatta was Dad's center his senior year. But before he was Dad's center, they were buddies. James owned a car, and he and Dad often drove around Pittsburgh doing what teenagers do when they have a car. Liatta remembers one football game in which St. Justin's was on its own 10-yard line and the ball was supposed to be snapped on the call of "58." Dad was in what we now call the shotgun. He called "58" but instead of hearing him, Liatta was thinking about when he was supposed to snap the ball, repeating "58" in his head. Finally, my dad yelled at him, "Hey, Mo, snap the god damn ball." He did, but it went over Dad's head. Liatta doesn't remember whether or not it resulted in a safety, but he does remember that my father didn't hold this against him. A couple of months later, they were able to laugh about it.

Dad was more than a leader; he was also tough. The year before Dad had another incident involving a gun, except this time his brother had nothing to do with what was almost a disaster. There had been a prowler in the neighborhood, so my grandmother had a gun in the house for protection. Dad inadvertently shot himself in the finger. No one today remembers why Dad had the gun in his hand. It went off—how or why, no one seemed to know then and still doesn't know today—almost ending my father's football playing days and career.

He put a splint on the injured finger, missing no game time. Even with a splint, he threw a ball while rolling left, across his body, jumping into the air, and going spread eagle about 50 yards down the sideline. The ball was right on target. That was the kind of player my father was. He played hurt and he overcame adversity, even when it was of his own doing. Whether he was well known as a local high school player or not, no one who knew him questioned his toughness.

****

High school wasn't just sports. It was academics and religion. That's why Dad and his siblings went to St. Justin's, to get both. He was an average student at best, like most of his friends. College wasn't the foregone conclusion that it would become when I graduated from Calvert Hall in the early 1970s. My Aunt Millie went to college one year at a local school in Pittsburgh, but then she got married and dropped out to raise a family. Dad wanted to go to college, but he also knew that football would have to help, both in terms of admissions and finances. After St. Justin's, many of his neighborhood friends went to work in heavy industry in the Pittsburgh area or joined the military.

The idea that my father, a first-generation immigrant, would automatically go to college was a stretch. Furthermore, life after high school graduation became more complicated because of meeting Dorothy Hoelle, my mother. She was a grade behind Dad and much more studious. She first saw my father in the library ironically and knew instantly that he was the one for her. She was from Brookline, where my father was originally from. Dorothy's family was by no means rich, just a bit better off. While my mom and dad had made eye contact and love sparks were crackling, their parents, particularly hers, weren't enamored with the relationship.

Years later, Mom asked an older cousin, Millie (but not my Aunt Millie and Dad's sister), who often came to visit us, why Dad's mom, Helen, didn't particularly like her. She mentioned that this had stretched back to the days when they first started dating. Mom even thought it was because one Friday night, she and Dad returned to his house after a date, only to walk in on Helen having sex with a boarder who she had taken in to help make ends meet.

But that wasn't it, although it involved sex. Before my grandfather (Dad's dad) died, he had an affair with Helen's sister, getting her pregnant. My father had a half-sister, also named Dorothy, who oftentimes played with Dad and his siblings in the yard on William Street. As Cousin Millie said, "You're just a constant reminder to Helen, 'There's another Dorothy in her life,'" a reminder that my grandfather had cheated on her.

What my father thought of all this he never said, but I don't think there's any question that it had an impact on him. His upbringing is oftentimes looked at from an economic perspective. According to his brother and sisters,

Dad was always quiet, but maybe there was a reason behind his silence. He learned that was the best way to survive in a household that was clearly dysfunctional, oftentimes crazy.

****

At St. Justin's, the students were forced to go to Confession and church. Dad participated like everyone else. He did what he had to do. He was taught by nuns, some good, caring teachers and adults, others not so positive. But my father went to school and got religious training. At the time, he and his friends didn't think much of it. It was something they had to do, and it appears my father did what he was supposed to do at school.

Even at home, the church was important. He went most every Sunday to church, whether he wanted to or not, mainly because his mother told him to get up, get dressed, and get to Mass. Dad's adult life was influenced by the events of his childhood. He was made to grow up fast in a lot of ways. He and his siblings looked out for each other; Leonard and Millie were in charge of Dad and Shirley. Dad had lots of freedom sometimes, like after school, but when it came to going to church, he had to do it. While he didn't talk a lot about these obligatory Sunday mornings, I always got the impression there was a deal struck between the children and their mother: they would get lots of freedom and she would be there if they needed help in exchange for doing what she asked, which she rarely did. Church was one of those requests.

****

Dad wanted to go to college, not because college was an expectation or because he wanted to climb to a higher socio-economic class than Mt. Washington or even Brookline. Throughout his high school years, my father was either playing sports or working, helping to deliver coal with his brother. He was good with his hands and had a strong back, so working hard and taking a low-wage job didn't scare him. College was a way to play the next level of football.

The Unknown from St. Justin's

He was obviously good, but not everyone knew that. He wanted to go to Notre Dame. Every good football player, particularly those who were Catholic, wanted to go there. It was the gold standard of college football and it was Catholic. Within his silence, Dad was a dreamer. He already had visions of playing pro football, not something many boys that age aspired to. Notre Dame would be the best and fastest route to his dream. He may not have been known in high school, but if he could go there and prove himself, he would be known far outside of the Pittsburgh area. It had happened to other Western Pennsylvania athletes like Stan Musial and Press Maravich, Pete Maravich's dad, who was an accomplished basketball player in his own right before he became Pete's father.

When people graduated from high school in the 1940s and '50s, they had a card made up, like a business card. Friends often wrote on other people's cards, the way people used to write in each other's yearbook. A teammate at St. Justin's wrote on Dad's, "John, you're going to be a great NFL player someday." At some point in Dad's pro career, this classmate traveled to the Colts' training camp and reintroduced himself. Dad was happy to see him. When the classmate asked if he remembered what he'd written on the back of Dad's card, Dad opened his wallet and pulled out that card. The man may have been lucky, but Dad's dream wasn't a simple flight of fancy, at least not to Dad. His classmates understood his dream even if they thought it was a stretch.

Dad was looking at Pitt, Notre Dame, and Indiana initially. A few other schools approached Dad and his mother about possibly playing, but his academics weren't strong enough. That's why Pitt was quickly rejected: Dad didn't score high enough on its entrance exam. Notre Dame didn't really give him much attention. A couple of Dad's friends have told me that they thought he actually went to campus in August 1950 and quickly realized that he wasn't very high on the depth chart. There's no evidence that this was true, except my father and his coach, Max Carey, probably realized this without my father having to go to campus. Instead, he ended up at Louisville, mainly because of luck rather than planning. Louisville, late in the recruiting process, needed a quarterback, and Frank Gitschier, the backfield coach, checked him out. Dad

29

came recommended by some fellow Pittsburghites, and because Louisville was desperate, they took him without seeing him play. That's how college recruiting occurred in those days.

It would be easy to talk about how Dad didn't take care of academic business, but in hindsight, colleges at that time were able to get almost anyone they wanted into their institution. The problem was his size. He was scrawny. No one had film of him to watch nor could they see his abnormally long arms and huge hands. No one, and I mean no one, could have predicted his leadership qualities. He'd never been on the big stage. Mental toughness takes time to evaluate and even longer to rate. Dad was a good seven or so years away from grading out high in the mental toughness area, at least on a football field.

It doesn't seem like anybody took the time to examine how Dad had overcome the loss of his father or the fact that he'd gone 22–6 as the starter at St. Justin's. Skinny is as skinny does, just like a winner is as winning does. Even college wouldn't reveal Dad's best qualities, persistence and resilience mixed with talent equalled positive results eventually. We know that now. But it wasn't a foregone conclusion then.

CHAPTER 4

Skinny (on a) Nobody

September 26, 1954
Los Angeles Rams 48, Baltimore Colts 0

This is not how Webb Ewbank envisioned beginning his tenure as the head coach of the Baltimore Colts. Not only did the Colts lose their opening game of the season badly, but it was also at home. The Colts weren't favored, a status that Ewbank wasn't used to having just come from being the No. 1 assistant to Paul Brown of the Cleveland Browns. In Ewbank's five years with Brown, Cleveland had made the AAFC or NFL championship every year.

On this particular Sunday, there would be no Cleveland Browns imitation. Instead, the Rams scored on the very first offensive play of the game on a hidden wide-receiver pass that went for 80 yards. The Rams sent in lots of players after the opening kickoff went through the end zone, basically shielding a wide receiver who stood next to the sideline, camouflaged among his teammates who were spectators. As the *Baltimore Sun* reported, "They [the Colts] were fooled by a kid's play and played like sandlotters the rest of the way."

When Ewbank was hired, he promised a championship within five years. Like Soviet Communism at the time, five-year plans were popular, and Ewbank came with a dictatorial reputation. That was Paul Brown's style, and Weeb learned it well. When he was hired, Ewbank promised that his teams would work hard and be graded on their performance on every play. Before he'd coached one game, he was quoted by the *Baltimore Sun* saying, "I think hard work will produce winners and we will surely put in the hard work. [Assistant coach Frank] Cuminskey has already told me that he should have signed for 25 cents an hour because he can make more than on his straight contract."

Obviously, Weeb got neither hard work nor a stirring performance from his team against the Rams that day. Even allowing for a fluke play on the first play doesn't account for a 48–0 score at home. The Colts were down 27–0 at halftime. As would reflect the rest of the season, the offense would gain 197 yards—measly considering the Colts were playing from behind—and the defense would give up almost 600 yards. The Colts would finish the season 3–9, and there was some concern that Ewbank wasn't the right guy.

As history would show, he was the right guy, and his five-year plan initially lacked some important components: a quarterback, a young speedy running back, and an offensive line to protect the quarterback and open holes for the running back. The Colts addressed the problem of quarterback, so they thought, in the 1955 draft by taking George Shaw as the No. 1 pick of the entire draft. They would later take Alan Ameche, also in the first round. In 1956, besides signing Dad to a free agent contract, the Colts drafted Lenny Moore to provide speed for the offense.

As Ewbank's plan slowly slipped into place, Dad was getting married, finishing up his senior year at Louisville, preparing to be drafted and later cut by the Steelers, and having his first of eight children. Little did anyone envision the 1958 season and championship. Lots of luck and taking advantage of that luck would play into the ascension of the Colts. It's easy now to see Weeb and Dad as destined for each other and their success, but that's too easy, the kind of thing fans do to create legends because there's no question that both Baltimore and America were waiting for someone like Dad to come along. Eventually he would, but the journey wouldn't be easy.

Ironically, it would take a narrow 22–21 win in the second-to-last game in Los Angeles for the Colts to get their third and final win of the season. Maybe that was an omen that things were looking up. Easy to see it that way today.

Skinny (on a) Nobody

Today by interstate, it's 372 miles to South Bend from Pittsburgh and 411 miles to Bloomington, Indiana. Louisville split the difference at 388 miles.

Google tells me that today it would take more than six hours to drive to any of these places. In 1951, it would have been a much longer trip. Beyond the literal distance, these places were another world away. College was yet another world away, even if he'd gone to Pitt. There's no evidence that my father left Pittsburgh except to travel for football and basketball games for St. Justin's. But because his mother had raised her children to take care of themselves, Dad was ready for whatever came his way.

He got to Louisville by car, driven by his friend, James Liatta. It was an all-day drive and they spent the night along the way. The next day Liatta dropped Dad off just like he snapped the ball to him a year earlier at St. Justin's. He was doing a favor, initiating the play, and once it was started, he moved on. Liatta returned to Pittsburgh. In many ways, Dad going off to college was his departure from Pittsburgh. He would return for a year after Louisville when the Steelers drafted him, but he rarely came home while he was in college.

The fact that my father was going to college now seems surprising, not because he wasn't a good enough athlete—clearly he was—but because books and classes and homework had never been his thing. His friends remember him as a decent student, just as they were, but not as a great one. His time at Louisville would prove this true again. Given that he had other motivations and ambitions, however, college made a lot of sense. He wanted to get out of Mt. Washington, down the hill, and living on a street that was paved. Who wouldn't? He wanted to see the world, at least a little bit of it. World War II was over and the Depression long ended. Money was no longer tight. The steel mills of Pittsburgh were working overtime producing the steel that America would drive and watch and build with. Jobs were plentiful, but Dad wanted something else. Part of it was playing football at the next level, but part of it was having opportunities that Leonard didn't have and his parents didn't even think about.

He was over not getting into Pitt. The real issue at Notre Dame probably wasn't his size: it was his lack of reputation. He played at the B-level at St. Justin's. It wasn't Beaver Falls or Aliquippa or Donora. Western Pennsylvania was already famous for turning out great high school athletes, not just football players. The area was the home to Josh Gibson, Stan Musial, Hack Wilson, George Blanda, Johnny Lujack, Bill George, and Arnold Palmer. Many more would follow. My father wasn't putting Pittsburgh on the map as a recruiting destination. It was already well established. It was because he was from Pittsburgh that a coach was willing to listen.

Louisville seemed a mid-major football program, but it really wasn't. It was a university trying to figure out its place in the bigger football world, just as Dad was doing the same. No matter what its place in the pecking order of the college game, it was the place that offered my dad a chance to play. Too small and too unknown combined with a feeling that he hadn't played against good competition in high school all worked against him. This would become a common theme throughout his life. What scouting and word of mouth didn't project was his toughness and his uncanny ability to lead, seemingly to become a different person once on a football field, and in particular, to become general-like in the huddle.

Getting into Louisville hadn't been any easier than his attempts to interest Notre Dame or test into Pitt. He struggled with his entrance scores, but once at school, he overcame that. Because of the low entrance test scores, Dad entered Louisville on academic probation, limited in the number of classes he could take. It was probably a good thing, but it would be the last time he was on probation. Louisville football at that time was nearly a joke—much different than it has become, in part because of Dad. The football players' dorm was an old Navy barracks, and the home field was a high school stadium off campus most of the time. Sometimes it was the Louisville Colonels' stadium, a minor league baseball affiliate. Wherever they played, it wasn't big time. It wasn't Notre Dame or the Southeastern Conference or the Yale Bowl with 60,000 people routinely filling large stadiums. But after the childhood that Dad had, these were small obstacles. While he had most everything he needed—don't forget that my grandmother drilled into Dad the difference between need and want, something that was drilled into me and I've drilled into my children, maybe not as successfully as Dad learned it—he hadn't been living the high life. While he understood need versus want, he still wanted stuff, not necessarily physical stuff but chances, like being a big-time quarterback, and he was willing to do whatever was needed to make it happen.

Louisville wasn't the same athletic school in 1951 it had been as recently as three years earlier. Football had been disbanded during World War II. It was restarted in 1946 and then as quickly deemphasized, maybe a reason Dad was able to go there. As Frank Gitschier had said, Louisville wasn't recruiting Dad. They didn't have any more idea what he was going to go on and become than anyone else. "We were desperate." Another word, in hindsight, would be lucky.

In many ways, Louisville wasn't so far removed from St. Justin's. While Louisville was deemphasizing its program, at least it would still have one; by the time Dad became famous in 1958, St. Justin's team was gone, long gone. Who knows, if it had survived until "The Greatest Game" in 1958, Dad certainly would have put St. Justin's on the map, and maybe it would still have had a team. How long the team would have lasted, however, is uncertain because St. Justin's as a school didn't survive. It closed its doors in 1974, and by that time, Dad was a household name.

****

In 2011 Louisville football finished 7–6, including a bowl game against N.C. State. The Cardinals played in the Big East Conference, a BCS conference, meaning that if Louisville had a great season—undefeated—it could have played for the national championship. Average attendance for its home games in a mediocre year was more than 39,000 fans. This a far cry from the less than 3,500 fans who came to games in 1959 or the approximately 7,000 fans who attended in 1957, just three years removed from when my father played there. Furthermore, Louisville has all the modern amenities today that are expected at a big-time program—lots of assistant coaches, training tables, athletes' dorms, and eight home games.

When my father arrived in August 1951, there was nothing like this. Most students at Louisville didn't live on campus; instead, they commuted. The football players lived in a Quonset hut. It was hot and lacked air conditioning. They were fed bologna sandwiches for lunch. While Dad's coaches talk about helping him gain weight, putting on about 30 pounds in his freshman year, according to their memories, Louisville didn't have much of a weight room. He was raw. That much was obvious. He started the season as the back-up behind three quarterbacks who had split time from the previous year.

Dad befriended another freshman quarterback, Jerry Nassano, who was from Thomas, a suburb of Cincinnati in northern Kentucky. Occasionally, they went to movies. They were down the depth chart together, and when Dad got the nod, first to play and then to start, Nassano had seen enough. He wanted to play and realized that he wasn't better than Dad. So he transferred to Western Kentucky University. Another big difference Nassano noticed was that while football mattered, it was mostly a way for him to get a free education. For Dad, football was much more: it was a ticket to the NFL. One day, early in their freshman year, Nassano asked Dad about his future, what he wanted to do after college. Dad responded that he wanted to play a couple of years of pro ball. Nassano thought, *Geez, funny that he can talk like that, playing the same position, and he's telling me he was going to play pro ball.* As for Nassano, he was realistic; he wasn't planning on playing at the next level. He never had the ambition for it.

Lots of people talk about Dad's confidence, a quiet trait that didn't come across as conceited or arrogant, even when he had no visible or tangible reason to believe he'd get to show it.

✶✶✶✶

There are lots of different kinds of intelligence. Clearly, my dad knew his way around a locker room and football field. As for the classroom, he was less accomplished. To this day, I'm not sure if my father's academic results—or the seeming lack thereof—were the result of not having the ability in the classroom or his not caring. Both his high school and college academic efforts were perfunctory, at best. His childhood friends report that he got by in the classroom. They admitted they weren't much different. College was more of the same.

Interestingly, I own a three-ring binder from one of Dad's college classes. I don't know how it came to me or why there aren't more. It simply is a snapshot into Dad's college life that simultaneously says a lot and nothing about his relationship with education. He was a health education major. The notebook is from a class taken it seems in the spring of his sophomore year. It's pages and pages of notes, meticulously taken by my father, in handwriting that almost looks like art. Just like when he signed autographs (or how he dressed), Dad was insistent on doing it "right," something he drilled into his children's heads. It was a type of first impression that Dad meant to do right. It ranked up there with solid handshakes and looking a person in the eye when you first met them.

There are blue checks from his professor and occasional pithy comments scattered throughout. The quality of the work is not the type of effort given by a student who doesn't care. At one point, he wrote, "Drinking Will Prevent Thinking, Thinking Will Prevent Drinking." The sentence is underlined twice in perfectly straight lines, darker than his usual writing. Nothing else is noted so dramatically.

Dad's intelligence throughout his life would remain a source of discussion among family and friends. He was a mish-mash of contradictions. He instinctively understood relationships and could read the weakness in the placement of the defense between breaking the huddle and walking to get under center. On the other hand, he didn't read much. The only parts of the paper he read were the comics and sports sections.

Mom read the paper, front to back, every day. There was more than one occasion when Mom and Dad were at dinner or a cocktail party and Mom was discussing a current event. Someone in the group would ask Dad a question, and he would have no idea what was being talked about. Mom would interject a comment to cover for Dad. It was subtle. Mom had the right touch in handling Dad; she could cover for him without openly and obviously embarrassing him. One time, he brought it up the next day. My parents didn't argue in front of us much, and I wouldn't have classified this as an argument.

"You made me look stupid last night," Dad said to Mom in the family room, thinking none of the children were around.

"No, you made yourself look stupid," Mom retorted. "You were the one trying to answer a question you didn't know anything about. I was just trying to help you out. It has been in the paper, John, and if you read anything besides the sports section, you might have known."

****

On paper, looking at the team's record at Louisville and Dad's statistics, it would be real easy to say he didn't have a very good college career. Other than his freshman year when the team was 5–4, Louisville had a losing record. His career record was 12–22. He passed for just more than 3,100 yards and 27 touchdowns while completing less than 50 percent of his passes. His best year was his sophomore year when he completed 106-of-198 passes for 1,540 yards and 12 touchdowns. His second-best year was his freshman year, almost comparable except he didn't get significant playing time until the fourth game. Again, on paper, it looked like he got worse as his career progressed. So getting drafted in the ninth round, on paper, seemed pretty generous, maybe attributable to luck or because it was the Pittsburgh Steelers and somebody local put in a good word for him.

However, there were reasons for the decline. The main one was that in January of his freshman year, the new president at Louisville decided to de-emphasize football. Dad had led the team to 5–4 record, but winning wasn't enough. The president wasn't in favor of getting rid of the program, only reducing its financial strain. Some of Dad's games had about 1,000 people in the stands and getting 8,000 was huge. Instead of paying for all educational expenses, Louisville would now only pay tuition, no room and board or book expenses. These were expected to come from the community. Furthermore, the president tightened academic standards. Louisville now had two problems: very few quality players and not enough players to overcome injuries that naturally occur. Although the school was de-emphasizing the sport, its schedule, set a couple years earlier, was still competitive and organized as if Louisville was moving up the big-time ladder rather than down.

The second big issue that limited Dad was injuries. Just like at St. Justin's, besides being a star quarterback—and maybe star is too strong a word at this point in his career, at least he was considered the best player on the team—he sometimes played safety, punted, kicked off, and returned kickoffs. Injuries limited his senior season to the point that he didn't even pass for the most yards.

A few games encapsulated Dad's career at Louisville. The first was his freshman year against St. Bonaventure. The *Louisville Courier-Journal* reported before the game that Dad would be starting even though he'd played sparingly through the first three games. He didn't start, and he didn't enter the game until the start of the second half with Louisville trailing 6–0. He wound up throwing three touchdowns, the last putting the Cardinals ahead 21–19. At one point he completed 11 consecutive passes. Louisville thought it had won, but there was a controversy over the time on the clock, which gave the Bonnies enough time to kick a field goal to win 22–21.

Interesting, the *Louisville Times'* follow-up story focused on the controversy and only mentioned Dad once, well into the story. The quarterback for St. Bonaventure was Ted Marchibroda, who would circle Dad's life. He would be one of the three quarterbacks who would beat out Dad for a job in 1955 when Dad was drafted and tried out for the Steelers. Marchibroda later would be a Colts head coach, a couple years after Dad was traded to San Diego, and he would be the first head coach of the Baltimore Ravens in 1996, an organization Dad initially had conflicting feelings about. Nonetheless, Dad led his first comeback—almost—against a team that was quarterbacked by a talented future NFLer. It was still too early for anyone to know that about Dad.

Dad's very next game was against N.C. State, a team led by single-wing tailback Alex Webster. Webster would later play for the New York Giants against Dad in the 1958 Championship Game. Dad led the Cardinals to a 26–2 upset, played on a frigid early November day. This game and another later in the year against Houston revealed Dad's gambling mentality, his philosophy about calling running plays when the other team thought he was going to throw and throwing when they thought he was going to run. He led Louisville to a 35–28 upset, the second in a row, by passing for 240 yards and four touchdowns. One of those touchdowns, in a story that has been mythologized as having happened while playing semi-pro ball in Pittsburgh, involved a fourth-and-2 call. The Cardinals were on the Houston 40-yard line when Dad called a pass play. His running back said to him that he could get the two yards necessary. Dad responded, "You run the ball when I call your signal, and I'll call the plays." Maybe he did the same thing with the Bloomfield Rams, I don't know. But I do know he told more than one teammate with the Colts to shut up—probably not that nicely—in the huddle or when he thought he knew what play should be called.

There was a slaughter against Tennessee Dad's junior year—except he and Louisville got slaughtered. Though not as strong a team as in previous years, Tennessee defeated the Cardinals 59–6 in a game where Louisville finally scored in the fourth quarter on a 23-yard run by Dad. Statistically, the teams appeared to be relatively even, but it was a matter of superior athletes beating up on less superior athletes. Except for one person: Dad. The *Louisville Courier-Journal* wrote after the game, "He was the chief Cardinal on offense and was outstanding on defense. When he was hurt while running to the Tennessee 16-yard line in the final period, he came off the field with an ovation from the Tennessee stands."

The Knoxville, Tennessee, paper *The News-Sentinel* reported, "John Unitas, Louisville's lanky quarterback, stole the show. Hailed mainly as a passing star, the 6'1", 185-lb. Unitas was a terrific performer.... He not only directed the Cardinals' attack brilliantly, but passed expertly, punted well, ran like a halfback, kicked off, and tackled like a demon." It also reported a standing ovation when Dad left the field late in the fourth quarter. After the season the Tennessee coach called him the best quarterback the Vols had faced that year. Dad remembers the game for something else, and while my father never liked losing—probably hated it, in fact—he could live with it. Except for one thing: showing someone up. During the Tennessee game he felt that happened. While Dad called the Tennessee game his longest day in college, he also didn't like watching the Vols' coaches on the sidelines telling the first stringers to change out of their uniforms into street clothes and watch the second half while the reserves finished off Louisville.

Being the best player on the field wasn't the result of Dad having a career game against either St. Bonaventure or Tennessee. Even in college, long before Dad had solidified his spot as a master of the comeback and as a player who managed to pull out wins when many times games appeared to be unwinnable, people who were playing against him saw something special. Dad played against Andy Nelson of Memphis State, who later became a teammate with the Colts and an acquaintance with a reputation for playing the game hard and on the edge of being out of control. More than 50 years later, Nelson commented that the day when his Tigers played Dad's Cardinals, Dad was the best player on the field. Nelson wasn't surprised when Dad later went on to his stellar NFL career. Nelson saw what it took that Saturday, November 8, 1952, when Louisville lost to Memphis State on the road 29–25.

While on paper both Dad's academic and athletic time at Louisville seem suspect, it held an important spot in his heart. While he never spoke much to me about college, he did have a dorm named after him at Louisville in 1975. Furthermore, in the late 1980s when he decided to start a foundation to award high school football players some scholarship money and honor the best senior college quarterback in the country, he initially presented the award in Louisville. As with many things my father saw as important, he let his actions speak louder than—many times in lieu of—his voice. Dad didn't have to tell you how he felt most of the time; the way he behaved and the focus and time he put into a relationship or event or job did the talking for him. Clearly, he didn't see his time there as wasteful or negative. Instead, it was a time of some difficulty that prepared him for the future, both the uplifting moments like the 1958 Championship Game when he needed to be cool under fire, and the rocky moments, like the breaking up of his marriage to my mom. He didn't always handle the pivotal moments right, but he was willing to face them.

The biggest problem Louisville and Dad had during much of his final two years was lack of protection. He learned—or maybe it's intrinsic to his nature—to stand in the pocket as it broke down and hold his ground. Maybe the greatest quality his future Colts' teammates saw in him other than his leadership—his willingness to stand firm and tough—was already revealing itself. That characteristic is not an easy thing to judge in practice or when a game is going well, but Dad had it. It took others who made football decisions, not his opponents on the field, longer to realize it.

CHAPTER 5

Marrying Tough

November 25, 1956
Baltimore Colts 56, Los Angeles Rams 21

Dad's serious first NFL game experience was quickly forgotten. Just more than a month earlier, he had come into a game in the third quarter against the Chicago Bears on the road and threw his first pass of the game for an interception, setting up one of the great trivia questions of all time: to whom did Johnny Unitas throw his first touchdown pass? The answer is J.C. Caroline, a defensive back for the Bears, who intercepted that first pass and returned it 59 yards for a touchdown.

Now a month later, Dad was at home in a game that didn't mean a lot. The Colts came into the game 3–4 and the Rams 2–6. Both were playing for respectability. Memorial Stadium wasn't sold out, but there was a solid crowd of 40,321 fans.

Dad was a rookie, replacing the injured George Shaw, who was no slouch. The year before, Shaw had been drafted out of Oregon as the overall No. 1 choice. Not only was he an All-American in college football, but also in baseball. His senior year, he led the country in total offense. But Shaw blew out his knee in the third quarter of the Bears game and was lost for the season. He was drafted to lead the Colts to championships; Dad was brought in to be a back-up, or at least that was Ewbank's plan at the time. Like most other football "experts," Ewbank knew that Dad was talented and had a strong arm, but he didn't foresee the Hall of Fame career that really got off the ground in this start against the Rams.

The temperature was 41 degrees at game time. Earlier in the week, as late as Thursday, Baltimore had felt almost like early fall as the temperature pushed 70. This particular Sunday, however, winter was on her way. It was foggy with spits of rain and sleet.

Dad had his best day of the season against the Rams. He was 18-for-24, passing for 293 yards. Dad scored the second Colts touchdown on a one-yard run. Later in the first half, he would throw for three more touchdowns, the game a blow-out by halftime with the Colts leading 42–7. He threw two of the touchdown passes to Jim Mutscheller, who ended up gaining 112 receiving yards. Alan Ameche ran for 162 yards, and the Colts totaled 574 yards on offense. It was their best offensive showing of the season. It was such a blow-out that Gary Kerkorian replaced Dad in the fourth quarter and threw his only two passes of the season, one for the final touchdown of the game.

Kerkorian had been the starter for the Colts in 1954, leading them to a 3–9 season, only to be replaced by Shaw in 1955. When Dad arrived in 1956, Kerkorian was relegated to third string. Dad need not have worried about pushing Kerkorian out of his backup role: Kerkorian would quit football to go to law school and eventually become a California superior court judge.

Kerkorian would return to football in 1958, but at that point, Dad was firmly cemented as the starting quarterback of the Colts. The blow-out against the Rams showed flashes of what football fans later came to expect from Dad on most Sundays, helping to turn football from a smash-mouth, run-first offense to a passing game with precision patterns and timing as the primary offense. The only thing missing was a late drive to pull out a seemingly lost cause because, on this day, the Colts didn't need that. That would come a couple of years later—on national television—and my dad's legend as a football player would be cemented.

Marrying Tough

My father's life officially got more complicated in 1954. Most people who examine, write, and dissect my father's life tend to look at the 1958 "Greatest Game Ever" as the moment—the first big step—when he went from being

44

John Unitas, football player, to Johnny U, the legend and sports and cultural icon. And while that was important, 1954—late November to be exact—is when he married my mom, Dorothy Jean Hoelle. The NFL and football part of my dad's life was probably out of his control. He would need a great deal of luck to succeed as a player, like Weeb Ewbank sticking with him and seeing a special talent, but getting married and starting to live a grown-up life was a decision that Dad had control over. It was a life he chose. And it would be the pattern of contradictions in his life that would settle over him until he died in 2002—success in one area while failing in another.

My mother and father had been dating since high school. My father had gone off to college at Louisville, not spending much time back home. While my dad chose to marry my mom, circumstances beyond his control helped him make the decision. My mother wasn't sitting at home pining for her quarterback boyfriend. She may have been a cheerleader, a year younger than Dad and more outgoing, but she was no stereotypical 1950s stay-at-home, soon-to-be-married woman. She was working in downtown Pittsburgh. Just like Dad's mom, she had two jobs. Women didn't generally go off to college, at least not working-class women, and that was the kind of family Mom came from. They may have had more money than Dad's family, but they weren't much better off, even if they thought so.

Mom worked for the phone company, and her other job, the job she truly loved and was good at, was with John Robert Powers working in its cosmetics department. JRP was, and is, a modeling "school" that employed predominantly women, mainly as models. Mom wasn't a model, but she was good at the cosmetics aspect of modeling because she had a flair for glitz and style and fashion. JRP wanted to put her on a career path in management. They wanted her to go to New York City to a one-year training program. Naturally, her parents were worried. New York, particularly when compared to Pittsburgh, was the "big, bad wolf."

My father, probably understanding Mom better than her own parents, wasn't worried about her getting eaten alive there. He knew she wouldn't. Instead, he was worried that if she went to New York City, she would see that there was so much more out there. She might meet a man who was "better" than Dad. He both understood Mom's aggression and also his insecurities. Mom figured she would take the offer and live in New York while Dad finished at Louisville, and then they would both return to Pittsburgh. She figured they could then figure out their lives from there.

Instead, Dad called Mom's parents and begged them not to let her go. "Please don't let Dorothy take that job because if she goes to New York City, she will never marry me," Dad told her parents. They talked her out of the job, and Dad convinced her to get married, which they did on November 20, 1954, just after Dad's senior football season was over. They got married the Saturday before Thanksgiving and had the reception in Mom's parents' basement. A lot of Dad's friends didn't go to the wedding because they had to work that day.

The next day, they drove to Niagara Falls for a honeymoon, but it wasn't as long as planned as Mom stayed in the bathroom most of the time because she was scared. Finally, cutting the trip short, they came back to Pittsburgh, and Dad returned to Louisville.

****

My father faced complications and cemented the personality that would eventually become his legend in 1955. My sister, Janice, was born in Pittsburgh. She was premature by almost two months. Neither her delivery nor her first few months were easy. Dad missed most of it because he was still in Louisville finishing up his senior year.

Janice was born in May, and my mom almost died having her. Mom lived with her parents at the time, even though she was married. When she went into labor, my grandparents took her to the hospital. The doctors came to my grandparents and said, "It's either your daughter or the baby." My grandmother told the doctor to save her daughter because she didn't know the baby, and Mom could always get pregnant and have another child. Miraculously, Janice survived. She now claims that she looked like a tadpole, and maybe she did, but she blossomed into a beautiful and wonderful sister. Mom was bedridden for two months, and even though Janice had survived birth, her troubles still weren't over. She couldn't put on weight. She weighed 3-1/2 lbs. at birth. While in the hospital nursery, she wouldn't take food and lost almost a pound in two days.

My grandmother marched into that nursery, scooped up Janice, and walked out of the hospital with nurses chasing after her, saying, "Mrs. Hoelle, you can't take that baby."

"The hell I can't. She's my grandchild, and I'm going to take care of her."

My grandmother, grandfather, and Great Aunt Neina fed Janice around the clock, an ounce of formula every hour, regardless of whether she wanted or needed it. Aunt Neina created a formula that she could stomach. While Mom was bedridden and recovering, she didn't know what was going on. Everyone pretended everything was okay with Janice, so when she needed ointment on her raw and unformed skin, they said they were giving her a bath. Eventually, Mom got better and joined in the feedings. By the time Janice was six months old, the danger was past and she was a pudgy little thing.

Probably the most interesting aspect of this story is how stubborn my grandmother was and how take-charge she was in the face of a crisis, in a very public way. My father isn't the only member of the family who is a leader, and clearly I come by much of my stubbornness naturally.

****

As most everyone knows about my father, he was drafted in the ninth round of the 1955 draft by the Pittsburgh Steelers. Scouting in those days wasn't as sophisticated as it is now; Raymond Berry, who as a Colts wide receiver became famous as the receiving end of Unitas to Berry, was a 20th-round pick in 1954. Probably, in the case of my dad, there was no scouting other than talking with coaches on the phone, seeing statistics in the newspaper, and knowing my father from his days playing high school football in Pittsburgh. He was the fourth quarterback in Steelers preseason. He might have even been the third, but Vic Eaton, who would make the team as the third-string quarterback, was also the punter. Advantage: Eaton.

The back-up quarterback, a man who had and would continue to figure prominently in Dad's life was Ted Marchibroda. This was his second season with the Steelers, and he was also their first-round draft pick in 1953, the fifth pick overall. He knew the system, and even though he spent 1954 in the army, he had more experience than Dad. Finally, Marchibroda was considered a hometown boy, too. He was born in Franklin, about 80 miles north of Pittsburgh, close enough to be considered "native" and another example of the famed output of Western Pennsylvania football. Advantage: Marchibroda.

Finally, there was the incumbent starting quarterback, Jim Finks, a 1949 draft choice for the Steelers. Clearly, he had years of NFL experience. Advantage: Finks. It seems reasonable that Dad didn't make the team.

There was a bigger problem than getting cut. Even Dad knew he was a long shot. Dad always had a problem with the way he was treated by the Steelers. His complaint wasn't about whether or not he should have made the team; rather it had to do with not being given a chance, a realistic chance. He didn't appear in a single exhibition game against other teams. But there may have been more happening behind the scenes in Pittsburgh, some of which Dad picked up on. A couple of Dad's high school buddies have talked over the years about how he felt that some of his older teammates intentionally worked against him. They didn't block as hard, run pass patterns as crisply, and dropped very catchable passes. My father never mentioned this to me, but over the years some of his Colts teammates have talked about some of the shenanigans they would engage in to protect their jobs or a place on the team of a longtime teammate. Sometimes it wasn't about protecting their jobs as much as it was about misdirecting the other teams in the league. As Artie Donovan explained, "Most of the guys that played, like our defensive line, we knew how good we were. There wasn't a young guy [i.e., rookie] who was going to come in and take our place right away because they didn't know the system." What the veterans would do, instead, is report immediately to Ewbank how good a rookie was; the Colts would cut him immediately because if they waited until the end of training camp, other teams would figure if he made it that far, he's close to NFL ready. Cutting a player early meant team officials thought he wasn't very good. Nobody would pick him up and the Colts could hide him on the "band squad" or the taxi squad as it came to be called in Cleveland where Paul Brown, Ewbank's mentor, hid players by giving them jobs driving taxis.

Although my father made it to the end of the Steelers camp, no team picked him up. He hitchhiked back to Pittsburgh, saving the $10 bus fare because he had a pregnant wife and baby girl at home. But the real reason for not spending the money is because Mom loved Popsicles, and $10 could buy a lot of those. He was supposed to take the bus from St. Bonaventure, New York, where the Steelers had their preseason camp, 218 miles away. It was also where Marchibroda first went to college to play football before the school disbanded its program.

Surprisingly, the Steelers would finish 1955 at 4–8 and Finks would retire from the NFL. It was another losing season for the Steelers, one of many since joining the NFL in 1933 as they had made the playoffs only once. While the Colts would go on to win three championships and play in two other Championship Games during Dad's playing days, the Steelers wouldn't make the playoffs once during that time. As for the other players who beat him out, Marchibroda would play two more years before retiring as a player, and Eaton wouldn't play in the NFL again. Dad hadn't even started on his 18-year career yet.

****

When he arrived back home in Pittsburgh, Dad thought his dream of playing in the NFL was probably done. There had been a bit of interest from the Cleveland Browns as they pondered the possibility of life after Otto Graham. There was discussion he was going to retire, but the veteran returned for the 1955 season. Dad found a job on a construction crew being the "monkey man," which required him to climb sometimes as high as 125' on a pile driver to apply lube. He also played for the Bloomfield Rams, a semi-pro team owned and quarterbacked by a local guy named Chuck Rogers. They represented a neighborhood on the north side of the river in Pittsburgh, opposite where Dad grew up. They played on a field underneath the Bloomfield Bridge that had little grass and on which a coat of oil was sprayed to keep the dust down. There has been much discussion and mythologizing about how much my father got paid by the Rams—$3, $6, $12, or $15 (some players on the team did make $15, but not Dad until late in the season)—but according to both Rogers and Uncle Leonard, he got paid $3 per game along with all the beer he could drink at a local pizza joint. Dad's talent would lead Rogers to give up his role as starting quarterback, and Dad would lead the Rams to an undefeated season and the Greater Pittsburgh League championship. While the GPL wasn't the NFL, it was damn good football. Keep in mind that the NFL still wasn't paying great money, and Pittsburgh and surrounding areas were a hotbed for football talent. Dad now had a bigger reputation in the area, whatever that might be worth. He'd stayed sharp, playing good football under trying physical conditions.

Part of my dad didn't know what to do about not making the Steelers, and part of him was pragmatic. He was married now with a child and another—me—soon to follow. It's hard to follow dreams when there are mouths to feed. Uncle Leonard constantly reminded him that he didn't go to college simply to drive trucks or climb pile drivers (imagine doing that at 50, but then again, Dad played pro football and by 50, getting out of bed was a 10-minute production). Dad had approached Uncle Leonard about driving a truck for him, but he said no, that getting cut wasn't the end of the world, and that Max Carey, his high school coach, could probably help him for next season. Carey was Dad's contact with Cleveland, which obviously didn't work out.

Instead, Rogers became his contact with the Colts. But it was Mom who made Rogers' assistance stick. Rogers wrote a letter to Don Kellett, the general manager of the Colts, seeking a tryout for Dad and a defensive lineman, Jim Deglau of Turtle Creek (12 miles from Pittsburgh) and Wake Forest College, but the tryout was mainly for Deglau. Even with the letter and tryout, it took Mom's persistence to make things happen for Dad.

After the tryout, Kellett said he would call. Mom and Dad lived in a tiny apartment (they had finally moved out of Dad's in-laws' house) with baby Janice and Mom pregnant with me. When Kellett called, Dad wasn't home from work. Mom said that he'd be home later and to call back then. Dad came home from work, and Mom said, "Hey, Mr. Kellett called from the Baltimore Colts and he wants to talk to you."

Dad said, "I'm going bowling tonight. Tonight's my bowling night."

"But you have to stay home and get this call."

He said, "I don't think I'm going to pursue this any more. I've got a wife and baby, a second baby on the way, I can't be chasing these dreams when I've got mouths to feed." He knew where his responsibilities lay.

Mom said, "Oh, no, we're not doing this. If you think for one minute that you're going to use these kids and me as an excuse because you're too afraid to continue pursuing this dream, you've got another thought coming. You're going to talk to Mr. Kellett and you're going to go after this because I don't want to wake up 5, 10, 15 years from now and you looking at me saying, 'You got in the way of pursuing my dreams.'"

Dad being Dad, he went bowling anyway so Mom took the call from Kellett. "I'm sorry he couldn't be home, but he's very interested."

He said, "I'd like to send over a contract."

She said, "Okay, send it over." He sent it over, and she signed it with Dad's name and hers, and that's who signed that contract, the famous contract that went up for auction and sold for an undisclosed amount (but estimated between $20,000 and $30,000) in February 2007. I'm pretty sure Dad didn't even see that contract for years.

****

Three important events in my dad's life happened in 1956. First, getting a tryout and making the Colts. Second, George Shaw getting hurt and Dad replacing him for the rest of the season. Third, my birth on July 9, 1956. I like to think that my being born is the most important of those three (and maybe it is), but without the other two, I was still going to be born but probably wouldn't be writing this book, or if I were writing a book, not many people would have even a passing interest.

What is important about my coming into the world is, in many ways, I'm the last thing connecting my mother and father to Pittsburgh. Shortly after I was born, my mother loaded Janice and me in the car and made the drive to Baltimore. We would return occasionally, and there's no question that what my father later became—a great NFL quarterback—was established in Pittsburgh. But after 1956, my father became a Baltimorean. He didn't know this at the time and also didn't know it wouldn't take long for him to become a household name. All six of his remaining children would be born here. He would own and live in six houses. He would play 17 years for the Colts, and while he would finish his career with one last season in San Diego, he was a Colt through and through. Even more important was how he became the symbol for the people of Baltimore. He would do business in Baltimore during his playing days and long after them. He would eventually die here and be buried in Baltimore County.

****

Colts' training camp was held that year at Western Maryland College in Westminster, 37 miles from downtown Baltimore and 209 miles from Pittsburgh. Dad was the third-string quarterback in camp, and he was given opportunities in team scrimmages and exhibition games. The first preseason game was in Hershey, Pennsylvania, against the Eagles. Dad got to play, and so did Raymond Berry. It would be because of this game that the legendary 12-year relationship between two future Hall of Famers developed. At one point in the game, Raymond, now in his second year and worried that he wasn't going to make the team, dropped an easy pass. He thought he was going to be cut the next day. He wasn't.

Raymond's response and the only remedy he knew: work harder and longer. Little did Raymond or Dad know at the time, but they had each bumped into someone else who valued the same two things: hard work and faith. They started the routine of staying after practice for an hour or so, sometimes until it got too dark to see, working on pass routes and timing. George Shaw couldn't do this because his arm couldn't take it, but Dad could throw all day long. One day, Ewbank casually said to Raymond, "Keep working with Unitas." Ewbank saw in them talent, ability, and potential. He also saw hard work and toughness. By the end of training camp, both Raymond and my father were in different places than they were at the end of the previous season. While Raymond caught 13 passes in 1955 in 12 games and Dad didn't even play in the NFL, both knew how tenuous their places were on an NFL team. But as the Colts broke camp in Westminster and prepared for their opener against the Chicago Bears, Raymond was the starting left end and Dad was the back-up quarterback, having passed Gary Kerkorian.

****

As with most things in life, luck played a part in my dad's career. He was lucky to have found Raymond who was willing to work after practice as hard as Dad was. He was lucky to have bumped into Weeb Ewbank who was willing to wait and see how Dad developed (Ewbank did this with lots of players), and he was lucky that once he made the team, starter George Shaw got hurt.

Everyone needs luck sometimes. It's what you do with that luck that defines a career. Dad jumped on that luck, but it also required something else: perseverance, a trait he had shown already. He had competed through injury, bad teams, and getting cut. In hindsight, it's easy to figure out what made my father a success, but at the time he was barely past being a kid (although he'd never really had the opportunity to be a kid growing up). He had responsibilities far beyond football. He had a wife who loved and supported him.

In hindsight, I can only wonder why others didn't see earlier what most football fans came to see eventually: my dad's greatness. He made the team and appeared in every game early in the 1956 season leading up to the

Chicago Bears game when George Shaw got hurt. It has been reported that Dad's first official pass in the NFL was completed to Caroline, the Bears' cornerback who returned it for a touchdown. It was Dad's first completed pass, but he had thrown incomplete passes earlier in the season in limited duty. It seems to be a more interesting story if that was Dad's first pass, but it wasn't. Sometimes—and with Dad, a lot more often than not—reality gets in the way of a good story.

Dad struggled early in the Bears game. When he entered in the third quarter, the Colts were only losing 27–21, and Caroline's return made the score 34–21. Not long after the interception, Dad fumbled a handoff, which led to a Bears field goal and the score was 37–21. Although the Bears lost their first game of the season to the Colts in Baltimore, they were in the midst of a seven-game win streak. The game got so out of hand that George Blanda, the Bears kicker and back-up quarterback, played most of the fourth quarter, throwing three touchdown passes. Blanda is another western Pennsylvanian, having been born and raised in Youngwood, 37 miles from Pittsburgh.

Ewbank had no choice but to send Dad out the next week. The Colts were 1–3, and he needed to find out what Dad could do. Privately, Dad wasn't sure he had what it took. The next week the Colts played the Packers in Baltimore. Dad's mom, Grandma Helen, stepdad, Howard Gibbs, and older brother, Uncle Leonard, came down from Pittsburgh to see his first NFL start. Early Saturday, October 27, the day before the game, Dad and Uncle Leonard went for a walk. Dad admitted to being nervous, and who wouldn't be. His myth probably doesn't allow for this, but it's true. Uncle Leonard told him not to be afraid of anything. "You're going to be the boss in there," Uncle Leonard said, "Don't let anybody tell you otherwise. You be the king in there. Anybody says anything, tell them to be quiet. You're running the show. You're the one who's going to get the blame, and naturally, being the quarterback, if things go well, you'll get the credit."

It was an ugly passing game against Green Bay, but the Colts won. These were not the Packers who became a nemesis for Dad and the Colts. They would end the season 4–8 (in 1957 they went 3–9 and in 1958 1–10–1, which would lead to a new coach in 1959, Vince Lombardi). Dad only threw for 128 yards but Lenny Moore had 185 yards rushing, and the team rushed for 318 yards total. If Dad's life were truly a Hollywood story, he would have led the Colts down the field late in the game for the winning touchdown. While the Colts scored late to win, it was on a 79-yard run by Moore. But now Dad had his first start and NFL win under his belt.

Many of his teammates were already pretty sure what they had in this free-agent rookie quarterback. Raymond has said that although Dad started poorly against the Bears, he still went about his business, ending with a pretty respectable day against a team that would eventually win the Western division and play in the NFL Championship Game. What Raymond saw that day in Dad was a certain mental toughness and confidence that couldn't have been determined in drills or scrimmages.

Jim Mutscheller recognized Dad's mental toughness. After the bad game and loss to the Bears, the Colts were riding the bus to the airport. Mutscheller was sitting in a seat behind Dad and Walter Taylor, the Colts' beat writer for the *Baltimore Sun*. They were talking about the game, and Dad was explaining to Taylor what he did wrong and what he needed to do to improve. The tone was matter of fact. There was no sense of fear. As Mutscheller pointed out, the entire team had a bad day. "Geez," Mutscheller said, "we don't have a lot of confidence because we weren't a really good team, and we hadn't developed a lot of attitude or cockiness or whatever you want to call it. And he's just sitting there as confident as could be. That's when I first became impressed with John, with his mental attitude."

Typical of Dad. He wasn't going to say much. He wasn't going to toot his own horn. He would answer questions matter of factly. As he would do with much of his career and life, Dad would quickly put the past behind him, looking forward, but not too far forward, simply to the next game against Green Bay where he would get his first NFL win as a starting quarterback.

But not even Dad could deliver a Hollywood ending right away. There would be no championship that year. The Colts finished 5–7 although Dad's record as a starter was 4–4, including the game against the Rams, his best day to date in the NFL. It would also include a big win in Cleveland the week after the Packers game in which Dad went 5-for-14 for a total of 21 yards. He was now 2–0. That streak ended the next week when the Detroit Lions blasted the Colts 27–3. His teammates were also noticing that Dad didn't need to play well for the team to win. He had more than a great arm and statistics. There was something intrinsic that his coaches and teammates saw. It wasn't worth analyzing because he was young—who knew that he would turn into the greatest quarterback of all time?

Even with a losing record, not all was negative. At the Colts' final game that year against the Redskins, Dad was named the Colts' Rookie of the Year, finishing ahead of Lenny Moore. No longer was it just Dad, Mom, Uncle Leonard, and a few childhood friends from Pittsburgh who recognized that Dad was the real deal. He was a legitimate NFL quarterback; the *Sun* reported that he was maybe the greatest investment in team history, costing three cents, the amount of the stamp for the mailed contract.

Also announced on the same date was the NFL Player of the Year—the New York Giants' Frank Gifford, a man the Colts would hear more from in the future. And he would hear a lot more from the Colts, particularly Dad.

CHAPTER 6

Picked Off the Sandlots

August 28, 1955
Los Angeles Rams 23, New York Giants 17

It was a preseason game—meaningless in many ways—being played in Portland, Oregon, a typical exhibition game to get the starters in shape and spread the NFL game to cities that didn't have a pro team. The Colts, for example, usually played a game in Hershey, Pennsylvania, during Dad's career. They also played a game in Louisville, for obvious reasons. Artie Donovan's last game played as a Colt was a preseason game in Roanoke, Virginia, after which he asked Alex Sandusky to pull off his jersey, a ritual they generally followed after every game because, as Donovan said to him, "It's the last time you'll pull it off." After Sandusky had done it, Donovan cried.

But this game between the Rams and Giants is remembered not for playing a preseason game in an unusual place. Instead, it will be remembered for its unusual ending. For the first time in NFL history, a game was decided by "sudden death" overtime. As part of a promotion to sell tickets, Harry Glickman, now considered the father of pro sports in Portland and one of the original owners of the NBA Trail Blazers, got the NFL to agree to allow overtime if the game ended in a tie—not because it was a new rule, but because it was a preseason game. It was about the last thing he expected.

More than 22,000 people attended the game, which featured three future Hall of Famers: Tom Landry, Frank Gifford, and Norm van Brocklin, a graduate of the University of Oregon. Van Brocklin led the Rams to victory in overtime. Paul "Tank" Younger scored on a short run a little more than three minutes into sudden death. News of the overtime was reported the next day in the *Oregonian*, the largest daily paper in Portland. "The Rams, the winner of the original toss at the start of the game, were lucky enough to call the fall of the coin again, and, quite naturally, received." Few liked the way overtime was set up.

But it had been in the rules since 1941, when the overtime rules for playoff and Championship Games were implemented and a manual of the NFL rules was published for the first time. There are lots of misconceptions about overtime, particularly in the 1958 Championship Game. But even today, it's often reported that the overtime rules were first published in 1974. That's not true. In 1974, the overtime rules were changed from the original 1941 rules. The big change is that overtime was added to both preseason (even though the Rams and Giants played it in this 1955 game, but that was with permission from the NFL) and regular season games, but allowing for only one overtime period. Ties would then still be possible in the preseason and regular season but not playoffs or Super Bowls. The rules have been changed since then, the most recent was in March 2012 and included different rules for regular season games and playoff games.

Even in overtime, the Rams scored with most of their starters playing. Unlike today's preseason games in which starters either don't play at all or play sparingly, and you'll almost never see them in the fourth quarter much less an overtime period, Van Brocklin and Younger were on the field during the extra period. Both of them would go on to make the Pro Bowl that year.

Picked Off the Sandlots

My father was born and raised in Pittsburgh, and while I was also born in Pittsburgh, I don't remember my time there. It became a place where I occasionally visited relatives, but other than that, I have as much in common with Pittsburgh as I do with New York, which means not much. Both cities are rivals, just like Washington and Philadelphia to some degree. But Pittsburgh is a sports rivalry, one that has really developed in the last 15 years since the Ravens have come to town. New York, on the other hand, is a city we simply don't like on any level.

We Baltimoreans—insultingly called "Baltimorons" by outsiders—don't like the way the larger cities to the north and the nation's capital to the south look down on us. Visitors to the city in the 1950s and '60s didn't see the Inner Harbor or Camden Yards or M&T Stadium; instead, they drove through downtown past the Block, renowned for its burlesque shows and Blaze Starr, and the harbor full of unloading ships. On the site where two fancy hotels stand today was the McCormick Spice Company. If the weather wasn't too hot, downtown smelled of cinnamon. If it was too hot, it smelled of rotting fish and raw sewage. Outsiders saw us as less sophisticated, or not sophisticated at all. While all of the Northeast was an ethnic melting pot, Baltimore was home to lots of Eastern Europeans. Industrial, yes. Working class, absolutely. Both of those we could live with, but it was descriptions such as dirty, poor, and crime-ridden that got our goat. It was also the fun poked at our twangy Southern, Eastern European accents. We were late to the major league sports scene: the Orioles arrived in 1954 from St. Louis, not a reincarnation as the Cardinals but as the Browns, historically one of the worst, if not *the* worst, team in Major League Baseball history. The '54 Orioles lost 100 games and didn't have their first winning season until 1960 when they were developing the baseball equivalent of Dad in Brooks Robinson.

The Colts arrived not once but twice. They came out of the All-America Conference in 1950, already feeling a bit inferior, and survived one year. They reappeared a year later after the Dallas Texans failed, and again the city felt like it was on the receiving end of leftovers. The Colts in their reincarnation had losing records the first three years, and it wasn't until 1957 that they managed a winning record.

Baltimore was—and still is—a major city with a chip on its shoulder. In the early '50s, it was hungry for recognition and to be able to stand up with—if not as an equal at least close to it—New York, Boston, and Washington. It was looking for winning teams and heroes to thumb their noses at the snobbish outsiders. The city didn't know it yet, but in Dad it was on its way to finding that hero.

****

The Colts opened their exhibition season every year with a Blue-White scrimmage at Memorial Stadium, ostensibly to raise money for charity. Scouts from the Philadelphia Eagles called it nothing more than "a glorified scrimmage," but attendance was more than 40,000 fans. The year before, Dad had entered the game probably needing to have a good game in order to make the team. He did. In 1957, Dad's spot on the team was secure.

There's a saying in golf that you can't win a major until you lose one. That's often true in any sport. Football teams—and the Colts were no exception—needed time to gel, opportunities to find that final missing piece, and game experience to know the difference between winning a close one and losing it. The Colts learned that valuable lesson in 1957. The team finished the year 7–5, and it was a season of streaks. They won their first three games, lost their next three, won their next four, and lost their last two. If they had won their last two, they would have won the Western Division. Losing the final games is an example of the team not yet understanding how to close out the season, not yet believing in itself the way playoff-bound teams must. They had the highest point differential in the league, second only to the Cleveland Browns, winners of the Eastern Division. On paper, Baltimore was very good. It's easy now to look back at that season and say, "Hey, if only the Colts had won their second to last game against the 49ers, they would have been in a playoff with Detroit for the division title."

I don't think I ever heard my father say, "That's a big *if*," but it's the kind of thing he would've said. They didn't win their last two, and regardless of Donovan saying that the Colts should have won four consecutive NFL championships beginning in 1957 and ending in 1960, they didn't. The game that probably made the difference was the Lions game in Detroit on October 20. In blowing a huge lead, the team learned a great lesson about how to come back.

The Colts raced out to a 21–7 halftime lead, mainly behind Dad's passing in the second period. He threw only three passes but completed all three for 145 yards. He also drove the Colts down the field at the beginning of the second half on their opening drive, throwing his final touchdown of the game to Lenny Moore. Alan Ameche had a number of good runs. After scoring this third-quarter touchdown, the Colts missed the extra point, but at 27–3, what was the worry?

The worry should have been holding onto the ball, as the Colts lost three fumbles in the last 20 minutes of the game, and all three turnovers led to Lions points. Furthermore, Cotton Davidson—drafted as a possible quarterback but beaten out by Dad—punted horribly, averaging a mere 35 yards.

Ultimately, it doesn't matter what happened or who was responsible. It would be easy to say Dad wasn't responsible as he was 16-for-21 for more than 200 yards and four touchdowns. Although I never heard Dad talk about this particular game, I did hear him mention that football is a team game: you win as a team and lose as one. Three days after the loss, the *Baltimore Sun* ran a column labeling the loss "jolting" and comparing the disintegration in the fourth quarter as the equivalent of Sputnik suddenly falling from outer space. This was said almost tongue in cheek, but later in the same column, C.M. Gibbs theorized it had more to do with complacency.

The team learned that a game isn't over until it's over, and this would be important the next season. As Weeb Ewbank said after the game, "Make one mistake in pro football and you're dead."

****

The Colts always finished their season—when the league was 12 teams—with their two final games on the West Coast, playing first the 49ers and then the Rams. They stayed out there for more than a week, often arriving at the hotel in Los Angeles at the same time the previous team would be packing up to leave. This tradition started with the Colts' rebirth year, 1953, and continued through 1961 when the NFL expanded to 14 teams. Some years they played the Rams and/or the 49ers in Baltimore the two weeks before the trip to California.

As one would expect, it was a tough trip. The Colts arrived in San Francisco needing a victory but losing late in the game, again. This time, it was 49ers rookie John Brodie coming off the bench late in the fourth quarter and throwing the winning pass in the final minute. Dad had another good game, completing 23-of-37 passes for 296 yards. It was the 10th time the Colts had traveled to San Francisco, and it was their tenth loss. So close, but not quite, as close only counts in horseshoes, one of Dad's favorite expressions. (I later learned that he was routinely the Colts' training camp horseshoe champion.)

The loss set up a three-way tie for the division lead, basically forcing the Colts to win in Los Angeles. If they did win, and so did Detroit and San Francisco, the Colts would get the bye to determine who would play Cleveland. But that didn't happen; instead, they were blown out, ending a productive season but ultimately disappointing one. The team had taken an important step—a winning season—but there was still room to grow, and everyone knew it.

Dad had emerged as the starter, having such a good year that he was named to the Pro Bowl. He led the league in touchdown passes. The lack of a great quarterback in Baltimore was over. I'm sure Dad wasn't happy with just missing out on the playoffs, but the team was certainly moving in the right direction. After all, at the beginning of the season the so-called experts had the Colts projected for last place in the Western Division.

****

Heading into 1958, the team needed to take that next step and make the playoffs, the first time ever in Baltimore's brief NFL history, but an important milestone nonetheless. As we all know, the team didn't simply make the playoffs, they upset the New York Giants in the "Greatest Game Ever Played" to win its first championship. But as Artie Donovan claims, there are two problems with the 1958 Championship Game against the Giants. First, the Colts were the far better team and should have won the game easily. Second, that as "great" games go, it wasn't a well-played game and that the game earlier in the year against the San Francisco 49ers, where the Colts came from behind and scored four touchdowns in the second half to win 35–27, was a far better contest.

I'm not here to argue with Artie. He has his reasons for his opinions, but I will say that the 1958 Championship Game is the game that truly began the legend of "Johnny U." It wasn't started by a particular person or by a conscious decision; instead, it was the beginning of a long run that cemented the fact that my father is the greatest quarterback of all time. But there was also the making of Dad's legend with his teammates, which was probably more important because it allowed for Dad to be the leader he was in that Championship Game, starting with the "two-minute drill" even though it would be years before that term was officially coined or stats kept for comeback wins.

The Colts got out to a blistering start that season, winning their first six games. They were good and they knew it. The team squandered the opportunities of the 1957 season, but lessons had been learned. The team also reflected its leader, Dad, and quietly went about its business. Their first loss came in the seventh game against the Giants, a game that was played without Dad. He'd gotten hurt, much worse than was reported in the papers at the time, in their previous game against the Green Bay Packers, a 56–0 blowout. Except it almost wasn't. If a team wins 56–0 and then loses its starting quarterback for what looks like might be the rest of the season, it's no longer a blowout. Dad had a punctured lung and broken ribs, injuries bad enough that he had to be taken from the game in the second quarter at Memorial Stadium to Union Memorial Hospital, about a half mile away. It looked bad and it was bad, but in the long run, it wasn't as bad as it could have been. Dad missed the Giants game and the following game against the Bears.

Interestingly, in the Giants game, it took a fourth-quarter field goal to beat the Unitas-less Colts 24–21. And then the defense pitched a shutout against the Bears in a 17–0 win with George Shaw again taking over for Dad.

Dad returned for the team's final four games, which they split 2–2, but the Colts ended up losing their final two games—the infamous two-game road swing through California—although those results didn't matter as Baltimore had already locked up a Championship Game berth by coming from behind to defeat the 49ers at home 34–27 in the game both Dad and Artie called "the greatest game ever."

Locking up this berth required a victory that many of the Colts I've talked with still remember vividly. The Colts were down 27–7 at halftime. As one player said, "We were bad on offense and probably worse on defense." It became two games in one: the bad first half and the second half, probably the best football the Colts played during their run between 1957 and 1960.

At halftime, Ewbank came into the locker room and didn't explode. He wasn't that kind of coach. He said little, which is one of the reasons he and Dad got along. He kept it simple, which according to Lenny Moore was just what the team needed: "Alright. We know what we have to do. I'm not going to say anything. We know what we have to do, and you guys have to get out there and do it. Other than that, it's all over. Just get yourselves together because we know what we have to do. And fellas, we can pull this out. We can do this." Everybody sat quietly until later, just before the end of halftime, splitting into offense and defensive groups to talk. It was probably the second-best speech the coach ever gave. The best would come later in the season.

Coming back against the 49ers wasn't easy. At the time, San Francisco's offense was centered around what was called the "Million Dollar Backfield" and included three future Hall of Famers: Y.A. Tittle, Joe Perry, and Hugh McIlhenny. But the Colts did come back, with Dad throwing for 229 yards and the Colts' final touchdown to none other than Raymond Berry. Lenny and Jim Mutscheller still talk about how that game gave the team much-needed confidence, the kind of intangible confidence that great teams have, as it moved forward. As Lenny said, the defense figured out a way to stop that 49ers backfield and gave the ball to Dad who went to work. Lenny is being modest here because he had a 73-yard touchdown run to put the Colts ahead for good. As Mutscheller stated, "Usually, when you're down that much in a pro football game, you don't come back, at least not at that time. Nowadays, they seem to do that sort of thing." The Colts did come back, and they did it against a very good team. That could only do one thing: inspire confidence.

****

During the regular season, the Colts led the league in scoring and points differential while having the second stingiest defense. It was a team that did everything well except for the kicking game. They led the league in takeaways. Dad, Raymond, and Lenny all were named first-team All-Pro along with Gino Marchetti. Naturally, Dad went to the Pro Bowl.

The Colts had a magical year, and winning the championship only added glitz to an already wonderful season. It settled the argument about which team was the best in the league. The Giants had ended their season 9–3 and won a play-in game against the Cleveland Browns 10–0. New York also had the best defense in the league.

Before the Championship Game, Ewbank gave what was probably his greatest speech. It was in the same place that Knute Rockne told his 1928 Notre Dame Fighting Irish to go and "win one for the Gipper" over Army. But Ewbank went in a different direction. He developed the theme around how most of the members of the 1958 Colts had been rejected by other clubs and now it was time to gain a measure of self-respect, to show those responsible for giving up on them that yes, they most emphatically could play in the NFL. Of the 35 men on the roster, 14 had been released outright or put in deals almost as afterthoughts. Dad had been released and signed as a free agent. Big Daddy Lipscomb had been claimed off the waiver list from the Rams for $100. Ewbank went around that locker room, stopping before each player and making a comment. To Carl Taseff, a cornerback and roommate of Don Shula's in college, he said, "Cleveland didn't want you. If there are any more like you, well, I'll take them."

To Dad he said, "Pittsburgh didn't want you, but we picked you off the sandlots."

****

The facts of the game are all out there. I was three years old when the game was played. I don't remember the game, and I wasn't there. Whatever I know about the game is from the facts that anyone can know. The game itself, for most of it, wasn't "the greatest game ever;" as a matter of fact, it was a sloppy affair that neither team seemed to want to win. The Colts jumped out to a 14–3 lead and had a chance to make it 21–3, the reason Artie believes the game shouldn't have been that close. However, the Colts were stopped inside the Giants' 10-yard line from taking that commanding lead. Instead, the Giants came back to take a 17–14 lead, setting up the final two-minute drive that required an extraordinary situation to keep the Colts' hopes alive.

There is the play. "The Play." And I'm not talking about Jim Mutscheller's almost touchdown—instead he slipped on an icy patch on the field—that would have won the game in overtime (where a lot of people wonder why Weeb Ewbank didn't kick a field goal) or Alan Ameche's game-winning touchdown run. (My dad had his thoughts on this issue that I will get to.)

Late in the fourth quarter, the Colts were down 17–14 and facing a first-and-10 from their own 31. Dad called time out. He then called two plays, like he always did in late-game situations, bringing his team back from the brink of defeat. The first play he calls is 76ZL, a square in. When Raymond came to the line to run the 76ZL split out from the offensive linemen, he noticed that Harland Svare, the Giants' outsider linebacker, had positioned himself right on top of him. As Raymond said in his Texas drawl, his country vernacular toying with the depth of his knowledge of the game, "You ain't goin' to run a 10-yard square in with a 250-lb. linebacker wrapped around my neck.

"It's at that point that the days and days and hours and hours of preparation—I studied the Giants' defense for two weeks—was put to the test." The longer Raymond talks about this moment, the thinner his accent becomes. "I saw in the films where the Giants did this one time: walked that back out on top of the split end. I went to John before we left for New York and talked to him and explained, 'If we have a square in when the backer's out, it won't work.' So we agreed to convert the square into a linebacker slant. We had plan A and plan B. Then we discussed it and forgot about it. We didn't talk about it anymore."

Lo and behold, at a pivotal moment in the game, what Dad and Raymond had practiced and discussed two weeks earlier came up. They hadn't talked about when this would happen, only if it happened. Raymond realized that the play called is plan A, but the situation now calls for plan B. He sees it, but does Dad? "Svare walks out. I look at John, and I'm not sure he looks at me. Does he remember what we agreed on?" All Raymond could do was hope, so he ran the linebacker slant, and clearly Dad remembered because he hit him on the slant, which Raymond caught six yards off the line and ran 18 yards more to get the ball to midfield. Suddenly, the game had shifted.

The Play has been mentioned many times by many people in many books, but most people—Mark Bowden in *The Greatest Game Ever Played*, for example—mentioned it because of its nature of changing the tenor of this particular game: the Giants had the Colts with their backs to the wall. Victory seemed imminent for the Giants. It's also been mentioned because if Dad and Raymond hadn't practiced the possibility of changing the play at the line of scrimmage—which did happen—about three weeks earlier, who knows how the game would've ended.

The Play worked, obviously, and as they say, the rest is history.

As I've learned from watching Dad and hearing stories from his teammates, history, as in this one play, is never simple or about luck. But there's more to this story. And if it's really history, it also tends to be far more complicated than people later want it to be. This pass play is no different.

According to Raymond, this play changed his pro football life. "That particular drive was the most important in my entire pro career. The conversation of the square in to the slant was the most important play in my career. It opened the door to the next two completions. We wouldn't have gotten the championship, anything, without that completion. And it's because we planned for that eventuality."

Whether that's true for my father or not, we'll never know, but this became an example of how my father thought and reacted under pressure. No one at the time made a big deal of the play. Neither the New York nor the Baltimore press made much of it as anything more than a play that altered the game, and neither said anything about how it altered Dad's and Raymond's careers.

Much has been made about some oddities of the overtime, that neither team nor the officials knew what to do initially. Overtime, and the rules concerning it, were on the books and a preseason game had already used it. Yes, the players didn't know the ins and outs of the overtime rules, just like today, most fans—and even players—don't know the intricacies of determining ties for playoff spots. The idea that the players were shocked to know that they had more action ahead of them is a myth. As Dad said, "We just never thought it would happen, or what it would mean." He acknowledged that players had talked about the possibility but only in the abstract. Also, because Gino Marchetti had broken his ankle late in the game, Dad was the Colts' representative for the overtime coin flip. He called tails and lost.

Also, the game was interrupted by a "fan" running on the field, although he was actually a hired gun of NBC who was sent to delay the game while the TV crew figured out why the game wasn't being broadcast. Ultimately, what was important about the game for the development of pro football was that it was on national TV. Finally there was a huge viewing audience for professional football, and with an incredibly tight game this was not the time to lose the telecast. NBC needed a few moments and had an underling run on the field.

****

But there's still more. Later in overtime on the game-winning drive, there was a pass to Raymond that, according to him, he was the third option. On an important third-down play, Dad threw to Raymond for a 15-yard gain. "I was the third-choice receiver on the play," Raymond told me. "First Lenny, then Jim [Mutscheller]. I was doing what we called a 'come open late' pattern. He came to me on that, and I can tell you, in 12 years of playing together, it was the only time that happened with that play. Just like the change [earlier in the fourth quarter] to the linebacker slant play."

****

There's no question the 1958 Championship Game was a great contest and was made bigger by the fact it was nationally televised and went to overtime. Pro football was at that tipping point, ready to move up in status from an ugly stepchild when matched up against college football and from the runt of the litter when compared to Major League Baseball, to becoming their equals and eventually surpassing them. It needed myths and legends. The game itself became one of those legends, but the "Greatest Game Ever Played" wasn't known by that name immediately. Mark Bowden, a fellow Baltimorean and Calvert Hall graduate (he graduated in 1969 while I graduated in 1974), credits Tex Maule of *Sports Illustrated* with giving the game its mythological moniker. Maule, in his article about the game published on January 5, 1959, never uses the term. He describes the game to the point of hyperbole—"But for the 60,000 and more fans who packed Yankee Stadium last Sunday for the third week in a row, the moment they will never forget— the moment with which they will eternally bore their grandchildren..." He never uses the term "greatest game ever." The closest he comes to that is the last line of the article, when he quotes a player about what the game means, who says, "It's the greatest thing that ever happened."

Hollywood would have my father saying that, but it wasn't my father. The facts don't always work out the way we want. Instead, Raymond Berry, who was the MVP of the game, catching 12 passes for 178 yards, said that.

But it wasn't just myth-making and television and football outsiders and what they wanted to see. The viewers, whether on TV or in the stands, know the facts about what Dad did in that game, the decisions he made at the line of scrimmage or while standing in the pocket in a less-than-full Yankee Stadium (sorry Tex Maule, but there probably weren't 60,000 people there that day). As dusk turned to night and thick darkness, as stadium lights of the 1958 shined not as bright as we are used to today, the myth and legend began. While games labeled as "the greatest ever" have their moments, what they really need is a person to become the symbol for that game. In the case of the 1958 championship, it was my father who had the right personality to match the quality of play on the field. Dad became the myth of the "Everyman," becoming the greatest quarterback of all time. But it's not simply luck or god-given talent, although they both play into it, that make the Everyman the great man. Sometimes, a person such as Dad needs an opportunity and a stage, a door that appears locked to open a crack, and my father not only pushed that door open, but he jumped through it and slammed it behind him. The John Unitas who'd grown up quiet and under-noticed was now on his way to becoming a household name.

As a result most people saw Dad in a new way, having been introduced to him at the pinnacle of the sport as the quarterback of an NFL championship team in a game played in the media capital of the world on national television in the first regular season or Championship Game ever to go into overtime. It hadn't been easy for him to get there, nor would it be easy as he moved forward. Here was my dad making the big play under immense pressure as if he'd been doing this his entire life. In a lot of ways he had, but very few people had noticed until that game.

CHAPTER 7

No Longer a Secret

Sunday, October 30, 1960
Baltimore Colts 45, Dallas Cowboys 7

As someone who came of age and really started following pro football in the late 1960s and early '70s, it's hard to imagine that the Cowboys were a new franchise in 1960 and didn't win a game. By 1966, the Cowboys would be a winning team, recording 20 consecutive years with a winning record until 1985, still the longest streak of that nature in NFL history. They also set an NFL record for most consecutive sellouts at 160. Not just home games in a row, but all games in a row, and the 160 games features 79 consecutive sellouts on the road. It's not for nothing that they came to be known—and still are—as America's Team. But the Cowboys weren't always good and they weren't always America's Team.

In late October 1960, the Colts came into the Cotton Bowl struggling a bit, 3–2 overall, having lost to the Packers and Lions on the road. The day was 65 degrees, and the Cowboys were simply terrible. Dad wasn't. He was fabulous in this game, throwing four touchdowns in the first half, three of them to Raymond and all three longer than 50 yards.

But what was most interesting about the 1960 Cowboys beyond what most people already know—it was Tom Landry's first season, for example, and a rough one to be sure—is that a little known Cowboy, Dave Sherer, was their punter. He not only had a good second year as a punter, but in this particular game, he punted five times for a 45.4 yard average. He did his part to help his team. Clearly, it was the defensive backs who couldn't stop Dad and Raymond, as Sherer would put the Colts deep in their territory, and then Dad would just as quickly hit Raymond for a big gain and touchdown. But what is even more interesting about Dave Sherer is that as a rookie he played and punted for the 1959 Colts and averaged almost 42 yards per punt.

Too often, in discussions of games, seasons, and careers from this time period, the focus is on the superstar, my dad, Lenny Moore, or Raymond, for example. In 1959, all three would be named first-team All-Pro and Dad would win the MVP. In 1960, all three would again make the Pro Bowl with Lenny and Raymond earning All-Pro honors. The 1958 Championship Game featured 12 players and three coaches who would eventually make the Hall of Fame, including Vince Lombardi and Tom Landry. Clearly, they deserved their recognition, but success was also due to players like Sherer, the mostly unknowns who make up the majority of a team even in the days when teams only carried 33 players. Eight rookies played on the Colts in 1958 and only four in 1959. Even with all the Hall of Famers on these two teams, there were lots of teammates who weren't going to become household names. Without them and their small—and sometimes large but generally unnoticed—contributions, the Colts don't win two championships.

Although he was a second-round draft choice, Sherer wasn't well known, not even in Baltimore. He lived a few blocks from Memorial Stadium and stumbled upon a room for rent from a police commander who charged him $9 a week. For Thanksgiving that year, he almost spent it alone in Baltimore until Jim Mutscheller invited him to join his family. He was a young man fresh out of SMU having a good time.

But Sherer went from playing on the best football team in the world in 1959 to playing for the worst in 1960. Adding insult, he would play his old team at home and lose badly. What's ironic about the situation is that Sherer asked for it. While he enjoyed playing on the 1959 Colts, he was engaged and lonely in Baltimore. After the 1959 championship season, he heard about Dallas getting a franchise. He approached Ewbank and explained how he was from the Dallas area and about to get married. He was open to the Colts exposing him in the expansion draft, which they did. He was taken by the Cowboys.

When Sherer explained his situation to Ewbank, Weeb was sympathetic, but it's easy to forget that the Colts almost lost the 1958 Championship Game because of poor field goal kicking. As Weeb developed his squad, he mixed young with experienced, offense with defense, stable players with characters, speed and athleticism with good hands and reliability. The one area where the Colts weren't great was the kicking game, particularly punting. Sherer in 1959 had been a godsend, improving the average distance of the team's punting by about seven yards per kick. As Sherer said, "It was different back then. In those days they tried to accommodate you." Just as Dad found what he was looking for after he was cut, so did Sherer, spending that one year in Dallas before retiring from football and settling into real estate in the area.

Nonetheless, Ewbank looked at Sherer and said, "You know, I've spent five years finding a punter, and finally I've found one, and you want to go home." That's all anyone was looking for in the NFL: a home. Sherer found his by leaving the Colts, and Dad found his by coming to them. It worked out for both.

No Longer a Secret

If the hardest thing to do in team sports is repeat, then I find it crazy that there hasn't been a lot of discussion about the Colts' 1959 season and championship. It's arguable, at least from the perception of the viewing public, that the Colts snuck their way to the championship in 1958, and yes, they benefited greatly by the overtime win and the fact it was on television. The incredible win and unusual circumstances allow people to forget that no one, except the Colts themselves, thought they were championship caliber. But there's no way they snuck into a championship the next year. As a matter of fact, they almost didn't make it and had to win out over their last two games during the regular season to quality for the playoffs. They may have just made it in terms of winning enough games and when they won them, but they weren't fooling anybody about how talented they were. And they were talented. And Dad was running the offensive show in his own quiet way.

The win in 1959 was on home turf, the first world championship at home for Baltimore since the late 1890s when the original Baltimore Orioles won championships in the National League. Two things about the Orioles' championships: they didn't have to defeat the winner of another league, and it wasn't long after winning those championships that the team folded in 1899. Those late 1800s wins somehow seemed tainted. Not so in 1959.

My father was firmly established as the quarterback. The Colts were his team, but it was a team that was filled, as the 1958 team, with lots of experienced veterans. He wasn't doing it alone nor did he have to do it by himself. They had the right mix of youth, experience, talent, and a championship under their belts. The 1958 Championship Game opened America's eyes to the Colts and Dad, but it would be the 1959 season that would cement them into place. Obviously, no one knew this heading into the season.

It wasn't going to be easy to repeat because in some ways the Colts were experiencing a hometown hangover after their win on December 28, 1958. The celebration went from wild to mob and almost tragic (although it didn't) very quickly. After winning the game, Dad was invited to appear on *The Ed Sullivan Show* in New York, but he turned it down so he could be with his teammates. He was offered $700 by Frank Scott simply to stand up and acknowledge Sullivan when introduced. Dad was even on his way to the CBS studio when he changed his mind and headed for LaGuardia.

Think about that. Dad had a chance to go on one of the most popular TV shows of his day, a show that would have thrust him even further into the public consciousness, and he didn't. Today, victorious athletes generally either make the rounds of the morning talk shows—the *Today Show, Good Morning America, CBS This Morning*—and the late night talk shows, or they get asked where they're going after their important victory and say, "Disney World." While Dad wasn't perfect, here's a great example of choosing his team and loyalty over money and fame. While the choices in his life weren't always between loyalty and money and/or fame, they were often between his friends and their feelings and what was best for them, and what was best for him personally.

This time, instead of the money he would have received from appearing on television, he got a riot at Friendship Airport (now called BWI). Thirty thousand fans turned out to welcome the team home from New York. The number would have probably been much higher except for the 20,000 fans who went to the game, mostly by train, and were still returning home. The team was informed as they were preparing for arrival that the airport was overwhelmed with fans and that they might have to land in Washington. They didn't, but it was out of control. Joe Croghan, a local sportscaster, was trying to report from a specially constructed stand, but too much was going on around him for him to be effective. Fans had climbed on top of a police cruiser, and the weight collapsed the roof until the car looked like a crushed tomato can.

Plans were quickly changed. They weren't going to the terminal; instead, the team would be taken directly to Memorial Stadium. Because most south-bound roads leading into the airport were clogged with fans still trying to get to the airport, the team headed south instead of north, an end-run around the congestion. What no one knew as the bus worked its way through the crowd was that six or seven teenage boys had climbed on top of the bus, clinging to the top by their fingertips as the bus eventually made it through the crowd and on to the highway going 50 mph. The police escort saw this, and pulled over the bus at a church. They pulled the kids off the roof like plucking apples from a tree. Dad was asked to get off the bus and talk with them, which he did. They were put in the back of the cruisers, mostly for their own safety, and Dad found them to be "regular fellows." Then again, he found most people to be that.

The city was joyous, the desperation for a championship gone. The festive atmosphere wasn't just at the airport; the neighborhoods were the same way. Dad said the city had the feel of Mardi Gras or the end of World War II when people were running and screaming in the streets, no particular plan to their wanderings, no particular meaning from their screams. It mattered to Dad and his teammates. They lived in the city; they were a part of it. As he once said to me, "We felt we made a contribution. Not so much by winning, although that was important, but honest to God, by making so many people happy."

Finally, there's the money. While the Championship Game came with bragging rights, civic pride, and honors, it also included a check for $4,718.77. The Giants got $3,111.33 each. What did Dad do with his money? It became the down payment on a new house in Campus Hills, a section of Baltimore County not too far from Towson where other players also lived. Mom and Dad were pushing their roots deeper into the community.

New York may have won—and continues to today—many championships, but after 50 years, Baltimore reveled in the victory, not for days, but months. Some people still talk about that 1958 December Sunday as if it were just last month. A first love dies hard. In the days following the game there were civic banquets and receptions in their honor. There was no parade. Dad and Mom went to New York to accept an automobile for being named Most Valuable Player in the game as voted by the editors of *Sport* magazine. The ceremony was led by *Sport*'s editor-in-chief, Ed Fitzgerald, who less than 10 years later would co-author a biography of Dad, a book in which I don't even think Dad was interviewed. It was more myth-making than reporting, but that's what fans wanted in their heroes. It's still what we think we want today.

****

The second championship has been treated like a second child: you still love him or her, but for the casual fan, the ecstasy has worn off a bit. Raymond Berry has said that the 1959 season gets short shrift. He's constantly asked about the "best game ever played," rarely about the 1959 game. "I don't think that anyone's ever asked me about the '59 season. It gets no press, and that's the way it's been for a long time." Raymond chuckled a deep-throated, Texas infused laugh. "That's why I'm laughing. I guess the 1959 season gets over-shadowed by the 1958 season that nobody ever pays attention to it." He has a hard time describing the season. He can only do it in general terms, and it's not like Raymond to forget important or interesting facts.

****

Great teams aren't built in a season, and truly great teams—and Dad's Colts of the late 1950s has to be seen one of the NFL's great teams—won two championships because they were built for the long haul. In retrospect, maybe the question to ask about the late 1950s Colts is why they aren't in the discussion about great teams of all time? They were the last championship team before expansion, the last championship team before the league went from 10 teams from 1945 to 1949, 13 in 1950, and 12 from 1951 to 1959, all of which was happening against the backdrop of the upstart AFL raiding the NFL of talent.

Maybe the best example of Ewbank's talents can be seen in an example that didn't work. Even as it wasn't working out, Weeb knew that it would, but for another team. Fuzzy Thurston played as a backup on the 1958 Colts championship team, only appearing in four games that year. Before the 1959 season, he was traded to the Green Bay Packers, even though Weeb knew he was trading away talent. One day during preseason, Ewbank gathered the team.

He said, "Well, fellas, you can see that empty chair there. That was Fuzzy's. I had to send him on to Green Bay. I know a lot of you don't like it, but I can't wait on him. We've got to get down to our limit, and I've got to go with the guys we have now. Alex Sandusky and Art Spinney are our two guards, and I've got to go with them. Fuzzy's not quite there; he was coming on, but he's not quite there. And I don't have the time.

"It is a question of either or—do we keep him, or do we send him and give him an opportunity to go somewhere else, and that's what I did. I didn't like it even when I did it, but my, my, my, I can't wait on him because we've got to get down to our final numbers and we've got to have the guys in there who belong in there doing it for Unitas."

Even as Weeb was trading away Thurston, who he knew would go on to a fine career, Ewbank has to be credited for seeing something in my dad that neither Notre Dame nor the Steelers saw. If a coach or general manager does this with simply my dad and Thurston, it's fair to see it as luck. But Ewbank did it with many others, beginning with Raymond Berry who was slow. While Raymond might be the first to tell you that he was lucky to have Dad for his quarterback, Weeb is the one who decided to keep him in 1955 as a rookie before Dad was even on the Colts. Raymond played in all 12 games that season and was fifth on the team with 13 receptions and no touchdowns. Not the statistics of a future superstar and Hall of Famer. Maybe it was his relationship with my father—it worked both ways as you will see—that allowed Raymond to achieve greatness, but there's no question that Ewbank gave him the opportunity when others didn't see potential. Raymond didn't even think he would make the 1956 team, the same year Dad was a rookie. Dad was brought in as a backup and had no say as to who should make the team—as he would have in later years. Furthermore, Dad was as much on the cusp of making or not making the team as Raymond.

The entire offensive line was comprised of guys who either hadn't made it for other teams or guys who switched to positions Ewbank believed would be a better fit. Buzz Nutter was picked up from the Redskins. Alex Sandusky was moved; the most natural of the offensive linemen was Jim Parker, and he was a great one. Ewbank, having learned his managerial style under Paul Brown, was logistical and organized. Many of his players say he ran the best practices they ever experienced. He was a players' coach, not meaning that he let them get away with whatever they wanted to do. Instead, he listened to them; he asked the veterans about practice and what needed to be worked on. He never asked them if practice was hard, because it was. It was both hard and hot, but that wasn't going to change. Ewbank made sure that what they sweated over on the practice field under the hot July and August Maryland sky was exactly what needed to be worked on.

Once the games started, Ewbank's relationship with the players changed. He wasn't a good game manager, but he didn't have to be because he had Dad. Whenever I ask one of Dad's teammates about Dad's relationship with Ewbank, they almost always tell a story that involves a big play in a big game. It doesn't matter which game. Ewbank sent in a player, and Dad asked the newly arrived player, "What he say? What play does he want run?"

The player quickly responded, "He said, 'Get a first down' or 'Score a touchdown.'"

It's become a joke among the offensive players that Ewbank relinquished control of play to Dad, and it's the great coach who knows enough to let talent be in charge. Dad would jog over to the sidelines late in games, the score close, his gait slow and measured as if he had little energy left, as if the importance of the moment, underscored by the intensity of the crowd, was happening somewhere where Dad wasn't; in contrast, Weeb would be pacing and ranting. His rants were meant to call specific plays. Some of the Colts refused to listen to Ewbank once the game started, that's how out of control he seemed.

By the start of 1959 the Colts knew what they had and had learned to work around weaknesses and toward strengths. Not everyone liked Ewbank, but they played hard for him. He had managed to create a sense of distance that let the players feel like they were in control without sacrificing discipline and hard work.

****

On the field and around the NFL, 1959 signaled change. Obviously, the champion didn't change as the Colts repeated, but transition was in the air. It was the 40th NFL season, but only the first season for Vince Lombardi, who inherited a 1–10–1 team and led the Green Bay Packers to a 7–5 record. In doing so, he was voted Coach of the Year. Like Dad, Lombardi seemed old school in that he stressed discipline and execution rather than trickery and new-fangled ideas, clearly both Dad and Lombardi got their message across in a world and culture that was shifting.

Bert Bell, the commissioner of the league, died on October 11 while watching a game at Franklin Field in Philadelphia between the Eagles and Steelers. My father had a great deal of respect for Bell, something that can't be said about his permanent successor, Pete Rozelle. Maybe, as it pertains to my father, the most important link to Bell is his bringing on Carroll Rosenbloom as owner of the Colts during their second appearance in Baltimore in 1953. Bell had been Rosenbloom's freshman football coach at Penn. He convinced Rosenbloom that buying the Colts was a good investment. And it was.

Personally, I had my own connections with Rosenbloom and his family. In the mid-1960s, I worked with Bell's son, Steve, who was an administrative assistant with the Colts, during training camp.

The 1959 team had only four rookies on it: Jerry Richardson (current owner of the Carolina Panthers), Hal Lewis, a little used back from the University of Houston, Alex Hawkins (who would later become a dear friend to my dad), and Dave Sherer, the team's punter. It was a veteran team, but Ewbank and the front office were always looking to improve.

The biggest weakness in the 1958 team was the kicking game, both punting and field goal kicking. What sticks out most for Sherer, other than winning the championship, was how Dad handled meeting him as a rookie. Sherer wasn't returning from an off-season of reveling in not only winning a championship but also in beating hatred New York to do it, as most of his teammates were. Instead, he was late for training camp because he was playing in the College All-Star Game in Chicago. It pitted the defending world champions against a collection of college All-Stars and almost always drew a sellout crowd to Soldier Field. As was the tradition well into the '60s, preseason games, All-Star Games, the Consolation Bowl between the playoff losers for third place, and the Pro Bowl were taken seriously. The Colts easily won the game in a laugher, 29–0. This year-after-year game wasn't always a blowout. Up to that point the college All-Stars had won about a third of the time, and the last college win would come in 1963 when the college team upset a Vince Lombardi–led Packers team. According to news accounts at the time, Dad didn't play well but still threw three touchdown passes and completed 15-of-25 passes.

The blowout was so out of control that the sportswriters didn't know who to pick for the collegians' Most Valuable Player. One writer suggested the head referee because "he gained more yards than anyone else." Another suggested, more seriously, Sherer as he did have a fine game punting. In the end neither won, but Sherer did meet Dad briefly at a banquet. About a month later, Sherer would officially meet Dad when he arrived at Westminster. Even then, Dad and he didn't have much contact. It wasn't until after making the team that Sherer had a conversation. Dad initiated it. He approached Sherer: "Look, I wanted to be your friend earlier, but with so many people coming in and out of training camp, I hate to get close to anybody." Sherer appreciated the gesture. He had already seen how much command and respect Dad got on the field; it was the simple gesture off the field that gave him an idea of the man Dad was. He knew Dad was a great football player; now he saw that Dad was also a good person.

****

For Dad and the Colts, it was obviously a good year. When you win a championship, it overrides everything. However, unlike the year before, the Colts weren't going to fool anybody. There were no picks by the sportswriters to finish last in the division or even second to last. The Colts were a favorite and rightly so. After seven games, however, the Colts were only 4–3 with five remaining games against Western Division foes. That third loss happened on November 8 as the Colts dropped their game to Washington—a terrible team that finished the season at 3–9. The Redskins kicked a late field goal to break a 24–24 tie. If the low point the year before—and it's hard to have a low point when you've never made the playoffs and you've got a winning record—was when Dad had his ribs broken against the Packers, then this loss was the Colts' new low.

Players in any sport and from any era will tell you that there are basically two kinds of good seasons: the magical ones where nothing goes wrong and the ones that struggle along until a moment when everything turns to the positive. None of the players seem to know why 1959 was a struggle. Some players talk about how confident the team was, and that a confident team finds ways to win. In many ways, that sums up Dad: a confident man who usually found ways to win. But confidence alone won't do it.

There was a team meeting, players only, after the Washington loss and while there was no screaming and yelling or finger pointing, there was a collective sense that the team had to produce and now, or else there would be no defending its title. There were three leaders on the team at this point:

Dad, Gino Marchetti, and Art Donovan. In many ways, the team was Marchetti's; he did most of the talking at the meeting for two reasons: he had seniority, and he knew how to talk. Dad didn't like to speak much. He preferred to let his performance speak for him. Donovan finally ended the meeting.

Produce they did, winning their final five games, first defeating a much-improved Packers team 28–24 on the road in Milwaukee. Dad threw three touchdowns and passed for more than 300 yards. The Colts took a 7–3 lead in the first quarter, and Green Bay spent the rest of the game playing catch-up. Every time the Packers cut the lead to three or four points, Dad would lead a touchdown drive.

The remaining four games were all against the two West Coast teams, San Francisco and Los Angeles. The first two were at home, and the final two were the infamous West Coast swing where the team stayed out there for more than 10 days. All four games were blowouts. The Rams struggled that year, but San Francisco didn't. Whatever was said in that players-only meeting had worked. The Colts had their rematch with the Giants in Memorial Stadium, the team brimming with confidence and the results to back it up.

Before the game was played, Dad received good news as he was named AP Player of the Year for leading the Colts to the championship again and for throwing 32 touchdown passes, a record for a 12-game season. It was his first major seasonal award. He was also awarded the inaugural Bert Bell Memorial Award for the best player in the NFL. He easily outdistanced Jim Brown who placed just ahead of Charlie Conerly of the Giants. By the end of the year, Dad had also lengthened his consecutive-games-throwing-a-touchdown total to 37 games. The streak would end the next year at 47 games, a record recently broken by Drew Brees of the New Orleans Saints in an era where passing is the offensive name of the NFL game.

In winning the award, Dad established himself as one of the best, if not the best, quarterback in the league, and he provided fodder for future fans to debate the greatest seasons by a quarterback ever. He threw for just under 3,000 yards, which by today's standards doesn't sound like much. His more than 2,800 yards in 1959 was the second highest total for a season, behind only Sammy Baugh's 2,938 yards in 1947. In 1960 Dad would throw for more than 3,000 yards, the only time any quarterback threw for more than 3,000 yards in a 12-game season. This was also before blocking rules for linemen were liberalized, and defensive backs were limited in their physicality with receivers, opening up the passing games. Furthermore, the Colts were the top offensive team in the league, scoring 374 points, an average of more than 30 points per game. No other team scored more than 290. In other words, Dad had one of the greatest quarterbacking seasons ever.

But what made the season even better was winning the championship. Dad's teammates universally state that he didn't care about stats; he only cared about winning. He didn't care how he won, who he threw to, or who got credit, just as long as the team won. Heading into the Championship Game, the Giants clearly were looking for revenge. Frank Gifford, their star halfback and future *Monday Night Football* announcer, argued that the Colts were "old." That didn't go over well, and while some members of the team were creeping toward the older side, the offensive position players weren't, particularly the big three: Dad, Raymond Berry, and Lenny Moore.

****

The game was close, just like the year before, until the fourth quarter. The Colts led 7–6 at halftime on a pass from Dad to Lenny. Both teams—newspapers reported it as coaching blunders—chose to go for first downs within easy field goal range and failed. The game turned on three interceptions in the fourth quarter, the Colts scoring 24 unanswered points to make the game a rout at 31–9. The Giants added a touchdown late once the game was clearly out of reach. The Colts had just won back-to-back championships—it was only the fifth time in NFL history since the Championship Game was instituted in 1933 that had been accomplished.

On paper, the game reads like a typical game, up and down the field, coaching miscalculations, defensive plays and offensive plays, one team—in this case, the Colts—getting unexpected and inspired play from a relative unknown, Johnny Sample, who intercepted two passes and returned one for a touchdown. And in that sense, it was a typical Championship Game, not as close as the year before, but exciting and unpredictable.

The game was so much more for the city of Baltimore. It was a coming-out party. The year before, the Colts had surprised almost everyone but themselves, and even most Baltimoreans. This year, the city was ready. While the game was televised, the NFL Championship Game was not the Super Bowl we know today. I don't remember the game at all. I was a little over three years old. I didn't go to the game.

But lots of people I've since met did. They talk about the noise. Not the noise of the PA system playing rock and country music; not the noise of an electronic scoreboard urging the fans to clap or highlighting a thermometer that registered how loud the crowd was. There was no tailgating. It was a different fan experience, maybe more passionate because the fans were part of the experience. There wasn't external stimulation; the only stimulation was the game itself and fans feeding off each other. Six cheerleaders were on each sideline, holding up large cutout letters that spelled "Colts."

Mike Gibbons, executive director of the Babe Ruth Museum and Sports Legends Museum in Baltimore, was at the game and remembered, "Johnny Unitas was clearly the ringmaster of the whole thing. He stirred all that. He made it go. When he took the field, when he was introduced, you'd never heard a sound like that, ever, EVER. And you never will again. You think Ray Lewis' intro is loud, and it is, but it's nothing like that." That noise lasted the entire game, Baltimoreans first urging their team, not long in the city, to victory and then celebrating their first local championship. No need to go to the airport. No need for Dad to lecture some young boys who were clinging for dear life to the roof of a team bus. As the *Baltimore Sun* explained, the crowd in 1959 was joyous just like it had been filing out of Yankee Stadium a year earlier, but not nearly as drained. Because the win hadn't been as tense, Baltimoreans had more emotional energy to celebrate all over the city, chanting and spelling out the Colts' letters late into the night.

For the people of Baltimore, a bond was formed. At the Sports Legends Museum, the exhibit on the Colts is called "Almost Religion." To many people, those 1950s and early '60s Colts were not simply something to root for and follow; instead, the teams were almost mystical. Today, the NFL seems almost like a religion, but the connection between teams and fans isn't as close as it was in 1959. Whatever the Colts were to the fans, Dad was at the center of it, maybe the ringmaster as Gibbons called him or maybe the magician who never thought the Colts were out of a game. Dad represented the heart of a bond between a team and the people of a city—seemingly strangers, but only seemingly.

CHAPTER 8

Central Casting and Reality

November 13, 1960
Baltimore Colts 24, Chicago Bears 20

In the last minute of the Colts' eighth game of the season, Dad threw a touchdown pass to lead Baltimore to another come-from-behind victory. The win kept the Colts in first place at 6–2, and as an AP article stated, "all but knocked the Bears from playoff contention." Depending on which newspaper you read, Dad either threw the winning touchdown with 42 seconds left, or according to Cameron Snyder, the Colts beat writer for the *Baltimore Sun*, Dad threw the pass with 17 seconds left. It doesn't really matter except that either way, Dad, with much help from Lenny Moore who caught the pass and his offensive line, led his team to another stunning victory.

As seems to be the story with Dad's career, foils and friends are constantly popping up in his career. In this game, it was J.C. Caroline, the Bears' defensive back who intercepted Dad's pass back in October 1956 to become the answer to the trivia question, "Who caught John Unitas' first regular season pass?" It doesn't matter that it was to the opposition or that it was returned for a touchdown. Since then, Dad had won two world championships and now had the Colts in first place in the Western Conference, a half-game up on the Vince Lombardi–led Green Bay Packers.

The statistical facts of the game aren't very important; the teams were even in terms of total offense. No box score or summary of the stats could show how brutal the game was. Late in the fourth quarter Dad was tackled twice, once while in a pile-up and the second time by a rushing Bill George that resulted in a cut on his nose and blood dripping from his face mask. Snyder, who had covered Dad since his beginnings with the Colts, wrote, "Never in his career with the Colts has John taken such a physical beating and never has he been more glorious. Skeptics have said John can't be rated with the all-time greats because his tenure has been too short. But even his severest critic must take a bow to his courage, poise, and deadly accuracy as a passer."

Snyder wrote this the day after the game, and two things jumped out. First, even in writing a news story about the results of the game (not a column or opinion piece), Snyder referred to my dad as John after his initial reporting of him as John Unitas. Every other Colts player is either called by first and last name or last name only. Second, Dad had been in the league only four and a half years (he had won two championships) but there was already a discussion about where he belonged in the pantheon of quarterbacking greats.

There was no love lost between the Colts and Bears. George Halas had a tough reputation—in 1960 he was the longest-standing coach in the league, the owner of the team, and a direct connection to the founding of the NFL. It can be argued that he was the founder of the NFL, having coached every year since its inception. When the NFL merged with the AFL, the trophy for winning the newly named NFC was called the Halas Trophy.

Halas represented the past: brawn and strength. Dad represented the future: intuitive play-calling and precision pass routes. The Bears that day out-rushed the Colts, and the Colts out-passed the Bears.

After connecting with Lenny to win the game, Dad showed emotion and celebrated. Many of his teammates have told me that they couldn't tell by looking at Dad after a game whether he'd won or lost. But because of the brutal nature of the game and the long-standing bad blood between the teams—or maybe Dad was simply happy to win a game on the road basically on the last play of the game—he celebrated. "The usually stoic Unitas, who must have Indian blood to take such a beating as he received today, jumped in the air and flashed his arms around a couple of times when Moore reached lovingly up and pulled in his pass seven yards deep in the right side of the end zone."

The celebration was short-lived and premature. Dad and the Colts may have won that day, but the cost was too much, as they wouldn't win for the rest of the year. Dad wasn't the only one who got hurt. The cost of the win throughout the Colts' lineup was enormous.

The Hollywood fantasy was coming to an end. Dad's seemingly charmed NFL life—five years now—since late 1957 was going to be more realistic and typical: full of injuries and the Colts having to redefine themselves as they moved forward. This game had taken its toll on an aging Colts team. Dad was in his prime, but others weren't. And because Dad was willing to stand in the pocket and take a hit, he was also willing to plug away at everything he did. Pain and injury wouldn't stop him. It might slow him down, but he was tough, not different from his teammates and opponents. He was simply the face of pro football now, his every move watched.

CENTRAL CASTING AND REALITY

When I was a teenager, like all teenagers, I didn't think Dad knew much; furthermore, I didn't care that Dad was a famous quarterback. I also didn't think my mom knew much, either, and other than being married to Dad, she wasn't famous, didn't want to be famous, and wasn't working on becoming famous. Now that I have two adult children, I realize that not only do parents know a lot, but that life gets harder as you get older. Children complicate marriages. Fame complicates relationships. Age complicates. Nowhere does this become more obvious than in sports, particularly football.

The dream my father appeared to be living—the classic rags to riches story—couldn't stay on the tracks forever: that only happens in movies. In many ways, by 1960, it seemed that Mom and Dad had been picked from central casting. While I often look at my father and think that he looks rugged, I don't necessarily think handsome, but he was the perfect person to fill a need with Baltimoreans and Americans more broadly. While we idolize grace and good looks—Cary Grant, Joe DiMaggio, and John F. Kennedy all come to mind—we also want an everyday coolness under fire, a ruggedness and toughness of face and body, and someone who has over-come the fates and elements to be someone better, someone who has risen from where he started. In other words, we want someone who was born without being blessed.

Dad answered that need. The United States was changing. By 1960 the last 15 years had been basically peaceful and prosperous. Underneath the peace and upward mobility were the rumblings of change. People needed strength and stability; they needed a sense that the old way wasn't dead; they needed to know what they'd loved and counted on for the past 15 years wasn't gone. Flash and style were nice, but many people still needed simple substance. While Dad was simple, he was no simpleton. Although he appeared to be starring in his own fantasy dream film, the film turned in a different direction in 1960. It was only football—no one died—but the old days were over. To the average fan, Dad was unwavering, the silent but strong type, and a man interested in two things: his team and wins. He didn't care how those things happened as long as they did, and if they didn't, he knew that the sun would come up the next day.

★★★★

Off the field, the Unitas family was now six people strong. While Mom was put on this earth to be a mother and parent, Dad not so much. Maybe he wasn't as involved a father as we would have liked—particularly now that we were old enough to understand that he wasn't around all that much—because of his job, his fame, or his lack of a model from his childhood of how to be a father. It wasn't that Dad wasn't physically around; rather it seemed that he was emotionally distant. He often drove us to school in the morning, even during the season, dropping off me and my sister, Janice, at our parochial elementary school, Immaculate Conception, in Towson, not too far from our house. In hindsight, Dad wanted us to have the same Catholic schooling that he did. Later on, my brothers attended the same school, and my sister and I went to Catholic high schools.

People don't ask me what my father was like because they tend to have formed their own opinion either based on the way he conducted himself on the field or from having met him personally. The number of people who've met my dad, particularly in Baltimore, is astounding. When I'm introduced to a stranger, often that person says, "I knew your father. I met him once." Strangers figure they "knew" him, meaning I think "understood" my father when, even now, I'm not sure I understand who he was and what he was about. They wanted a man who met their personal needs and expectations, that his outward actions and appearance were in line with his private life. I only wish that were true.

The early '60s were a time when Janice and I, in particular, were coming to understand my father as a person as best we could. To us, he wasn't a football player. We knew he threw a ball and generally spent Tuesday nights in his "study" watching game film, sometimes one of us sitting on his lap as he watched a play, hit rewind with the toggle switch he kept in his left hand, and watched it again. And again. And again. What he was hoping to gain, we didn't know. What we did know is that we were spending time with Dad.

In many ways he was of a different era: men made the money, worked hard, came home to a home-cooked meal, and spent their time outside of work and the home with other men. My father wasn't much for going to bars and drinking. If, after practice, Colts went out, Dad would join them for a beer or two before heading home. He wasn't the late-night partying type like Alex Hawkins or Jimmy Orr, even though he was friends with both. Instead, after dinner, always cooked by my mother—who could flat out cook—he retired to the living room to his chair with an ottoman and the newspaper. He always had a mug of coffee with plenty of sugar, so much sugar that it didn't taste like coffee. He also added milk, giving it an amber color. The mug was on a table between his chair and another chair where my mother, Dorothy, sat.

Instead of spending time literally with other men, he spent it with them through the sports section. As he would read, my brothers—Bobby and Christopher—and I would roughhouse under his feet. Usually, we were playing knee football, tackling each other. Sometimes we were wearing his shoulder pads and helmet, looking comical in equipment way too big. Just as he stood in the pocket as Doug Atkins of the Bears or Deacon Jones of the Rams was about to level him with a hit, he sat stoically reading, snapping the page of the newspaper over to the next page. He would glance over and encourage us to "tackle him hard" or "get him around the head." Bobby, if he didn't get his way with a call, would quit. Whenever he did, Dad would chuckle, but occasionally he would shake his head, disappointed. If not reading the paper, he was watching the news on television, again, noise about him, Dad and Mom seemingly enjoying their kids.

And just like the pocket and pass protection collapsing around him, and just after he released the ball, the hit was coming. When it got too much, like it once did with Jim Parker who claimed he couldn't block the man opposite him, Dad said, "Then go over to the sideline and we'll find somebody who can." Or the time Dad got leveled by an unblocked defensive line with a bone-rattling hit, and as he returned to the huddle, probably trying to clear the cobwebs, he asked the sinning blocker if he wanted to play quarterback and for Dad to block for him. The lineman understood: get the job done.

In the case with us children, we the pass rushers would hit him once too often and knew we'd riled him. That meant one thing: a spanking. Understand, I feared my father, not in an abusive way. He was the disciplinarian, the parent who wasn't around a lot so my mother used his absence as a way to get us to behave. "Do you want me to tell your father about this when he gets home?" Mom would ask, the tone clearly arguing that we didn't, so then we'd better stop misbehaving.

But as much as I feared my dad, I feared his hairbrush more. It was metal, silver, and shiny. It was solid and hard and when it hit me, it stung, a lot. This was the same hairbrush that he ran through his famous, iconic flattop, not doing much to alter his appearance. Today, I think about Dad and that hairbrush and chuckle. He didn't have much hair to brush. It was only after he retired that he grew his hair out and long, so that it fell flat against his scalp. In his twenties, it was always a crew cut. Too much roughhousing or not minding Mom meant the Brush. Up to his room and kneel next to the bed. He swung that brush hard and it hurt, and as he did it, he said, "It's meant to." And as he hit me, I didn't cry, even though I had a reputation as a crybaby sometimes. But around my dad, I had to be tough.

I wanted to be tough. I wanted to be like him. At least at the time I thought I did.

****

By 1960, the Colts were getting older, at least some of their mainstays, particularly on defense. Artie and Gino Marchetti had been in the league for about 10 years, plus both were older than the typical veteran because they'd fought in World War II, including Artie at the Battle of the Bulge. While the 1958 season was almost undone by Dad's broken rib, the 1960 season was done in by injuries. Between 1960 and 1965, the Colts aged and suffered major injuries to important components of the team. Further, it often takes players until they've retired to realize just how much luck is involved in winning a championship. Even if you believe you manufacture your own luck, lots of things are outside the players' and coaches' control. Look at the shape of a football; sometimes the ball literally bounces the wrong way when you don't want it to. Even if Artie argues that they should have won another championship in 1960, they didn't.

Injuries have always been part of football. And they always will be. During Teddy Roosevelt's presidency, there was pressure to either reform football or outlaw it because of the fatalities incurred. In 1905 18 college players died and another 159 were seriously injured. The reality is that Roosevelt never threatened to outlaw football for two reasons. First, he couldn't, and second, he was a big fan of the game and two of his sons played at the college level. He did ask college presidents to look into making the game safer. Today, with concussions at the forefront of the NFL, the league is constantly tinkering, trying to make the game safer without losing its essence, but I think they're making it worse, leading to more injuries. Maybe that's the problem: as long as players stay on the field when they shouldn't—which Dad did on many, many occasions—it will be impossible to clean up that aspect.

Furthermore, not all injuries are reported and not all of them are serious enough to miss time. Dad had lots of injuries during his career, ranging from broken ribs and punctured lungs to torn Achilles heels to torn knee ligaments to damage to his throwing elbow. Those kinds of injuries meant missing games. He also had the "usual" bumps and bruises, things like contusions, dislocated fingers, and broken noses. These were painful and were what he would call an "inconvenience," but they didn't mean he would miss a game.

In 1956, Dad's first year, he was injured near the end of the season, but he didn't miss any games. I don't know why because it was pretty serious but he had just gotten his chance to play because of an injury to George Shaw, and the last thing he wanted to do was lose his position. Shaw actually started the game to test his knee but couldn't last past the first play of the second quarter. Dad came in and played through the pain, leading the Colts to a come-from-behind 19–17 victory that included a 53-yard touchdown pass on the game's final play. What Dad did, coming off the bench injured, is what a lot of players did (and still do). It goes without saying that the '50s were a different era. Technology and medicine, particularly the possibility of an immediate diagnosis, were different. When the Colts played at home at Memorial Stadium, Union Memorial Hospital was less than a mile away, so a player could be taken there, examined, and returned to the stadium to play if the injury wasn't serious.

Injuries and toughness go hand in hand. Playing through injuries, particularly because Dad played the most important position on the team, meant better continuity for the team and it meant having an advantage at that position. Every good team before expansion and the addition of the AFL had a great quarterback. Think about the situation today. When discussing possible championship-caliber teams, the list is usually limited to five or six, the ones with the best quarterbacks. Most teams in the '50s had a great starting quarterback, but there tended to be a big drop-off with the backup, mainly because of roster size. The backup quarterback always had other duties. The goal of defenses, after stopping the ball and keeping teams from scoring, was to get the quarterback out of the game. If you could get the quarterback out of the game, in essence you got the team out of the game. As Dick Szymanski, one of Dad's Colts teammates, once said, "He was the No. 1 meat." Because of rule differences—roughing the passer existed on the books but was rarely called—when the quarterback went back in the pocket and threw the ball, there was sometimes a half second lag while they were still watching the ball and a defensive lineman could still hit them. Whenever a lineman hit Dad, he would always get right back up and say something like, "Is that the best shot you've got?" The lineman would respond, "Ah, come on, John, you know I could've really decked you." Dad and the opponent would chuckle and get ready for the next play.

But maybe the most important facet of playing tough—playing injured—was what it said to your teammates. I've never heard a teammate of Dad's ever say anything but that he was tough. No one has ever questioned that about him. In hindsight, it might have been his undoing and shortened his life. In addition to being tough, many of his teammates talk about how he might have been the toughest player they ever saw or played with.

"One day he had his finger busted against the Chicago Bears," Szymanski told me. "One finger on his right hand was out at a 90-degree angle. He just went to the sideline, and they taped the busted finger to a good finger, straightening it out. He never missed a play." Another time, he had torn a knee ligament. When that happens, you don't walk off the field, you're either carried off on a stretcher (or on the back of a golf cart today) or hop off with a player on either side acting as props. On that day, Dad walked off the field. He didn't play again, and later that night, he was operated on, missing the rest of the season. It was that kind of toughness, according to Szymanski, "that everyone liked about him." As another teammate said, "He was a quarterback with a great arm with a linebacker's mentality."

This all has to be taken in the context that my father clearly wasn't a physical specimen. It was his size, supposedly, that kept Notre Dame from being interested in him. At Louisville, while the coaches liked his arm, they were worried about his weight. Job No. 1 for assistant coach Frank Gitschier was to put meat on his bones. Dad would work hard to keep weight on through his entire career.

Szymanski had played with the Colts before Dad made the team, went into the service, and then returned to the team with a few games left in a season after Dad was the starter. Szymanski had heard about him, and Dad was having a good season. But he'd never seen him. He walked into the locker room early upon his return and asked, "When is Unitas coming in?" Someone told him he was in. "What do you mean he's in? Where is he?"

Someone pointed to the first set of lockers and said, "That's him."

"That's not him," Szymanksi said. But it was. Szymanski went on, "If you ever saw John with a bathing suit on, you'd never think there's a great athlete. He didn't have that muscle body build. The reason John was a great quarterback is that he wanted to be a great quarterback. I didn't think he was the great athlete they were writing about in the papers. With John, if you put him next to the quarterbacks who were playing at that particular time—the Bobby Laynes and Norm Van Brocklins—as an athlete, John didn't stand out. He was a lean, not muscular, body. He just was. He didn't stand out until he got out on the field, and that's how he did it. One of the most important things that helped him more than anything else was he was a tough guy." Again, while Dad worked at being great, particularly with Raymond after practice, and was tough, there was much more than that. It seemed simple.

It wasn't.

And it wasn't just that Dad had the physical gifts needed to be a great quarterback. The NFL is full of stories of hot-shot quarterbacks with great arms, players who can throw the ball 75 yards on a line while on their knees. Or they can throw a 20-yard out that can break a receiver's hand if he's not careful. But great quarterbacking involves so much more than physical or mental gifts. Dad was smart enough to know with a veteran team that he needed to listen to his teammates. As he said about today's game not long before he died, he got his information from his teammates before they huddled up and "didn't wait to talk to the coaches on the sideline." His teammates trusted him because Dad trusted them. "If you don't have people working with you—to win—then they're working against you." When Dad got injured or was beat up, that sense of working together was affected. It wasn't just losing Dad's play calling or his ability to read defenses or throwing to the open receiver; the Colts also lost their general, a man who intuitively understood team chemistry and how important that is to leadership and winning.

Dad didn't put himself above anyone. He knew how fine a line it was between being a star in the NFL and playing on a grassless sandlot in Pittsburgh. Dad was good with his hands. So good, in fact, that he built the deck on our first house in Campus Hills by himself. Dad was a tinkerer. He was a doer. After getting cut by the Steelers, he talked about maybe becoming a health or physical education teacher. He also talked with Leonard about driving a truck, and there's no doubt if Dad had driven a truck, he would have been a darn good truck driver. My dad was great at anything involving using his hands, dedication, and preparation.

****

Teams can be undone by an injury to a star or they can be undone by injuries to multiple players, everyone missing games at different times so that the team lacks continuity and consistency. The latter is what happened in 1960. The eighth game of the season against the Bears took too much out of the team, inflicting nagging injuries across the entire lineup. When the Colts lost their final game to the 49ers to end the season, it also extended their losing streak to four games. Ewbank said after the game, "It's lucky we don't play next week. We couldn't field a team." The week before, the first game of their traditional West Coast two-game swing, not only did the Colts lose, but also Dad's streak of 47-game consecutive games with a touchdown pass came to an end.

Since the streak ended, the closest anyone came to it was 36 consecutive games until Drew Brees of the New Orleans Saints broke it recently. The game has changed considerably since Dad's playing days, and Brees plays in an NFL that resembles a 7-on-7 passing drill at times. Not that rating games gets at the essence of what a streak or moment means, but many pundits rate Dad's 47-game streak right up there with Joe DiMaggio's 56-game hit streak. Although Dad and I never talked about it, I'm sure he didn't mind that the streak was broken, but only if it were broken by a quarterback playing the game "right" and if the record-setting game was a win. Dad would have approved of Brees: he's not big and has overcome much derision early in his career to become one of the best quarterbacks currently in the game. On the other hand, his record-setting game came in a 31–24 victory over the San Diego Chargers. Dad never mentioned the streak to me, but that was like him; he wasn't big on individual records or accolades. What I'm sure bothered him much more was that the breaking of the streak resulted in losing a third consecutive game and putting the Colts on the brink of missing out of the Championship Game.

The seasons in 1961 and 1962 were similar to 1960. The team hovered right around .500 and was never in the playoff hunt. The club on the rise was Lombardi's Packers, and while Dad was selected to the Pro Bowl both years, they were down years relative to his typical offensive output. Finally, not long after their final game in 1962, Ewbank was let go as head coach with two championships under his belt.

As a *Baltimore Sun* writer said, "Ewbank has been on the hot seat so often calluses must have formed by this time." Ewbank was undone by many things: poor execution on the field, injuries, and even the claim that he stuck with his stars too long, including Dad. He was called unimaginative in his offensive design, but that wasn't new to the players; Ewbank had little to do with designing the offensive. The offensive line wasn't what it was back in the championship years, which had an effect on both Ewbank's standing with Carroll Rosenbloom and Dad's statistics.

Even Cameron Snyder, the beat writer covering the Colts for the *Sun*, questioned Dad's performance—this less than two years after raising the question of Dad's place in the pantheon of quarterbacking greats. How quickly, then and today, our heroes become our goats. It's easy to say today that that was Snyder's job, but sportswriters then had a different mentality than those working now. Snyder was infamous for sometimes filling in for injured players during Colts practices. In a 1960 column, he urged Baltimore fans to get behind the team because the team's apparent loss of confidence could only be overcome with positive support from the fans. That wouldn't happen today.

In the end, it didn't matter what the fans or reporters thought because Ewbank was replaced with Don Shula, a former Colt and only a five-year assistant in both college and the NFL. Shula was only 33 years old, three years older than Dad. Some players were older than Shula. When Marichetti was asked how he would feel if Shula, both younger and not nearly as strong a player, were to ever chew him out, Bill Pellington, standing nearby said, "That never stopped him from giving us hell even when he was a player."

The big concern with the hiring of Shula was that he was a defensive player and had spent the last three years as a defensive coach for the Detroit Lions. It was a change that would have a profound effect on Dad. Although the Colts started winning again within two years, Dad and Shula never got along. They had different personalities and different ideas about what the offense should be and who should be in charge of it. Maybe they didn't need to like each other because they did win together, but Dad wouldn't win another championship until Don McCafferty replaced Shula as head coach in 1970. The questions and tension between Dad and Shula persisted throughout their tenure.

****

At first, Shula's first year didn't look any different than Ewbank's last. The Colts finished 8–6, but they won their final three games to finish third in the division. While Rosenbloom mentioned a possible championship when he hired Shula, that wasn't in the cards. Dad had a great season, probably an All-Pro–caliber season, maybe even an MVP season except for the season Y.A. Tittle had with the Giants. Both Dad and Tittle's years have been listed in various rankings as the top 25 greatest years by a quarterback. Dad set a personal record with more than 3,400 yards, and he threw for 20 touchdowns and only 12 interceptions. But that's part of sports: you can play your very best and someone else can play better. Winning games and getting to Championship Games also helps. That's what Tittle did.

The win streak of three didn't last long as the Colts opened their 1964 season with a loss to the Minnesota Vikings, a team on the rise. But then Dad and Baltimore ran off 11 straight wins and finished the season at 12–2. As seemed to be the pattern, when the Colts won, Dad won more honors. He was picked for his eighth consecutive Pro Bowl and named All-Pro. He didn't pass for as many yards—only 2,800—but he was intercepted just six times. The Colts were going to their third Championship Game under Dad's leadership and their first since 1959. They had the No. 1–ranked offense and defense in the league. They were confident. Dad was named league MVP for the second time, and Shula won his first Coach of the Year honors.

The Colts were a touchdown favorite in the championship against the Cleveland Browns, but they were outplayed in every phase of the game, losing badly by a score of 27–0. The Colts were a team that had been winning because of confidence. During their final five games of the regular season, they had lots of turnovers but were able to overcome them. Against Cleveland, however, that wasn't the case. It was fumbles, an interception, and dropped passes that did in the offense. It was the running of Jim Brown that did in the defense. Finally, as evidence of the change that Dad had over the NFL, most teams, including the Browns, had a run-first type of offense, the run setting up the pass. The Colts, however, used the pass to set up the run. As Snyder reported in the *Sun*, "The Colts aren't basically a running team. The runners gain much better after Unitas has shaken the defense with passes…. The Colts tried to play it like the Browns did, but Baltimore has no Jim Brown. By the same token, Cleveland has no Unitas." Coincidentally, this would be Cleveland's last championship in any sport, whereas the city of Baltimore went on to win three World Series and three Super Bowls.

This wasn't the end of the road for Dad or the Colts. Better days were ahead, but even after the tough loss, there was something about the makeup of Dad that didn't let this kind of game undo him. While he was as intense a player and competitor who ever existed, he was always able to put losses, and wins even, aside and move on. As J.C. (John III), my son who never saw Dad play live, once said that his grandfather never showed emotion, except about two things: harm to other people or harm to animals. "My grandfather never showed emotion," J.C. said. "Never. Ever. I think it was the way he was raised—dare I say he raised himself—he lost his father at a young age. And Uncle Leonard was another tough-nosed guy. I'd never seen him show emotion until my grandfather's funeral. After he read the parable, he said, 'Watch after my baby brother.'" Emotion was a strange thing to Dad. Events happened and there were results, and then it was time to move on.

That's what he did. He didn't go hog wild after either championship in 1958 or 1959, and he wasn't going to go in the other direction because of an upset in 1964. He had a family to support, an off-season in which to recuperate, and next year to work his magic again, if it was meant to be.

CHAPTER 9

Awed by the Fans' Awe

October 28, 1979
Cincinnati Bengals 37, Philadelphia Eagles 13

Cincinnati was slogging through a horrible year. It was in years like this that a player found out how much he really liked playing football. It wasn't the games as much as the practice, travel, and time away from home and family. Fans watch a game for a little more than three hours, but there's so much more going on behind the scenes, almost all of it is fun and fulfilling when the team is winning and in the playoff hunt. But that wasn't the Bengals in 1979. They entered Week 9 of the season with a 1–7 record while the Eagles were 6–2 and on their way to a season-ending tie with the Dallas Cowboys for first place in the NFC East. It wasn't a close game, and the win for the Bengals did nothing to turn around their season. They would end up 4–12 and in last place in the AFC Central.

Instead, the game was interesting because it was one of three where Archie Griffin rushed for more than 100 yards in his career. Many NFL running backs, like quarterbacks, play multiple seasons without really doing much, but, at least from the average fan's perspective, Griffin's career should have been much better. Against the Eagles he rushed for 103 yards on only six carries, one of his runs resulting in 63 yards. In other words, it was close to a career day, but it proved what experts had thought all along.

If Dad came into the NFL with no expectations, then Archie Griffin was the opposite. Griffin was a football icon, maybe not an NFL one, but he was royalty in football conversations for many people. Although he wasn't drafted until late in the first round—he was considered too small to be an every-down running back—he was the first two-time winner of the Heisman trophy. Not only that, he was the first junior to win the award. But unlike Dad who was an okay college player and became a great pro, Griffin lived his life the other way. His college career reads a lot like Dad's pro career. He left Ohio State as the all-time leading rusher in NCAA Division I history. He's one of only two players to start in four consecutive Rose Bowls. His career record at Ohio State was 40–5–1. Obviously, his pro career was a different story as he rushed for 100 yards only three times and didn't gain as many yards in seven pro seasons as he did in four college ones. His highest single-game total was 246 yards in his sophomore season. He never had a day like that in the pros.

Nonetheless, he left the NFL and has done very well for himself. He received his MBA, was president of the OSU alumni association, and has been on numerous boards. He overcame expectations and pressure.

Just like his son, Adam, who has done the unthinkable: he has not only decided to play football, following in his father's footsteps, but playing his football at Ohio State where his dad is considered perhaps the school's greatest player. The difference between Archie and Adam is that Archie didn't start playing because he thought he would end up great. He probably hoped that. Adam, on the other hand, knew what he was getting into when he decided to follow his father. In an article about Adam playing at Ohio State, the opening sentence states, "It's not easy being the son of an icon."

That might be an understatement, particularly when thinking about how a teenager handles living life in his father's shadow. I don't know how Adam did it, but he obviously thrived because he led his high school football team to a state championship, and while many college coaches thought he was too small to play big-time college football, Ohio State was willing to let him walk on and then offer him a scholarship when one became available.

It's rare when sons follow their dads into football, probably because dads know what might be in store. It has happened—Howie Long and his sons come to mind—Adam had to know what he was doing and getting into. He'd lived 18 years as Archie's son, a shadow that falls big around him. When I was 18, I knew what it was like living in a large shadow.

I had some first-hand experience of what the football life was like, not just the life of being the son of a star. In 1965, I spent the entire preseason with Dad at the Colts' training camp, getting an in-depth look and understanding of what life in the NFL was like. It was beyond fun, at least for me, because I wasn't wearing heavy practice jerseys drenched with sweat in 100-degree summer heat, getting yelled out by an assistant coach. I was grabbing lemonade and cups of water for Dad and his teammates. It was an adventure, not a testing ground. It was also the chance to spend quality time with Dad without any of my siblings around or Mom telling me what to do. Adam Griffin is probably saying that playing football at Ohio State is more than a teenager could ask for. I will do him one better: at nine, I got to hang out with overgrown boys playing football during the day and sometimes playing pranks on each other at night, even if I had to pick up dirty ankle tape and smelly jocks.

AWED BY THE FANS' AWE

As I grew up, I don't remember football interfering—maybe not the right word, instead I'll say overlapping—very much in my life. Dad played, but when he was home, he was a father, even if he was a little distant. Mom went to most home games, the Colts putting wives and families at about the 50-yard line but near the top of Memorial Stadium. Dad got two tickets to games, so Mom usually took one of the kids. I guess I went, but I don't remember particular games. Many times Uncle Leonard would come down from Pittsburgh with Eileen, his wife, and babysit us while Dad played and Mom watched, and then after the game, go to the Green Spring Inn or the Valley Inn, for a postgame dinner. If Uncle Leonard couldn't come, then Harvey Weeks, a big Colts fan who became friends with my parents, would watch us. Harvey remains a friend of the family, particularly with Janice, to this day.

Johnny U and Me

****

In 1965 I had my first real experience with Dad and football. I had just turned nine, and Mom and Dad decided it would be a good time for me to go to preseason with Dad at Western Maryland College (now called McDaniel College) in Westminster. Preseason then wasn't what it is today. Dad had no physical involvement with football once the season ended. He attended community events as a representative of the Colts; he played on Colt basketball teams with some of his teammates; and he played softball, both in leagues and with his teammates next to the Valley Inn. But there were no OTA (organized team activities), some voluntary, some not. There was simply preseason with a slate of games.

Training camp is what it sounds like—a time to train. Most of the players, including my father, had off-season jobs. While NFL players made decent money, they weren't going to make that kind of money forever. They needed to work in the off-season to both supplement their income and prepare for life after pro football. Jim Mutscheller sold insurance, a job he still does to this day. Jobs got in the way of training. Dad didn't really lift weights, but he did do curls in the basement and punched a speed bag. Veterans came to camp oftentimes overweight, and spent the more than eight weeks there losing weight. Besides getting in playing shape, camp ideally molded the team into a cohesive group. Teams generally played six preseason games, which was reduced to four in 1978. Unlike today, starters played much longer into the preseason games as they were getting ready for actual game conditions. Today, in the third and final preseason games, fans will be lucky to see starters in the second half.

Training camp was long. Lots of players reported out of shape and fat. Some had clauses in their contracts about weighing a specific amount. It was also a time for players to get away from families, to hang with the guys, their teammates, and be the juveniles that locker rooms and all-male environments tend to make a group of men. Under the sweltering Maryland sun and amid the humidity of July and August, there was tension at camp. For some it was all serious because they needed to make the team; for others, like Dad and Raymond, it was a time to fine tune and bond.

****

For me, that summer, it was a time like no other. It was freedom and hard work and a chance to watch how grown men, particularly those other than my dad, behaved away from their wives and children. It was also an exploration, an athletic romp among their rooms and personal items, like going down to a creek to catch insects and bugs and find lost treasures half buried in the sand. Except I wasn't at a creek: I was living in a dorm with a chest of drawers full of girlie magazines and countertops scattered with cigarette lighters, decks of cards, shaving kits, and beer bottle tops, possibly secret talismans into the insights of how these behemoths lived, men who would tell jokes that mentioned women's titties, forgetting I was there, who farted and belched without worrying if Mom would say, "Johnny, must you?" Instead they laughed and did it again. But until I'd experienced training camp, I was like everyone else who probably heard the word "camp" and ignored the word "training."

****

It was a typical July day, and I remember driving to Westminster, about 45 minutes from our house near Towson. It was hot, but it seemed during my childhood all summers were unbearably hot. Dad always drove up the day before practices officially started so he could get settled. The car windows were down, the breeze trying to take the edge off the heat. Dad rested his arm on the window sill, his right hand on the steering wheel. In the trunk were a couple of suitcases, and some hang-up clothes of Dad's were blocking the rear window, rippling. Dad didn't look any different than he did when he drove me to school. The radio was off. He whistled most of the way there, but he always whistled. I was excited, tapping my foot on the floorboard, squirming in my seat, sticking my head out the window, the wind blowing through my crewcut.

Occasionally, Dad would glance at me, a quick look that said, "Enough," and I would stop. I knew better than to ask how much longer. If I had, he'd have sighed, that long one that signaled disappointment and finally said, "We'll get there when we get there."

When we pulled up to the college, I saw lots of big buildings and expanses of grass between them. Most of the buildings the Colts would be using formed a quad. I now know that these brick buildings, which then seemed so big and majestic, weren't really all that special, but to a nine-year-old boy off to spend seven weeks with his father and no other siblings and no mother constantly fussing over him, everything seemed grand. I didn't know fancy hotels, but if I had, they would have looked like McDaniel College.

In addition to tall buildings and lots of space and grass, a crowd was waiting next to the parking lot as we pulled in—hundreds, maybe even 1,000 people, standing rows deep on the curb surrounding the parking lot. They were chanting his name, standing respectfully at the curb, waiting. As Dad eased the car into his space, the fans broke out in applause, clapping and cheering. There was no rush at the car, no stampede to get at Dad. Just a loud, orderly mob, patient and adoring. The ones closest to us thrust pieces of paper and pen at him, politely asking for an autograph. Voices yelled questions, "Are we going all the way this year, Johnny?" To most questions, Dad nodded or grinned. He patted a little boy, maybe five, standing engulfed in his father's arm and torso, on the head. Once he'd taken the suitcases out of the trunk and given me my load to carry inside the dorm, he said loud enough for people five and six rows deep to hear, "Not right now. Hands full, but I'll be back out in a little while." He smiled. He meant it. "Let me get settled." The crowd parted and Dad and I walked toward the building, an occasional hand pat on Dad's shoulders. They didn't even notice me.

★★★★

Even today I'm awed when I think about that arrival. Here were hundreds of fans waiting for Dad, and when they saw him, they applauded. I understand the reverence fans have for players on the field; I understand going overboard for a team or player, particularly when you pay money for a ticket to see them. If nothing else, that ticket is for the action on the field. But on this particular July 1965 day, these people were waiting for one reason: to see the players, particularly my dad. Dad loved every minute of it. "You better enjoy it," he told me when I was an adult with children, "because one day you won't be recognized."

Pulling up to Western Maryland's parking lot was a lot like Christmas Day for him, with both fans and his teammates. That first day was a get-adjusted day, say hello to teammates who haven't been seen in more than six months. I knew my father was an "important" man, but I didn't know he was this beloved until that moment in the Western Maryland parking lot. After we got settled in the room, all clothes put away in drawers and shoes lined up in a closet, Dad did go back outside, chatting and signing autographs for more than an hour. I stayed in the room, watching out the third-floor window, taking it all in.

My role that summer was to do whatever Peter Seiden, then 14 years old, told me to do. And we did a lot. We set up the lockers, making sure every player had the right equipment. The footballs had to be blown up. During practice, we chased errant passes and kicks. We moved tackling dummies around and brought water to the players. The real work began when practice ended. We had to clean up the locker room, picking up the sweaty, dirty jocks, socks, and towels from the floor. Once the locker room was clean, we set up for the afternoon practice before hustling over to the dining hall for a quick, late lunch.

It wasn't the work that made the summer so special. Part of what I loved was rooming with Dad. Because of his position and length of service, he got a single room that I shared, me on the top bunk and Dad below. We were right next door to Raymond, who even then was beginning to feel like an uncle. While Dad wasn't with me all the time—he did have to get ready for the upcoming season so he wouldn't let all those adoring fans down—he knew what I was up to. He usually ate with teammates, and I ate with my friends who included Don Shula's kids, Coach John Sandusky's son, Gerry, and Donnie McCafferty, whose father would later become head coach of the Colts and lead them to the 1971 Super Bowl win.

What made spending all this time with the team unusual was how much it felt like a family. I was right in the middle of the locker room all the time. The players treated me like I was an important member of the team. They respected me, helped me, and also played jokes on me. They did this to all the kids helping, not just to me because my dad was John Unitas and he was the quarterback. Seiden remembers that the players made sure on preseason road trips that someone was taking care of our going out to dinner. On off days, the players made sure we had something to do, or they would take those of us who didn't have fathers there home with them.

That summer I also got to go with the team on its away preseason games, flying for the first time on a charter plane with the team. It was like heaven, beyond cool. I felt like a real adult. In hindsight, a couple of the Colts' games were played not only as exhibitions for the team, but also for the NFL to see if a particular city was NFL caliber. Baltimore defeated St. Louis 22–10 in New Orleans, and more than 75,000 attended that game. The Saints joined the NFL in 1966 and played their first season in 1967. The Colts also played a game against the Steelers in Atlanta, defeating Pittsburgh 38–10. The Atlanta Falcons would debut the next season, 1966. Probably because Dad played in this game—he didn't play the week before because of a sore elbow—an attendance record was set in Atlanta. They also played a game in Detroit.

The one that stands out the most was going to Atlanta but not because of the game. The Beatles movie *Help* was showing down the block from our hotel, and it was a big deal, probably a bigger deal for Peter than me. Peter had already become like a big brother, and for a teenager, the Beatles were almost as big as knowing Johnny Unitas. We really wanted to see it. When Dad approached us to ask what we were up to, we mentioned that we really wanted to go see *Help*. Without hesitation, he said, "Let's go."

Later during the trip we got into trouble because of a trick we played on some of the players and coaches. One of my favorite things to do during training camp at Western Maryland was to snoop on the players. If I got a free minute or two, usually when the players were in meetings (when they were practicing on the fields, we were expected to be there), I would go into their dorm rooms. Like most curious nine-year-olds, I didn't have any goal in mind. I wanted to see what these players were really like. I would take in what they had on top of their dressers, maybe check out what kind of cigarette butts they had in their ashtrays. Occasionally, I would go through a drawer or two, but I always made sure to leave the room just as I found it. Other than discovering that a lot more players smoked than I thought (athletes smoked then, some openly), I found lots of *Playboys*, some hidden, most on the night stand next to the bed. Thinking about it, I don't find it surprising, but for a nine-year-old, it was heaven. Knowing that the players liked pictures of beautiful naked women, Peter and I bought a deck of cards with nude women on the front. We left the deck lying about the lobby of the hotel, so players—and little did we know, some of the coaches—would pick them up. There was a catch, however, when you touched the deck, you got shocked. Naturally, the players weren't happy. It was okay for them to play jokes on us but not the other way around.

The Beatles movie aside, Peter doesn't remember one singular moment where he realized my father's greatness, but said it occurred over time. However, he does remember the first time he ever met him. Peter was at his first training camp. He came a day early with his father, and Dad was already there. Dad walked up to Mr. Seiden—they knew each other from a previous business encounter—stuck out his hand and asked how his dad was. At that moment, Peter realized that Dad was just another decent, humble person. As he said, "I know John Unitas thought he was the best player in the NFL, the best quarterback. He had that kind of confidence. But as a human being, he was no more, no less important than anybody else."

One day during training camp, thinking he was doing Dad a favor, Peter learned what it means to be a ball player off the field. That day about 200 fans were milling just outside the gym waiting for players to come out. Since there was a side door to the gym, a lot of the players would take that and avoid the crowd of autograph seekers. Dad didn't take the side door. He went out the main door, right into the crowd. Peter saw him trapped, so he called to Dad that he had a phone call. Dad came back into the gym and said, "Where's the call?" Peter explained there was no call, that he was getting him away from the crowd so Dad could use the side door.

Dad stared at Peter. "Don't you ever do that again. I love these people. Who are you to deny somebody the opportunity if they want to meet me and sign an autograph?"

Peter got that message, and he got so much more. "As you work around the ball players, live with them and eat with them, travel with them, you just deal with them as human beings and get to know them not as football heroes, but as human beings. John was no different than anybody else. He always took the time to see how I was doing, always took the time to say hello and chat. Occasionally, I got a little homesick and he tried to perk me up. That's just the kind of guy he was. At some point, you say this is a good guy, and it had nothing to do with being the Babe Ruth of football."

****

The Colts won all five of their exhibition games in 1965, one of two teams to go undefeated. The other was the Minnesota Vikings, the Colts' first opponent in the regular season. It was a game that encapsuled Dad's career in many ways. He threw two early interceptions that led to a Viking 10–0 lead, and then he threw two touchdown passes to help the Colts erase the deficit. He had up-and-down games; he had up-and-down years. However, when people look back at his career, they tend to remember only the positive. It all seemed so magical, like the comeback late in the 1958 Championship Game and the drive for a touchdown in overtime.

There were lots of moments like that, but there were also moments in the early '60s when Cameron Snyder of the *Baltimore Sun* was questioning if he still had it, if Dad was the right man to run the Colts. Fans—and sportswriters—tend to be fickle. They only remember what you did yesterday, sometimes not that long, what you did on the last play. Players, my father included, tend to take the long view of the game. Remember, it was Jim Mutscheller sitting behind Dad on the bus after a game in 1956 when the Colts had lost and Dad hadn't played particularly well that convinced Mutscheller that Dad was the real thing. Obviously, players constantly talk about the next moment, the next chance, the next game, but there was something in Dad's voice, maybe a quiet confidence, that projected something greater than simple words. If it was true in 1956, it was still true in 1965.

CHAPTER 10

Luck Runs Both Ways

September 10, 1978
Oakland 21, San Diego 20

It was a routine early-season game in many respects although Oakland and San Diego, two former AFL teams, had no love for each other. In hindsight, the game was even more routine than it first appears. Both teams finished the 1978 season at 9–7 and out of the playoffs. Oakland had made the playoffs the year before, and San Diego would win the Western division in 1979. But 1978 was a typical NFL year for both teams: barely winning records, and if they'd had a few more breaks both teams might have made the playoffs. Since the days of Bert Bell as commissioner, his legacy had been the idea of parity for the league. He didn't want the NFL to be Major League Baseball with the New York Yankees generally dominating because of financial advantages. Under Pete Rozelle, parity was happening.

It was a typical San Diego September Sunday, 71 degrees and sunny. The Chargers took an early lead on a Dan Fouts touchdown pass. Fouts and Dad played together Fouts' rookie season and Dad's final season. Fouts had turned out to be the player Dad predicted he would be. Early in the fourth quarter, San Diego took a solid 20–7 lead. Kenny Stabler, another Alabama quarterback in a long line of great Alabama quarterbacks, fired a touchdown pass to make the score 20–14. With 10 seconds left and Stabler on the Chargers 24-yard line and about to be sacked, he intentionally fumbled the ball forward (on film and hindsight, it was a forward pitch, not a "fumble"), running back Pete Banaszak picked it up about seven or eight yards away and he clearly pitched the ball forward again. Dave Casper, standing on the 4-yard line, tried to pick up the loose ball and instead, kicked it. His kick, which appeared to be the only inadvertent event of the entire sequence, punched the ball into the end zone where Casper fell on it for a Raiders win.

Outraged fans and the media called for something to be done. The NFL didn't overturn the Raiders' win, but as it is inclined to do, the NFL implemented new rules to make sure this didn't happen again. By the 1979 season, the NFL had enacted what came to be called "The Ken Stabler Rule" after the events in that September 10, 1978, game that was now known as the "Holy Roller" game. The rule stated that only the fumbling player on a fourth-down play or in the last two minutes of the half could advance a fumble. Any other offensive player recovering the ball returns it to the point of the fumble. There would be no more last-second fumbling shenanigans to win a game late. Interestingly, this rule would be amended again at least twice, once in 1988 and 2002.

Just as John Adams, our second president, once said that "We are a country of laws, not men," the NFL holds a similar outlook. Unlike Major League Baseball, which has had only one major rule change between 1975 and 2008, football is constantly tinkering with its rules. Some of them involve what occurs on the field, others involve television and playoff formats (television again). It seems that while baseball is about its history and consistency, the NFL is about adapting to what consumers want, and by 1978, clearly the consumers were the growing numbers of fans. What the fans wanted was lots of offense and fairness.

Often, NFL rule changes are the result of an action that took place on the field. That's what happened in the 1978 Holy Roller game. Unlike NASCAR, for example, that will change rules within days, even hours sometimes, of a driver discovering a loophole in the arcana of its rules, generally the NFL waits until the off-season when the second most important committee meets—the competition committee. Naturally, the most important is the broadcast committee.

For Colts fans, particularly in 1965, they wished the competition committee had seen fit to anticipate problems instead of react to them. And once

Baltimore lost the Colts to Indianapolis, Baltimoreans discovered that the competition and broadcast committees weren't actually the two most powerful committees; instead, it was the expansion committee. Dad would later have a few things to say about both. But first he would live through an interesting 1965 season, as he would get hurt toward the end of it and watch as he coached a running back turned quarterback and almost pulled off a monumental playoff upset except for the lack of the competition committee's foresight.

Luck Runs Both Ways

The 1965 regular season was now in full swing. I was back to school, and Dad was back to being Johnny U. No longer was he only mine, at least as far as the family was concerned. He still took me to school, but I wasn't sleeping in the same room with him, occasionally the two of us eating together at a table in the Western Maryland cafeteria during preseason where all his teammates and my summer friends could see me, alone with my dad. Now, I had classes to attend and creeks in the backyard woods to dig around in with neighborhood friends, and he had a regular season to play. While I saw the adoring fans and the efforts they made to see Dad arrive at training camp and to watch preseason practices, it still didn't register that Dad was bigger than me or the family or even Baltimore. I don't know whether or not it had truly registered with him, either.

****

Clearly, the Colts had responded to the upset loss to the Browns in last year's championship. They were back on track. Part of the reason, according to many of Dad's teammates when referring to Dad's effect on them, was his steadying influence and his ability to look forward while learning from previous mistakes without dwelling on the negative. Great kickers have that ability; they don't remember the previous miss. Great quarterbacks also have it. Although the Colts would lose their next game to the Packers on the road in a 20–17 heartbreaker, they would then run off eight consecutive wins followed by a tie on the road to the Lions. After 11 games, they stood in first place in the Western Division at 9–1–1.

To win a championship a team needs luck. The Colts got lucky in Detroit when the Lions could have kicked an uncontested free kick from the Colts' 42 with less than a minute left, but instead chose to throw one pass and missed on a 50-yard attempt. A poor coaching decision salvaged a tie. There was no guarantee the Lions would have made their free kick, but they'd have had a better chance.

In their next game at home against the Bears, the Colts were unlucky. In the second quarter, Dad threw an incompletion to John Mackey, and as he was throwing, two Bears rushers hit him high and low simultaneously, bending his leg backwards and injuring both knee ligaments and cartilage. He had surgery that night to repair the damage. This was Dad's second major injury of the year, and only the third of his career. Earlier in the season he missed the second Vikings game because of a back problem, and in 1958, he missed two games because of a broken rib and punctured lung. Dad was having another MVP-caliber season, maybe statistically his best to date, and later he would be named first-team All-Pro even though he missed the final three games of the regular season and the playoff game against the Vikings.

Gary Cuozzo, Dad's backup who started the second Vikings game and led the Colts to a 41–21 win, would now have to quarterback the Colts through their last three games while sitting on a half-game lead in the Western Division over the Packers. Dad's injury also led to a roster situation. Rosters could not be changed for the last two weeks of the season, and whatever roster was used during that time was also the playoff roster. There was a possibility, however remote, that Dad could make it back for the January 2 Championship Game. Shula had to decide whether to keep Dad on the roster and hope he recovered and the team got to the championship or find another quarterback to sign. That quarterback would have been George Haffner who was currently on the taxi squad and had never played in an NFL game. Or, the Colts could keep Dad on the roster and use Tom Matte, now a running back, who played quarterback at Ohio State under Woody Hayes. Shula decided to use Matte as the back up, but did place Dad on the inactive squad while elevating Haffner.

More bad luck would follow. In the second to last game of the year against the Packers—an important game because if the Colts won they would win the division—Cuozzo got hurt. He separated his shoulder and he, too, had to have surgery and was placed on the inactive list, meaning neither he nor Dad would be eligible if the Colts made the Championship Game or the Playoff Bowl, a 1960s idea of playing the two second-place teams from each division in Miami for third place. Matte would now be the starter in the final regular season game against the Rams, a game the Colts had to win to secure at least a tie for first-place with the Packers. Just to be sure, the Colts signed Ed Brown, a veteran who had last played for the Steelers, off the waiver wire for $100. Neither Haffner nor Brown would be eligible if the Colts made the Championship Game.

****

The Colts needed a win against the Rams in Los Angeles and at least a tie by the Packers to end up in a tie for the division. A Colts win and Packers loss would have given the Colts the division outright. The Colts upheld their end of the bargain, and they did it by having Matte throw only two passes—both incomplete—and alternating series with Brown, who had just been signed the day before. He only threw five passes, but completed three of them, including a 68-yarder to John Mackey to tie the game before winning on a field goal with less than four minutes left. It wasn't pretty football, but it worked. Tommy Bell, the head official that day, said to Matte after the game, "I can't believe you won." Even during the game, he helped Matte and the Colts out. He would come up to the huddle and say, "Stay in the huddle; it'll run out. Don't make any mistakes. You've won the game." The Packers also cooperated by letting the 49ers score in the fourth quarter to tie the game and force a playoff game between the Bart Starr–led Packers versus the Unitas-less Colts, now to be quarterbacked by Matte, who still hadn't completed a regular season pass.

To understand the playoff game against the Packers, it's important to understand what my dad did during his time recovering from surgery. First, let me tell you what he wasn't doing; he wasn't sulking. Instead, he became another coach, helping Matte prepare to be a full-game NFL quarterback. Matte had joined the Colts in 1961 after playing at Ohio State. He was a running quarterback there, and he came to the Colts as a great athlete. Ewbank liked players who could do multiple things, particularly at the skilled positions. Lenny was equally effective as a rusher or a receiver, in the backfield or flanked out as an end. While Matte wasn't as fast as Lenny, he had the similar multiple-skill set. He didn't think it would ever involve playing quarterback, however.

When Matte arrived at Colts training camp, all he knew about Dad was his legend. He had watched both the 1958 and 1959 Championship Games but didn't understand what pass offense was all about. At Ohio State the passing game was about a receiver finding a dead spot and settling in it, and Matte would throw the ball there. With the Colts, however, everything was based on timing and progressions. Patterns were spread out so the receivers came open in 2.3 seconds, then 2.5, then 2.7, and finally at 3 seconds. This was not only different for Matte, it was new.

Dad understood that, and he understood Matte. He had never taken a snap in practice until both Dad and Cuozzo got hurt. Bobby Boyd, later to be Dad's business partner in the restaurant business, had played quarterback at Oklahoma, but he didn't want to do it. According to Matte, Dad always played to a player's strengths. If it hadn't been for Dad, Matte wouldn't have lasted a year in the NFL. Because Dad trusted Matte not to fumble, to run proper routes, and to be where he was supposed to be, Matte stayed on the team. The first thing Dad did was convince Shula and Don McCafferty, the offensive coordinator, to keep things simple. Don't try to run an offense built for Unitas because Matte's not Unitas, he told them. Instead, build an offense for Matte. That meant rollouts and quarterback draws. One of Dad's mantras was KISS, "Keep It Simple, Stupid." Next, Dad stressed the fundamentals. "Make sure you get the snap. Make sure you get the snap." Dad understood that you had to start simple and keep it simple. Without a good exchange from center, nothing else mattered. "If there's nobody open, don't throw it because most of the plays are designed around short, quick passes." Matte's job was to take care of the ball and whenever he could, he was to run. The rest of the game plan was to play great defense. The Colts did this against both the Rams and the Packers.

In the playoff game, the Colts ran their Matte-designed offense to perfection. Matte did everything he was expected to do. He threw the ball 12 times, completing five of them. The Colts ran the ball 47 times, controlling the clock. It was cold in Green Bay that day and 22 degrees at game time. The Packers ran 80 total plays, the Colts 59. The Colts jumped out to a 10–0 lead at halftime, but it was the defense that gave them the one touchdown. It also got Bart Starr out of the game, and the Packers had to go to their backup quarterback, Zeke Bratkowski. Don Shinnick picked up a fumbled pass reception—on Starr's first pass of the game—and returned it for a touchdown. As Shinnick was racing toward the end zone, Starr attempted to tackle him and injured himself, returning only to hold on extra points and field goals. Bratkowski, while a back up, was no stranger to the position. He entered the NFL in 1954. He was a career second stringer, not unlike Cuozzo, although he had one year where he started most of the season. The dropoff in ability from Starr to Bratkowski wasn't close to the one from Dad to Cuozzo or especially Dad to Matte.

The Packers rallied to tie the game and send it into overtime. The difference was turnovers—four for the Packers and only one for the Colts, a fumble. Additionally, Matte was sacked just once. The offense and Matte did their jobs; they kept it close and didn't lose the game. Both the coaches and team knew that having a game plan of keeping the offense simple and relying on the defense would probably result in a low-scoring game. They were right. They needed Matte to give the Colts a chance, and he did that.

However, in the end, the Colts lost in the worst way possible—the officials made a couple of bad calls. Colts to this day still talk about Don Chandler's field goal with less than 2:00 remaining in the game. His kick, which some eyewitnesses said was at least 3' wide of the goal post, was declared good and sent the game into overtime. They saw it as wide right and claim that if you pay close attention to the game film, you can see Chandler immediately hang his head and swiping his kicking foot at the dirt—the actions of a man who knew he'd missed the field goal. Other reports even had the rest of the Packers walking dejectedly off the field. After the game Colts defensive tackle Fred Miller said, "If that field goal was good, I'll eat the football." The tying field goal wasn't mentioned in the *Baltimore Sun*'s write up of the game the next day, but it was mentioned by Bob Maisel, the *Sun*'s columnist, who covered the game. Later, almost 14:00 into overtime with both teams having chances to score, Chandler kicked his second field goal of the game. This time there was no controversy. The kick was clearly good.

Before the next season, the NFL changed the rule about goal posts, mandating higher uprights and requiring a minimum of 20', another example of the NFL tweaking its product after the fact instead of anticipating problems. Colts claim this was in reaction to the missed field goal being called good. The new rule doesn't take away the loss or give the Colts another chance. It's another example of the fine line between winning, winning enough to get to championships, and winning championships. Everything has to fall into place. In 1965 it didn't. Boyd said after the game, "We lost. That's all that matters. I think I'd rather lose 503–0 than this way." It might have been Dad getting hurt or a missed pass by Matte, or it might have been a bad call—an unsportsmanlike conduct penalty against Billy Ray Smith on the Packers' tying drive late in the fourth quarter—but we'll never know, and at this point it doesn't matter.

At this point in Dad's career, he had to be wondering how many more chances he was going to get. He was 32 years old and had one of his toughest seasons in terms of injuries. The good news for Dad was that this wouldn't be his last chance.

CHAPTER 11

Questioning the Football God

January 29, 2012
AFC 59, NFC 41

More than 12 million people watched the 2012 Pro Bowl. Under a relatively new format, the game was played one week before the Super Bowl (not after, as it had been done in the past) with no players from either Super Bowl–participating team. Winning players, plus the players selected from the Super Bowls who couldn't play, got $50,000; the losing players got $25,000. From looking at the score, the second highest scoring game in Pro Bowl history, the game had to be exciting. But is that what's supposed to happen when the best players in a sport are put together, particularly in a sport like football where rules are amended to keep the preparation as simple as possible? No motion is allowed on offense and defensively, teams can't blitz and must play a straight forward 4–3 alignment at all times.

The game was close until the AFC scored four consecutive touchdowns to overcome a 35–31 NFC lead and blow open the game at 59–35. The four touchdowns were scored in a 13-minute stretch. The two teams combined for 57 completions in 99 attempts. All but one of the seven quarterbacks who played that day had a quarterback rating greater than 100. Since 2000, the game has become a high-scoring affair, teams routinely combining for 70, 80, 90 points a game, the scores looking more like something from an Arena football game.

Yet, the biggest problem isn't the high scoring. Fans generally like to see scoring, whether it's a football All-Star Game or another sport. Scoring is okay as long as the fans think effort is being put out. In this game, it was obvious the effort wasn't there. One news report of the game commented: "The game didn't get off to an especially thrilling start, with the players appearing to move at half-speed. One early run by NFC running back LeSean McCoy actually drew boos from the crowd for its lack of effort."

Reporters and announcers are paid to point out deficiencies, players are not. Shortly after the game, Aaron Rodgers, the league's reigning MVP and the player many people perceive to be the best in football, criticized the NFC's effort. While I'm not going to put Rodgers in my dad's category yet, he is a fine player on his way to a possible Hall of Fame career. As one news article said, "When the MVP speaks, people listen." The same could have been said about my dad although he didn't speak that much. Rodgers said, "I'll be honest. I was a little bit disappointed. I felt like some of the guys on the NFC side embarrassed themselves. I was just surprised that some of the guys either didn't want to play or when they were in there didn't put any effort into it." Just like Dad, Rodgers called it like he saw it and didn't mention names. I'm sure there's no reason to—the players he was referring to know who they are. "How far the mighty have fallen," would probably be one of Dad's comments if he'd been alive to witness the 2012 Pro Bowl.

There's been a great deal of discussion about how to "fix" the problem, how to make the Pro Bowl relevant. Dad would be shaking his head at this, wiping his hand across his brow, a tension building in his jaw. His eyes would burn, as if they were wicks to a candle or bomb, but he wouldn't explode. He might sigh heavily or simply leave the room, walk outside, and go to his barn to do work around the house. Riding his tractor always made the world seem more right. Not playing football the right way meant something—it was bad—and Dad's world was out of whack. If Dad needed to say something about effort on a football field, then the problems were far bigger than his criticism could correct. He wouldn't have let it get to that point.

QUESTIONING THE FOOTBALL GOD

Dad didn't make the 1965 Pro Bowl because of the knee injury suffered in the 11th game of the season. Surgery ended his year, and if you didn't make the game, you weren't a Pro Bowler. He played in every Pro Bowl from 1957, his second year in the league, until 1967, except for 1965. The players and coaches voted players into the game, unlike today where the voting is done by the fans.

On January 11, 1958, Dad played in his first Pro Bowl. He was the backup quarterback for the winning West side, playing behind first-team All-NFL-er, Y.A. Tittle from the 49ers. Although Dad wasn't the starter, he ended up being on the field when the West did most of its damage to win the game 26–7. Six Colts played in the game, and they all had a big hand in the win. Dad was 7-for-10 passing with two touchdowns, but the real star on offense was Dad's backfield mate, Alan Ameche, who would go on to score the winning touchdown later that year in the Championship Game. Defensively, the star was Artie Donovan. Looking back, maybe the Colts being as strong as they were in 1958 shouldn't have come as a surprise. Donovan has told me that he thought the Colts were the best team in 1957. They showed it in the Pro Bowl. The game, played in Los Angeles, was the largest crowd to see the Pro Bowl to that point.

Dad was named Player of the Game in the Pro Bowl three times. During most of his career, there was both an offensive and defensive Player of the Game. But to simply look at Dad and his numbers—the number of games played and stats in the games he played—doesn't get at the core of who he was. Pro Bowls were for the fans and players in terms of bragging rights. They were exhibitions, but they weren't. In the 1950s and '60s, players tended to play for one team. Rivalries were real. The Colts didn't like the Bears. Their games against each other were brutal. So Pro Bowls were one of the few times the players from opposing teams were around each other for longer than a Sunday afternoon. Furthermore, the two divisions didn't like each other, either. The Pro Bowl was a chance to settle once and for all who was better. That's why they weren't simply exhibitions, but even if they were, that's not how Dad treated them, mainly because he didn't treat anything that way. Simply stated, Dad loved football, but more important, he loved playing football. He loved competing and he loved winning, but I think he loved playing more than anything. He loved being with his teammates and opponents, some of whom would now be his teammates. The game itself mattered, and while he wanted to win every game, once the game was over, it was on to the next one. Missing the 1965 Pro Bowl wasn't the end of his career, nor was it even the beginning of his ending. He still had great years ahead of him.

Three times Vince Lombardi was Dad's coach in the Pro Bowl. In some ways, their being paired together was hooking up the two biggest names in the NFL. And they couldn't have been more different. Lombardi was very much like his legend—an intimidating taskmaster. Dad, who intimidated me and some of his teammates on occasion, was quiet, sometimes blending into the background of a locker room as if he were nothing more than a locker. Lombardi wanted people to fear him; I think Dad just wanted to get along, although getting along wouldn't and shouldn't take precedent over doing things the right way. They both wanted to win. It was simply a matter of how they reached that end.

No one talked back to Lombardi, and no one—and I mean no one—questioned him. He was the coach, and everyone else was somewhere below him. That would seem to include Dad. During an offensive meeting a few days before one of the Pro Bowl games, Lombardi was discussing how to set up the formation for a particular play. Lombardi said, "Okay, this is the way I want our offensive line to line up. When we call the play, we want our tight end to just move about a yard or so. Anybody got any questions?"

Lenny Moore, who told me this story, laughed a quick chuckle: "Johnny U raised his hand. 'Yeah, John?' Lombardi asked.

"'Well Coach, what's the purpose of just moving the tight end out a yard or so? It's doesn't affect anything.'

"'What do you mean, John?'

"'Well, you've got your linebacker out over the tight end. If you just move him a yard out, it doesn't affect anything. Why don't you just tell him to split, go three or four yards. That affects the linebacker. It's an either/or. He's got to do one thing or the other. So what's the purpose of splitting him a yard out because it doesn't affect the linebacker one way or the other?'"

Everybody, both players and other coaches, in the room glanced around, minds whirring as to what Lombardi might do. He would do something. He might blow up and rant and rave, a classic Lombardi scene. Or he might simply stare, his eyes narrow, his jaw clenched, the skin of his face taut, and the fact he said nothing said everything, everything bad. He did neither.

"'Yeah, John, we can do that.' John was the only one who had any changes and the only one willing to discuss this with Lombardi. It was sort of like telling God he was wrong. Even Bart Starr was in there." Moore laughed again, a heartier laugh. "What Vince says, that's it. You do what Vince says."

And Dad did, but only if it made sense. Doing it right was worth standing up for.

The Pro Bowl was only an exhibition, but no one, especially Dad, treated it that way. Later, around about 2000, if not sooner, the game had turned into something different and more like a bad circus.

But even Dad had his limits. Raymond tells the story of the time of the week of the Pro Bowl when he approached Dad about working on some particular patterns that Raymond had been looking at film and discovered possible moves that would work against the Eastern division defensive backs. Dad looked at Raymond and said, "Oh, Raymond," like he was exasperated. Maybe Raymond worked on those patterns, but he didn't do it with Dad.

****

While Dad was making a nice living playing football, the NFL hadn't become the financial juggernaut it is today. We lived in a nice house, my parents drove nice cars (sometimes free as a result of winning an award like being named MVP of the Pro Bowl), dressed nicely (I was voted "best dressed" while I was in high school at Calvert Hall), and went to well-respected Catholic schools. Mom wanted us to dress nicely because it was important how we looked. She never said it was to portray a public image, but now I know better. It was both for the image and because my mom simply knew fashion. She picked out our clothes, not just mine, but also my siblings'. Every fall and spring we went to the same clothing store, a mom-and-pop type store, Andrew's on Padonia Road not too far from our house. She didn't buy a shirt or coat for each us; she bought four and five shirts, pants, and a couple of sport coats. She would pay for the items with a check. A few weeks later as my father was balancing the checkbook, he would throw a fit. He didn't yell at Mom, but he might as well have from the searing look and his liberal use of "what in the hell is this expense" comments.

My father had lived through the Depression (although not the darkest and most difficult aspects of it) and he'd watched his mother work two and three jobs to make sure her children had what they needed. Money wasn't tight, but Dad always felt a little more was nice. He also understood the value of a dime, and while he wanted us to look good, he knew that if he didn't watch the finances, Mom wasn't going to.

The paycheck for winning the Pro Bowl was like that $10 bill I once found in my suit jacket sitting in a church pew bored on Christmas Eve. Found money, I call it, and Dad wasn't against it. Except in Dad's case, he didn't use it for himself. Unlike some Colts who were so sure they were going to win the 1964 championship that they had already spent the winners' check before the game, Dad was more frugal. Instead, Dad always gave his Pro Bowl check, in its entirety, to Immaculate Conception, the church we attended growing up, and the church where I would be married in the early 1980s. His Pro Bowl check was their $10 of found money, except it was a lot more.

While Dad went to church every Sunday growing up, he didn't wear his Catholicism loudly. Then again, Dad didn't wear anything loudly. As an adult, Dad's church going ways increased—improved if being a good Catholic involves how often you go to church—to the point where he basically went to church every morning once he retired. Because of his divorce from my mother, the Catholic Church ex-communicated him, yet he still found his way to church. If a Catholic church wasn't available, he would go to another denomination.

Questioning the Football God

I remember that my childhood Sundays were hell. Four of us children through most of the 1960s doing everything in our power not to go to church, but Mom and Dad straightening ties and re-tucking in shirts, mainly Mom. We would park at the bottom of the hill at Immaculate Conception and trudge up the hill, half bent over as if slaves going to the mines. Dad would be behind us, hissing, "Straighten up. Walk tall. Don't shuffle." It didn't seem to be enough to simply go to church; we had to walk in looking right. Now, that wasn't because Dad wanted us to look good in front of God; no, he wanted us to look good in front of the other parishioners. If Dad was playing on the road that week, Mom organized this by herself. As we got older, her resolve lessened. Some weeks we didn't make it to church at all.

Whether we were going or not, Dad did make it, even on the road. The Colts often went as a small group. One time they were in a Catholic Church in Green Bay, probably 15 or 20 Colts, easily recognizable as football players and NFL players at that, when the priest asked for a prayer for the Packers to win that day. The Colts sat through it grimacing, but as Artie Donovan, another Catholic, said, "Screw this guy. And we didn't put any money in the collection basket, either."

Lots of people thought they knew Dad, but I don't think so. We kids didn't know or understand him, and that continued even after I became an adult and worked with him. Janice thinks that no more than three people really understood him: Mom, Raymond, and Lenny, all in different ways and on different levels. Janice and I don't claim to have understood him, that's for sure. But for Raymond and Lenny, the level on which they connected, besides football and its nuances, was the spiritual, not necessarily religious although all three of them were that.

Raymond was born and raised in Paris, Texas, the son of a high school football coach. Like Dad, he wasn't highly thought of as a high school or college player. As Raymond said, he didn't catch many balls because there weren't many thrown to him. Maybe it was the not being appreciated or maybe it was knowing from an early athletic age that making teams and gaining playing time wouldn't be easy, but Dad and Raymond connected. At first it was through trying to make the Colts, but eventually it was through the love of the game.

"I loved to play football," Raymond told me. "I come to the Colts. I'm a receiver. I love to play this game. That's all I'm ever thinking about. My job's to catch passes. Then they pick up this guy off the waiver wire in my second year and his name is Unitas, cut by the Steelers. Then I link up with this guy. We play 12 years together. You know, I don't believe any of that's an accident. If you're going to be a receiver in pro football, and you get matched up with the greatest quarterback that's ever played, aren't you going to think about that a little bit as to how that happened. Frankly, there's no question in my mind how that happened. I think God had a plan. I was a part of it, and Unitas was a part of it. What all he had in mind, I don't really know, but there ain't no way in the world that could happen by accident, and I get to play 12 years with this guy. We think alike. We're both focused on nothing but the game. We both had the same work ethic. We talked football all the time."

On a deeper level Raymond and Dad, while friends off the field but in different worlds most of the time—Dad already had a family and Raymond wasn't married yet early in their careers—they found themselves to be soul mates. It wasn't a religious understanding like you might see today, a player kneeling after scoring a touchdown or thanking God for winning the game in the postgame interview; that's not how Raymond or Dad were. They didn't wear their ideals and beliefs on their sleeves; instead, they both wore them in their actions. On the field, they prepared properly and then had faith that their preparation would be enough. Faith, like pass patterns, is something that has to be practiced. Because of Dad's and Raymond's faith off the field, it was easy to have faith on it, especially when you'd prepared properly. Sometimes their on-field faith wasn't enough, but that's what faith is all about—the willingness to turn loose of control and if you've prepared properly, let the chips fall where they may. If they don't fall where you hoped, you get up and do it again. You come out for the next game prepared and ready.

Both men, like most of the players from that era, were humble. They understood that what they did was much greater than simply themselves.

Other people and powers played a role. While Dad got lots of credit, both good and bad, depending on the outcome of the game, he knew that it was far more complicated—not the game but understanding how it came to be and why the outcome was what it was—than how the public thought of it. Dad recognized that football was just a game, an important game not only to the Colts and his teammates, but the citizens of the Baltimore area. Regardless of what happened, win or lose, life would go on. Dad and Raymond were successful in their lives after football. Again, their lives weren't easy, but if the best definition of success is peace and serenity, then they pass. With flying colors.

Raymond won two championships with Dad and was elected to the Hall of Fame. He played in seven Pro Bowls. Dad won three championships, was also elected to the Hall of Fame, and he played in 10 Pro Bowls. Every time Dad played in a Pro Bowl, the church was rewarded financially. It was a small token, I think he would have said, for helping him gain the intestinal fortitude to get ahead in life, to having more opportunities than he ever thought possible. It was a way of saying thank you for the spiritual support the church had given his entire life, the foundation to overcome lots of adversity. Both did a lot more than they ever expected. It was never about being perfect. That's for saints. Dad was a great quarterback, but definitely not a saint.

CHAPTER 12

Mom as Mrs. Johnny U

February 5, 2012
New York Giants 21, New England Patriots 17

The Giants weren't supposed to win. They were 9–7, and the Patriots were 13–3. On paper it was a mismatch. But Super Bowl III proved that what's written on paper is nothing more than paper. The Giants had to win two playoff games on the road, both of them close. The Patriots, on the other hand, had an easier time getting into the playoffs, playing both games at home and defeating the Baltimore Ravens in the AFC Championship Game. Both teams took care of business to get to Super Bowl XLVI.

This particular Super Bowl presented some interesting twists when it came to the Baltimore Colts. It was the first Super Bowl being played in Indianapolis, which had become home to the Colts in March 1984 when Robert Irsay fled under cover of night and snow to relocate to Indianapolis. Robert had since passed away, but his son, Jim, was president of the Colts. Furthermore, Raymond Berry presented the Lombardi Trophy to the winner of the game.

As for the game itself, it was a back-and-forth affair with the Giants having to come back from a 17–9 deficit, finally taking a 21–17 lead with less than 1:00 left. The touchdown play was set up by New England to allow the Giants to score, and when Ahmad Bradshaw realized that the Patriots wanted him to score so they would have more time to come back, it was too late and his momentum carried him into the end zone. Tom Brady led a last-minute comeback that fell short, and the Giants hung on for their fourth Super Bowl win and eighth NFL championship overall.

****

Although it was an upset, the real fireworks of the game came afterward because Gisele Bundchen, Tom Brady's wife and celebrity fashion model, made comments, indirectly, about the Patriots and some of Brady's teammates. That's a big no no. Players' wives and children, even their mothers, are to be seen and not heard. Bundchen made her way immediately after the game into the bowels of Lucas Oil Stadium and while getting on an elevator, she responded to some Giants fans chants with a quote picked up by a couple of reporters. She cursed and then said she couldn't pass and catch balls thrown at the same time, seemingly referring to a couple of dropped balls, one in particular by Wes Welker that would have put New England in the red zone late in the fourth quarter and given it the opportunity to put the game away. It didn't happen, and the Giants took advantage of it. That's the way the game happens sometimes. The best team doesn't always win. The great players don't always make the great play. Football players know that. Coaches know that. That doesn't mean they like mistakes or even tolerate them. But they know they happen, and they happen to everyone, even the great ones.

Welker, now with the Denver Broncos, was Brady's Raymond Berry, a wide receiver who has done more with his talent than just about anyone in the NFL. In 10 seasons he has caught 841 passes, including more than 500 in the last five years. He has made the Pro Bowl five times and been named All-Pro twice even though he was never drafted. He has more than had a good career. He may be in line, with a few more strong seasons, to join Dad and Raymond in the Hall of Fame.

Gisele's comments were out of line. Welker acknowledged after the game he shouldn't have dropped the ball. But more important is the role that wives and girlfriends play, particularly in today's world of instant communication, and the feeling that fans have a right to know everything. Gisele isn't the first significant other to do this, and she won't be the last, but she's big enough in her own right to know that what she says matters.

In a lot of ways, Mom, who always spoke her mind, was lucky to be born and have lived when she did. She occasionally got in trouble for speaking her mind about Dad's teammates, but it never got broadcast much beyond the inner circle of players and their families.

Even today as I interview Dad's former teammates, there's a sense of family and loyalty that means some criticisms and comments just never get said. Not in the heat of the moment, like Gisele, and not even with the passage, in some cases, of more than 50 years. Having feelings is one thing; talking in public about them is another.

Dropped passes or not, no matter whose fault it is, the team—and that includes wives—doesn't talk about it publicly. That's a cardinal rule.

Mom as Mrs. Johnny U

It was late winter or early spring of 2000. I was at a dinner party, I can't recall the exact circumstances, but the specifics of where and with whom aren't nearly as interesting as what was said. Earlier in the year the St. Louis Rams had defeated the Tennessee Titans 23–16 to win Super Bowl XXXIV. I had watched the game as a casual fan. My father had not yet died, and he had watched the game, also as a casual fan. Having grown up the son of a football player, a star no less, there is a big difference between being a fan and truly being involved in the game. I think back to all those Tuesday nights with Dad watching film for hours, sometimes the same play for 30 minutes. Every fan thinks he knows what's going on. Almost always, he doesn't.

Wherever I was, someone was discussing Ray Lewis, who had been involved in, or was near, a bar fight that erupted outside an upscale bar in a fancy Atlanta neighborhood. Two young black men from Ohio were killed. We'll probably never know exactly what happened. At this dinner setting a couple of weeks or so later, a grown man said casually, "I don't care what happens to Lewis as long as he's on the field next year." He stopped for a second. "Okay, suspend him for two games, but the Ravens need him." Yes, that was true.

The Ravens did need him. He was, at the time, the best linebacker in football, the Johnny Unitas of defense of his era, in some ways. Being considered in the same class as my father didn't mean I wasn't flabbergasted. I didn't say anything. Didn't this man, a lawyer I think, know that these two dead men had families? I've learned that the adage that you can talk about anything at a cocktail party except religion and taxes is true, but not entirely true—you can add controversy in sports. The drinks didn't go down as smoothly for the rest of the night nor did the food taste as good.

I understand a fan's attitude about his relationship with the team. The team always comes first. Players, if they can help the team win, are given exemptions from having to follow society's rules that the rest of us have to follow because their prowess on the field excuses boorish behavior. It's true in all sports, but that doesn't mean it's right. As the son of a football player, there is another side to every story. Just like I wanted to say to the fellow at dinner, but was too cowardly to blurt out, "What about the two dead men's families? Maybe they have children? How do their mothers and fathers feel?" Just because Ray Lewis was a great linebacker doesn't give him a free pass. Maybe he wasn't involved, but that doesn't give fans a free pass to forget that football, even if it's the Super Bowl, is still just a game, and that there are lives behind the people who play the game, just as there are lives behind the people who follow and love the game. What appears simple to the fan's eye probably isn't. Fans forget that even though Dad could accurately throw a football a long way and he could perform under enormous duress with thousands of people screaming at him, he was still human. He still had a family that had needs; he still had a wife with whom he had to live a life. When the games were over, the stadium cleared out, and the broadcast over, he came home to us.

It wasn't always two-minute-warning thrilling comebacks. Sometimes, his life, and ours, was both routine and even dysfunctional.

****

Mom as Mrs. Johnny U

My father has a stellar reputation among fans, most of it deserved. Long before he retired, he understood his relationship with the fans in Baltimore specifically and the fans of the NFL generally. Fans like to feel connected to their teams and players. Seeing them on television is a start, but give them more and they will love you. Dad understood that. How? I'm not sure. Maybe it was hard-wired and he would have understood the personal connection in any job he undertook. Whatever it was, it wasn't something that he worked at overtly. If he did, he was subtle. He liked people. He liked talking to people most of the time. He'd grown up without luxuries and saw football as a way to avoid the steel mills. Without fans, there is no NFL. He understood that and he liked having fans. He liked interacting with them. And it came naturally. But just because he did these things didn't mean that my mom did them. Just because he wanted fans didn't mean Mom did. Or me. Or my siblings. He was thought of in a certain light—an image and myth of a man in control who could do no wrong—and while that image was generally accurate on the field, it wasn't always correct off it.

The bigger problem was that people expected my mother and the kids to be the same way. We weren't. Because we weren't, particularly Mom, fans made assumptions. If my mother didn't meet the fans' expectations of being a silent and understanding partner to my father, then there must be something wrong with her. Like any mother, she wasn't perfect, but she wasn't always what strangers thought, either. Like my father, she was complicated. Because he was complicated, she was often misunderstood. Sometimes, she was understood, but out of context. Regardless, most of it wasn't fair.

✳✳✳✳

My mother was a strong woman, a woman born before her time. In dealing with my dad's life, it's easy to forget how much influence my mother had on what he accomplished. She was strong headed, and in the 1950s and '60s, at least in some quarters, it was safer for wives to be seen and not heard. That wasn't my mother.

It's easy to forget that much of what she did allowed him to do what he did. They seemed a perfect match: he loved to play football, very much an old boys' club in the late 1950s and '60s (and probably remains so today). He could concentrate on the game and everything that went with that, particularly as quarterback. He could be a man's man. He clearly loved us as best as he understood that. His role, both as father and famous person, involved his not being around a lot. He didn't really have models for either role, so he made it up as he went along.

Mom understood her role as Mrs. Unitas, the wife of a pro quarterback. She hosted parties, she was expected to go to games and cheer, but she wasn't to impose herself into his preparations. That was okay with her. She liked entertaining. Thanksgiving was always a thrill ride because we never knew who was going to show up, and no matter how many seats were set at the table, it was never enough. Dad had football and everything that came with that, and Mom had preparations of her own: it was, and still is, called housekeeping and raising the children. She relished raising kids; she chose to stay home. Remember, she was the one with the job offer that forced Dad, long before he was an NFL quarterback and famous, to ask her to marry him. Once children came along, she was a mother first, foremost, and always. Sometimes, particularly later in my adulthood, that wasn't easy for me, but that was just the way it was, and there was nothing anyone could do about it.

Not only did it seem that was what she was put on earth to do, but she was really good at it. She kept the cleanest house I've still ever seen. Not only was it clean, with everything in its place, but also she seemed to do it with grace and ease. The things I remember about Mom are that the house always looked like a crew of housecleaners had just finished straightening up, but she had done the work herself. Amazingly, we had no limits as to where we could go in the house. She didn't keep up appearances by limiting three hyperactive boys to their rooms, kitchen, and basement. While we stayed outside whenever we could, we also played all over the house, rough-housing, racing, tackling, and fighting, the things that brothers do with one another, the things that tend to drive obsessively devoted moms to cleanliness crazy. Not Mom. Other things did, but not roughhousing in the house. She even ironed all of the clothes, including our underwear. As for Dad and us, she ironed his business shirts, sometimes his suits, our T-shirts, and even our socks.

The kitchen was her office. She kept it well stocked. We had three drawers expressly set aside for snack foods: one drawer was for the snack type options—chips and pretzels; another drawer was for cookies; and the last drawer housed the candy. While these were supposedly for us, Mom had a sweet tooth. She loved chocolate. She'd sit at the kitchen table, a cigarette always burning in a recently cleaned ashtray, her hands holding a cup of coffee. She liked her coffee black. She liked lots of it. Friends knew if her car was in the driveway, she was in the kitchen, a pot of coffee hot on the stove. We always had dogs, it seemed, and they would be asleep underneath the table, near her feet.

Her specialty was cooking. She didn't cook exotic meals; instead she did the simple things well. She cooked a great meat loaf. She was a product of her times: she prepared scrumptious food that, while simple to prepare, didn't taste that way. The idea of a mother as chef hadn't been popularized yet. She also cooked that way because that's what Dad liked. When it came to the home, he left Mom in charge, and Dad stayed true to his roots, all the while helping with the dishes. He had one small claim to being in charge. At the dinner table, he always made us drink our milk. When Janice wouldn't, he made her go to the basement to finish her dinner.

While Dad didn't seem bothered by the fame that increasingly surrounded him, it wasn't an idea that Mom latched on to or gravitated toward. No question she liked the spoils of fame and athletic success. While my parents understood what it meant to be a great professional quarterback, Mom also understood better than Dad that fame and being named All-Pro didn't get kids to school or dinner cooked or homework finished. On the surface, the way they went about their lives as mother and housewife and dad and quarterback seemed compatible. He was about being prepared and in charge on the field. While he sought advice about possible plays, once the team was in the huddle, all discussion was over. Mom worked the same way—preparation and hard work, and then when dealing with us, no gruff. She was in charge, but if you weren't in trouble, then she was available for conversation. Once I'd been caught, it wasn't a negotiation: she ruled the roost.

Their presence as parents lingered far beyond their being in the house and telling us what to do. Once when I was home alone, I was goofing off in the garage/driveway area. I was filling up glass milk bottles, the ones that used to be delivered to our house twice a week. There was a stack of them in the garage waiting to be returned to the milkman for reuse. At 10 or 11, why do boys do whatever they do? To this day, I still don't why I was playing with them. As I was filling up the second bottle, wet from the spigot, it slipped and I tried to catch it as it hit the driveway. Instead of glass and water, there was lots blood. I had cut my hand—I thought severely—so I ran into the house, leaving a trail of red behind me. I grabbed a kitchen towel, and now there was blood all over the floor and countertops in Mom's spotless house.

As I tended to the cut, actually making a bigger mess than I already had, I wasn't thinking about the injury and whether I needed stitches or if I might bleed to death, or my hand getting infected and then needing to be amputated. Instead, I was worried about Mom yelling at me for screwing around and dirtying her pristine kitchen. Finally, would she tell Dad and if so, what would he say and do? It was this kind of thing, a really dumb move on my part, that could set Dad off.

Looking back on it, how I tried to deal with this deep, bloody cut is funny. I put methylate on it, adding orange to the ever-growing mess. Next I put regular-sized Band-Aids on, at least ten, the red strings littering the kitchen floor, wax wrappers scattered like snowflakes. The bleeding stopped, so I cleaned up, I thought really well, but only as well as a 10-year-old can.

Now I was really scared, in a medical sense. I realized Dad was out of town for an away game. Whenever he played away, he usually left on Wednesday and didn't return until late Sunday night, long after I'd gone to bed. Since the blood was washed away, the Band-Aid wrappers in the trash, and two towels soaked with blood in the outdoor garbage can, I wasn't worried that Mom would be upset. I even hid the dirty tea towel deep under other garbage, just in case Mom decided to investigate.

My solution: redress the wound to make it less obvious and wash the methylate off my arm. Suddenly, Mom was home, grocery bags in hand. I didn't do the easy, casual, "Hi, Mom, I cut my hand and it really hurts and I'm scared." Instead, I played it cool. I didn't mention it. After Mom had put the groceries away, she noticed that I was hanging around in a way that wasn't like me. She asked what was the matter and then noticed my right hand and pinky finger. "What happened to you?" She didn't sound angry. I explained how I'd treated my injury without telling her how it happened. She didn't follow up with the how. I finished off by letting her know that she might want to buy more Band-Aids.

That incident is a snapshot. I was often left alone to do my thing. When I made a mistake, Mom knew exactly what to do. Dad wasn't generally around. If it wasn't training camp or traveling to away games, then it was checking on his bowling alley up the street he'd invested in or doing a photo shoot for an ad or speaking at Colts Corrals, the fan clubs of the team. He was always active in the community, so he might have been at Kernan Hospital visiting crippled children. He might have even been out having a beer or two with buddies or teammates. There were too many wild kids, myself included, for Mom to watch us all the time. When I made a mistake, which was often, my first thought was how much trouble was I in. But most of the time, Mom was too involved in a bigger problem to care much about my issues.

Mom made Dad's lunch every day when he was off to Memorial Stadium for practice and film or in the off-season when he might be on the road as a salesman's assistant. She always made the same thing: a bologna sandwich with mustard and chips and shortbread cookies. It was always in a brown bag on the kitchen counter next to our lunches. Dad never complained. Or if he did, he did it quietly. But that was my parents in a nutshell—simple people who liked simple things, but their idea of a simple life was becoming harder to keep that way.

****

Since this isn't a novel and I'm not giving away what most people already probably know, my parents eventually divorced. There's clear evidence that the marriage wasn't perfect. Even if they hadn't divorced, it wasn't a perfect marriage because my parents weren't perfect people, my dad's accomplishments on the field notwithstanding; they were complex people. Add my father's notoriety, and their marriage was even more difficult. The big issue it seems with my mother concerns her drinking and her drinking habits—what others thought she was doing but wasn't. I don't remember either of my parents drinking much when I lived in their house. Most people who truly knew my mother say she didn't drink much, an occasional celebratory glass of wine or champagne at a birthday party or Thanksgiving. At the same time, because people—usually strangers—have a certain image of what my dad was like—and it involves being close to perfect—the divorce must be someone's fault, so it must be Mom who wasn't the good wife. Strangers have heard rumors she drank too much, and some people who truly knew Mom now claim she never drank, or they never saw her drink. The truth is somewhere in between, coupling my mom's personality and Dad's fame. Myth mixed with fame and everyday reality often is a perverse combination in which someone, usually the lesser known—Mom, for example—gets hurt.

****

We lived in a typical neighborhood in that it wasn't typical. We weren't the only famous family nearby. Brooks Robinson, the Baltimore Orioles third baseman and Hall of Famer, lived on the street behind us. His boys are younger than me so I didn't hang out with them although the Harvey girls, who lived about three houses away, babysat them. The Harveys were in many ways our best friends. We were four boys and one girl, and they were four girls and one boy. The ages, except for Kenneth, my youngest brother, matched up pretty well with us. Our house, mainly because of my mother, was a hang-out spot. We had a pool in the backyard, a basketball goal over the garage, and a pool table in the basement. We had a father who wasn't around a lot so with lots of kids around, it was hard for just a mother to keep up.

We lived at the far end of a cul-de-sac. There were five or six other houses on the street. The Knights lived closer to the busy street where our little street ended. Mr. Knight, a radio personality, was the first Ronald McDonald to appear on television. His daughters were around our various ages, and Kim is now a local Baltimore radio personality. But not all was normal. One of our neighbors was a professor at Goucher College who had a son who was into drugs and drinking. He was a derelict who grew his hair long, a hippie kind of guy. He always was doing drugs, having parties. He was really into music. I mean, you didn't want to mess with David. He was a real badass. Knew jujitsu and karate. His father was a concert pianist, a brilliant guy who was also a major general in the army. He had his entire army garb, from uniforms to hats to medals, in the garage. David used to mess with it all the time. He'd wear the hats and play with the knives. There were even machetes.

It was scary to be around this guy because I never knew what he was going to do. His parents had no control over him. He'd do anything anytime. We'd go up to his room. He had lava lamps and black lights. He had tie-dyed blankets and his bed was up in the corner. It was a strange environment. Like most people, David intrigued me, but I didn't want to be him. I wanted to see what his life was like without having to live it. Just like Dad, I am conservative in many ways, and how I viewed and interacted with my neighbors way back when showed that.

We were kind of friends. He knew who I was, but he was older. He ended up dying from a drug overdose. Everyone has this wonderful image of Johnny U, and down the street from me, there's a guy who's going to become a heroin addict. He knew who my father was but he didn't care. He knew who I was. He didn't treat me any differently than he treated anybody else in the neighborhood. He treated us all like shit.

His hair, as much as anything, made an impression on us because Dad always had a crew cut. Dad was an adult product of the 1950s who had to watch his reputation, but we children were a product of the suburban '60s, featuring rock 'n' roll and hanging out in the woods, or around David's house regardless of how scary it was, doing stuff that we probably weren't supposed to do, like having BB gun fights, setting off fireworks, and building bonfires. All harmless at first, but as we got older, the woods became a place to drink and fool around with girls.

I like to think that I'm pretty straight-laced, and I guess I am. The older I get, the more I realize how much like my father I am in terms of discipline and behavioral expectations. That doesn't mean I was always like that. My father warned me not to get into trouble, and I tried not to, but living in a neighborhood where there were lots of kids, it was hard to always do the right thing. How much my father knew I was up to, I have no idea. I'm pretty sure my mom knew, but she had her hands full with lots of children and being Mrs. Johnny Unitas, a bigger burden than she ever expected.

My mother wasn't beloved the way my father was, even within the Colts. In all my years of dealing with my dad's teammates—at training camp, on the sidelines, at reunions, as manager of Dad's company, and sometimes as advisor in their retirement—I've never met or heard a teammate say anything remotely bad or negative about him. I have, however, heard players and their wives criticize Mom. Because Dad was the quarterback, there was a sense, not ever officially bestowed on her, that Mom was the leader of the wives. She was expected to meet and greet new players' wives and help them negotiate a new city and all that came with that, particularly with children. She loved doing that.

Raymond, for example, wasn't married when Dad started with the Colts, and he didn't get married until about five years later, after both were Pro Bowlers. He often came to our house for dinner, and after he was married, Mom helped Sally as she progressed through being a football player's wife, including taking Sally to the hospital when she had her first kid. It was the middle of the night, and both Raymond and Dad were at training camp in Westminster, and she called Mom who went into the delivery room with her. Sally describes Mom as someone who wasn't "a wring-your-hands, cry-baby sort of woman."

Unlike Gisele Bundchen, who criticized her husband's teammates and got caught by the national media, Mom did the same without getting caught by the media. The media was different then, not interested in the off-field lives of the players, much less their wives. The players and their wives knew Mom, however, and they weren't always enthralled by Mom's behavior. While it's easy to see that Dad was incredibly competitive, so was my mother. She didn't like losing any more than Dad did. However, they didn't handle it the same way. Dad moved forward from losses, immediately thinking about the next game or event. Mom, on the other hand, thought about it and figured out, at least according to her, what the problem was. She also wasn't shy about speaking up. She was more than willing to defend her man, and maybe that's why Dad didn't have to defend himself.

****

Whenever we went to one of Dad's games, we got dressed up, Mom especially. It was as if she were going to church—she wore dress suits, stockings, and heels. I have always been a snappy dresser, but on game day even more so. At one particular game where Dad hadn't played well, a fan sitting in front of me and Mom said, "I hope you're happy, son. Your father blew that game. He's a bum." Then he turned and walked down the aisle and out of the stadium. I just hung my head. Mom noticed that and came to me. Using her pointer finger under my chin, she lifted my head. Her eyes, while dark and deep and sometimes foreboding, now were a soft black.

"Are you upset about what that man said about your father? Let me tell you something." She seemed to be shouting, but she wasn't. It was a whisper, firm and clipped. She was angry, but only I knew. "Your daddy is the greatest quarterback to ever play the game and don't you forget that. Don't you ever hang your head or feel bad about the job your dad did. The reason they didn't win the game is because of the 10 other guys on the field."

Dad probably wouldn't have agreed with Mom, but Mom understood the nuances of children and what we were going through better than he did. He played quarterback and most of the time he won, sometimes he didn't, but no matter what happened on the field, it was time to think about the next game.

145

Unlike Dad while he played, Mom thought about how we were feeling. All five of us children are glad she did because if she hadn't, our family's dysfunctions—and every family has them—probably would have been much worse. Instead of another problem that Dad had to think about, Mom did it for him so he could focus on football.

CHAPTER 13

Who's in Charge?

September 15, 1963
Chicago Bears 10, Green Bay Packers 3

The Packers were defending NFL champions, having won the year before with a 14–1 record as maybe one of the greatest teams of all time. They were opening the 1963 season at home, but it wasn't the same Packers team because of the year-long suspension of Paul Hornung for gambling on football. Nonetheless, the Packers played the Bears tough. The Bears, while finishing third the year before at 9–5, were expecting to compete for the championship. It was a typical Bears/Packers game—lots of defense. There's a reason that this division today is known as the "black and blue" division; there's also a reason four years later why the Colts chose to be in a division with two California teams rather than in one with Detroit, Chicago, and Green Bay. A Colt once said about George Halas that "he didn't care whether he won or not, as long as the other team got beat up."

Little did people know at the time, but this opening game would probably be between the two best teams that year, not just the two best teams in the Western Division. Baltimore had an off year, finishing at 8–6, including four losses to the Bears and Packers. Often teams don't recover from an opening loss like the one the Packers experienced, but they did. They would only tie and lose one more game for the rest of the season, but it wouldn't be enough. Instead, the Bears would finish 11–1–2 and win the NFL championship, including another victory over the Packers. The question about the Bears was whether they had the offense to compete with the Packers because smart football people knew the Bears could compete defensively. They had five defensive players make All-Pro including Doug Atkins and Bill George. The Giants won the Eastern Division at 11–3 but had a bad 31–0 loss to the Steelers. The Giants didn't have to face either the Bears or Packers during the regular season although they played the Bears close in the championship.

****

The best teams don't always win championships. That's true in all sports, but rarely do great teams get left out of the playoffs. Probably that's what happened to the Packers in 1963. As anyone who follows football knows, this debate has been going on for years in college football because it lacks a playoff system. Today in the NFL, the argument tends to be made about teams making the playoffs when they shouldn't. In 2010, the Seattle Seahawks made the playoffs with a 7–9 record. That's what tends to happen when leagues allow more teams in the playoffs and the league is made up of more teams. The 1963 Packers were one of fourteen teams and only two made the playoffs.

If you Google the New York Giants, their official website lists only four championships in bold years, all of them the four Super Bowls they've won. Not listed are the four championships won before the Super Bowl started in 1967. Now the only way to recognize greatness in a team is by whether or not it won a Super Bowl. That also tends to be how arguments go about great teams that didn't make the playoffs; regular season records don't count without playoff victories just as NFL championships before the Super Bowl aren't looked at anymore as legitimate. For example, since 1992, only three teams with 11–5 records haven't made the playoffs. The argument here isn't whether a great team got left out because it didn't, but did a team that wasn't as good get in?

That's a different argument from the 1963 Packers. Or the 1962 Lions who were 11–3. Or the 1948 Bears whose only two losses were to the eventual division champs, and yet the Bears outscored their opponents by two and half times. Or the 1929 Giants who were 13–1–1 with seven shutouts but lost out for the championship to the 12–0–1 Packers. This was three years before a championship was played.

But worst of all is the 1967 Colts who tied for the best record in football with the Rams and who had to put up with a new rule change that didn't allow for playoff games to see who got in the playoffs. As the *Baltimore Sun* said after that 1967 season, the Colts were the best team for 13 weeks of the regular season. In 1963, the Packers were arguably the second best team in the league, but they got beat twice by the best.

In 1967, for the Colts, it's just too bad that season was 14 weeks long.

Who's in Charge?

After missing the end of the 1965 season and watching the Colts lose a tough game to the Packers in the playoffs, 1966 was a big year for Dad. When you're young, you think that the playoffs and championships will come in droves. Winning in 1958 and 1959 reinforced that. But it had been six years with no championships for the team.

But before the 1966 season could be played, the Colts had to finish the 1965 season by playing in the Playoff Bowl, a game between the second-place finishers in the two divisions. It was nothing more than another exhibition, but after the overtime Packer loss, this seeming exhibition took on greater importance. The Playoff Bowl—also another tribute to Bert Bell as it was called the Bert Bell Benefit Bowl—was created in 1959 and first played after the 1960 season for the most obvious of reasons—the NFL wanted more exposure on television now that the AFL existed and televised more of its games. Football game results would be determined by the play on the field, but the rules and types of games played would now be determined by television. No longer would decisions be based on what was best for the players or teams or the sport.

The Colts had played in the Playoff Bowl the year before, and Shula used it as an opportunity to let Tom Matte have some fun. Before the Playoff Bowl in Miami, Matte had thrown a total of 19 passes in parts of three games.

In this game, he completed 7-of-17 passes for 165 yards and two touch-downs. As a reward for Matte stepping in and almost taking the Colts to the Championship Game, Shula opened up the offense. This wasn't like Shula, who was a control freak generally but also a man who knew his team and what it needed. On that day in January 1966, he showed a side of himself that Dad had rarely seen.

There has been a great deal of discussion around my house and football historians about the relationship between Dad and Shula. Clearly, Dad didn't like him much, but I've never been able to figure out why. The most prominent argument about their tenuous relationship has centered around Super Bowl III and not getting Dad in soon enough. But they weren't getting along long before that game. Maybe it was that Shula screamed and yelled a lot. Dad didn't like screamers and hollerers. Dad believed that if you needed someone to motivate you to play well, then you shouldn't be playing at all. There's no question that Dad was the silent type and Shula was the opposite.

Bill Curry tells a story about coming off the practice field his first year with the Colts. It was July and hot, as Western Maryland College seemed to get when the Colts practiced. The team, under Shula, had been out in the afternoon for what seemed like forever to Curry. He said, "I felt sorry for myself. I had a five-week-old daughter, my girl, Carolyn, was in Atlanta. I didn't know if I was even going to make the team, and it was 1,000 degrees outside. I was so tired and dragging up the hill [to the locker room and dorms], taken my pads off and taken a shower. I'd already stayed out longer because I was the long snapper. I simply wanted to quit sweating, but you couldn't because there was no air conditioning. It was almost dark, but I noticed something moving on the practice field. It was Unitas and Berry throwing. It was Unitas' 12th season and Berry's 13th. Berry always carried a flashlight. They were throwing in the dark and the ball never touched the ground. I decided maybe I needed to stay out a little late, too. That's how you teach greatness." That is a difference between Dad and Shula—Dad figured his actions would do the talking or they wouldn't, but no amount of screaming could change that. Regardless of how they got along, Dad and Shula managed to win.

While 1966 didn't play out exactly as the team had hoped, it wasn't all bad. They finished the season 9–5, again second to Green Bay. Dad had a good year, earning his ninth invitation to the Pro Bowl. The season was close enough that before the last two games, Pete Rozelle had a coin flip between the Colts and Packers to determine who would host the playoff game if they tied. Unlike the year before when Green Bay won the toss, the Colts won it this year and would host the game on Christmas Day. Obviously, that didn't happen as the Colts lost to Green Bay 14–10, ending their hopes. Dad had a solid season; however, he wasn't his usual great self. There were lots of nagging injuries and he was still feeling the effects of recovering from knee surgery.

Green Bay would go on to win the first Super Bowl, and before the 1967 season, the NFL would expand again, the first time since the Cowboys and Vikings entered the league earlier in the decade. To accommodate more teams, an interesting rule change happened after the 1966 season that would have a great impact. With the addition of the Atlanta Falcons and New Orleans Saints, the NFL was now a 16-team league, and to deal with that, it created two eight-team conferences with each conference split into two four-team division alignments. The Colts were assigned to one of the Western Conference groups along with San Francisco, Los Angeles, and Atlanta. Management saw this as the easiest group of three, and Baltimore would no longer have to face Green Bay and Chicago twice a year. They also avoided New York, Washington, and Philadelphia twice a year. But the more important change was that there would no longer be playoff games for ties like there had been in 1965. Instead, ties would be broken through a predetermined set of formulas.

As luck would have it, this rule would come back to haunt the Colts. Dad had one of his best seasons in 1967, and it was his last really good one. He was named to his final Pro Bowl and named first-team All-Pro, also for the final time. It would also be Raymond's last year. He struggled, mainly from injuries, and only played in seven games while catching 11 passes. A special relationship, in so many different senses, had come to an end. Like Raymond has said many times, his relationship with Dad was much deeper than just football. They were friends but didn't do a lot together off the field. It was a connection of opposites as players—the highly technical and analytic mind of Raymond meshing with the highly intuitive and reactive mind of Dad. They loved to practice, but it was Raymond who decided what they practiced. He needed to feel the comfort of knowing that he and Dad were on the same page, while Dad needed the power to know that he would decide when to implement their practice skills in games. Both were simple men in that they wanted to win, but they had ethics that they adhered to. Football has always been a rough and physical game, and Dad and Raymond stood up to that roughness. But in many ways, other than being receivers of cheap shots and hard hits, they tended to not dole out physicality. They both beat other teams with their mental toughness, intelligence, and guile.

Eventually, someone was going to bring science to pro football—Paul Brown was already doing more studied approaches to the game with Cleveland in the late 1940s and early '50s—but Dad and Raymond turned an analytical, practiced approach to the game into an art form. They connected on a deeper, spiritual level that neither man could really talk about. It includes God, but not in the sense of reading the Bible together (even though Raymond is a religious man); it had more to do with how they saw the world and how they treated other people, regardless of their standing in the world. Humble is a word that comes to mind, an understanding that they were blessed by something greater than themselves. Neither Dad nor Raymond would have claimed that their greatness was solely because of what they did. They needed others and luck. Fortunately, they somehow found each other 12 years earlier.

****

As a team in 1967, the Colts had a great year, at least record-wise. They were preseason favorites to win the new division—called the Coastal Division—and they ended up tied for the crown. They opened the season with a team they wanted, Atlanta, starting its second year in the NFL. At halftime, at least considering the score, it would be hard to call the game an NFL game. The Colts led 31–7, scoring at will. On the first play from scrimmage, Dad hit

Matte with a 15-yard pass across the middle that Matte ran another 73 yards for an 88-yard touchdown pass. This was the very reason why the Colts wanted to be in the same division as the Falcons. The second half was a different story as the Falcons stormed back to almost tie the game. If Mike Curtis—later to become famous for clotheslining and tackling a fan who ran on the field from the stands—hadn't intercepted a pass near the Colts' goal line with 10 seconds left, things might have been different.

The rest of the season played generally how they thought it would: three blowout wins after the Falcons game, and then a tie with the Rams at home. The Rams were good that year, led by young Roman Gabriel at quarterback and the Fearsome Foursome—Lamar Lundy, Roger Brown, Merlin Olsen, and Deacon Jones—on their defensive front line. It took a couple of dropped passes, including one on the goal line by Ray Perkins and a controversial fumble call with less than two minutes, to help the Rams tie. Raymond didn't play because of injury. He might not have gotten open on the fourth-and-1 from the Rams 14 when Dad threw the ball to Perkins, but if he had, he surely would have caught it. Raymond has said that he can think of only two passes that he dropped in his career (he can remember the exact details of those plays) and only one pass when Dad overthrew him when he was wide open. Furthermore, the controversial fumble probably wouldn't have happened because Raymond wouldn't have had the ball stripped from him the way Willie Richardson did, at least according to the referee. The Colts were clearly the better team that day.

It was the following week that the Colts had a setback, one that would come to haunt them at the end of the year—they tied the 1–4 Vikings on the road. Other than the tie, the *Baltimore Sun* reported that Dad's arm was hurting from tennis elbow, inflammation in his elbow joint, and that it had been hurting off and on all season. This wouldn't be a story in 1967, but it would become important in 1968. Next, they beat the Redskins in Washington in a game that always had local bragging rights implications and followed that up with a narrow 13–10 win at home against their recent rivals, the Packers. In that game, Dad threw two late fourth-quarter touchdowns to lead the Colts back from a 10–0 deficit. While he didn't have great numbers, he completed the passes he needed to win the game.

After the Packers game, it was three blowout wins and then a close win over the Cowboys, an emerging power who would win the Eastern Conference Capitol grouping with a 9–5 record. On December 10, Baltimore would easily defeat the Saints to enter its final game 11–0–2 but needing a tie or victory to win the division. A loss to the Rams would give the Rams the title because the new tiebreaker, the recently installed rule, was about point differential in head-to-head games, and since they had tied their first game, a Rams win would give them the title outright.

The game was in Los Angeles. The Rams were a two-point favorite because of their upset of the Packers the week before. It was a game for the first half, but once the Rams took a 17–7 lead, their defensive pressure proved to be too much for the Colts, particularly Dad. He completed 19-of-31 passes but spent much of the second half on his back even when he did complete passes. Most of the players I talked to who played in this game and the 1965 Packers playoff game mention the 1965 game as harder to deal with, mainly for two reasons: it was close, and a referee's decision on a controversial field goal decided it.

The final game of 1967 against the Rams wasn't close, and it didn't matter what the refs did as the Rams were the better team that day, by far. Most of Dad's teammates had an intellectual answer as to why they didn't win. "The big play for us was John Mackey's catch. If he hadn't taken two steps backwards, we would have had a first down and gone in for a touchdown. That would have given us a 14–3 lead and they would have had to play catch-up football," according to Bobby Boyd. Mackey's explanation: "My cleats got caught in the turf and I stumbled backwards." Maxie Baughan, the Rams' linebacker, stated that they were prepared. "We had Unitas pegged, and how many times have you seen that done?" Much of the strategic discussion after the game centered on how much time Dad had—or didn't have as was the case on this particular day—to throw the ball. His normal 3.5 seconds was shortened generally to 2.6 or so, not even enough time for receivers to finish their routes.

Dad was more philosophical. Again, he showed that once a game was over, it was time to move on. Snyder commented in the Sun that while Dad was "cold and calculating in victory," he was "warm and gallant in defeat." Dad saw the game a bit differently. While he discussed plays that could have gone differently, passes he probably shouldn't have thrown, and ways he tried to help his offensive line deal with the Fearsome Foursome, he also saw the loss in the bigger picture. "The man upstairs is in control. We weren't supposed to win." As he was leaving the locker room, he stopped at the door and spoke to Carroll Rosenbloom, the Colts' owner, "I'm sorry. I tried to get it for you, but I just couldn't do it."

It was the third time in the '60s that Dad and the Colts had played a big game and lost: 1964 27–0 loss to the Browns in the NFL championship, 1965 13–10 loss to the Packers in overtime, and 1967 final regular-season game against the Rams. Green Bay would go on to hammer the Rams, and ultimately, the Packers would play the Oakland Raiders in Super Bowl II and win easily 33–14. The Colts had great hopes for 1968.

****

It's possible that August 25, 1968, may have been the day that saved the Colts' season. It was on this day that they traded for Earl Morrall, a perennial back-up quarterback who had spent the last three years with the New York Giants. The reason stated publicly for obtaining Morrall was that the Colts were worried about the condition of a young third-string quarterback's knee. In reality, they were more concerned about the condition of Dad's elbow, a problem that went back to the previous season. His elbow hurt all the time, but as Shula said, that had been true for some time. By 1968, Dad was 35 years old, and his body, particularly his arm, was feeling the effects of 12 NFL seasons. There was also a preseason game in Dallas in which Dad threw a pass, and maybe he hit his arm on his follow through on a defensive lineman's helmet, or maybe his arm was feeling the effects of practices, games, Pro Bowls, and time spent after practice with the now-retired Raymond Berry.

In an exhibition game against the Detroit Lions, Dad left the game early in the second quarter holding his elbow. He hadn't been effective while he was in the game, and after the game, Shula and other team officials stated that the injury wasn't serious. But it was. Two days later, the trade was made for Morrall. While Dad probably did hit a Cowboys lineman while throwing, his arm problems were mainly the result of lots of years of wear and tear. The newspaper account of the Cowboys game doesn't mention an injury, only that Dad played the first and third periods and a bit into the fourth, and Morrall the second and fourth, fairly standard use of quarterbacks at the end of the exhibition season. It wasn't until the team was leaving Dallas that Dad was spotted by reporters with an ice pack on his elbow, and finally acknowledging that his arm hurt. For him to admit pain was a big deal to the team, the press, and most likely, to himself.

The Colts, a preseason pick to finish second in their division behind last year's champs the Rams, opened their season against the 49ers. Two days before the game, Dad's status wasn't known. Shula announced that he would wait until as close to game time as possible. John didn't play against San Francisco that day nor did he play in the next three games. He didn't play until the fifth game of the season against the 49ers, even throwing a touchdown pass. Dad's return, even though it was during mop-up time in the fourth quarter of a blow-out, made headlines in the newspapers the next day.

Entering the Cleveland game undefeated, the Colts may have been looking ahead to their next opponent, the Rams. Whatever the reason, the Colts played poorly, so badly in the first half that Dad replaced Morrall at halftime. It didn't do much good as he was intercepted three times, and the Colts lost their only game until Super Bowl III. He didn't appear in another game until December 1 against the Falcons. It didn't really matter from the team's perspective as the Colts were on a roll. Not only was the offense the second best in the NFL, but the defense was ranked No. 1 in fewest points allowed.

While the team hummed along to another great season, Dad spent lunchtime of most days rehabilitating at Kernan's Hospital with team physical therapist, Bill Neill, who started with the team in its infancy in 1953. He watched Dad sign as a free agent and wait his opportunity, and when it came, jump on it. Dad was a quiet guy, a man without many friends, although he was friendly, according to Neill, a description I have heard many times. As can be expected of a guy who treats injuries, Neill spent a fair amount of time with Dad but said he didn't become friends with him, a friendship that would last the rest of Dad's life, until the injury in 1968.

Every weekday around 11:00 AM, Dad would go to Kernan and do his rehab exercises. According to Neill—although he's not officially a doctor—Dad was misdiagnosed in terms of what was wrong with his elbow. He had more than tennis elbow or tendonitis; instead, he had ruptured his medial collateral ligament in his right elbow. It eventually healed on its own, but the natural healing resulted in instability of that elbow. After rehabbing, Dad and Neill would go outside on the hospital grounds, Dad throwing, Neill catching. It was a stepladder kind of thing, each day throwing more reps and farther. "We started passing 20 balls, 30 balls, and eventually, he was humming them in," Neill told me. "He was throwing 50, 60, 70 balls with the accuracy and degree that I thought was necessary.

"Then the day came when I called Shula and said, 'We're ready for you to come examine John Unitas.' We met on Homewood Field [Johns Hopkins' football and lacrosse stadium less than a mile from Memorial Stadium] on a Saturday morning. John was there and he had one of his receivers and he threw all kinds of stuff to him. And Shula said, 'Yeah, he's ready.'"

Dad didn't play in the next-to-last game, a fairly routine win in Green Bay. However, he did play in the last game against the Rams. While the prognosticators had predicted the Rams as preseason favorites, it didn't quite work out that way, but just barely. The Rams entered the game 10–2–1, the Colts 12–1, so no matter what happened, the Colts had already won their division. Until the week before, it looked like a showdown similar to the year before would determine the Coastal Division winner, but the Bears upset the Rams, turning the finale into a "meaningless" game. It wasn't for Dad, as he played the entire second half, the longest he'd played all year, completing a respectable 4-of-9 for a touchdown with one interception. Morrall didn't have a particularly good day.

In the Western Conference championship, which neither the winners nor the losers received additional money for playing, the Colts defeated the Minnesota Vikings 24–14 in Baltimore on a muddy, soupy field. Neither team played well, and Dad didn't get in at all. As one of the Colts said after the game, "Last year we lost one game and had a poor season. This year although we've already won our conference it will be a bad season if we don't beat Cleveland." Again, not only did they beat Cleveland, it was a game in which the defense, the stingiest since the league went to 14 games, showed off its stuff, shutting out the Browns 34–0 even though Morrall didn't have a particularly good game. He didn't need to. That's the sign of a good team. Instead, Matte, playing in his hometown of Cleveland, scored three touchdowns. The Colts also avenged their only loss of the season, a 30–20 loss in which Leroy Kelly, a Morgan State graduate whose campus is about a mile from Memorial Stadium, ran for 130 yards. On this day, he couldn't even get 30.

However, the season wasn't over. The New York Jets were waiting in Super Bowl III, led by native Pennsylvanian and fellow Eastern European immigrant-tied legend, Joe Namath. The words of Dad's teammate about beating Cleveland also held true for beating the Jets. And as we know, the loss to the Jets wouldn't just define the 1968 season but would define the AFL/NFL merger and add importance to the Super Bowl. It might not have been the "Greatest Game Ever" like the 1958 games was, but it became the most important game since the formation of the AFL, and remains so today. It brought the tenuous relationship between Dad and Shula into the everyday discussion of NFL issues.

It would also become Dad's most controversial moment in his NFL career.

CHAPTER 14

Stiff-Arming Glam

September 16, 1950
Cleveland Browns 35, Philadelphia Eagles 10

The Cleveland Browns were the New York Yankees of pro football, a dynasty that lasted 10 years, only there was one problem: a perceived lack of competition. They had won four consecutive championships prior to 1950 in the All-America Football Conference. It would be easy to dismiss what the Browns had accomplished because much of their competition was inferior. In 1949, the last year of the AAFC, the Browns went 9–1–2, winning the Championship Game 21–7 against a very good San Francisco 49ers team. In 1950, three teams—Cleveland, San Francisco, and Baltimore (not to be confused with the Colts that would arrive in Baltimore in 1953) joined the NFL, ending the AAFC.

Naturally, fans and followers of pro football and sports in general considered the AAFC an inferior product. This was not, and still is not, unusual. The American League in baseball was originally considered inferior. A number of leagues have sprung up in opposition to basketball, baseball, and football; for example the ABA during the '60s in basketball, the Federal League in the 1910s in baseball, and the USFL in football in the 1980s. Established leagues are always assumed to be better, but the problem in the pro football after World War II is that it wasn't really on the radar except in the cities where it was played. College football ruled in the fall once baseball ended.

Not able to sustain a war between the NFL and the AAFC, three teams joined, and immediately, sports fans wondered just how good the Cleveland Browns were, the only champion the AAFC ever had. However, the Browns had always wondered this while they were winning their four AAFC champi-onships. Bert Bell, the NFL commissioner, clearly had a sense of humor or his finger on the pulse of what people wanted because the first game scheduled in 1950 was Cleveland on the road against the defending NFL champion Philadelphia Eagles. Maybe both. And in the first game of the season, the question many people had—how good were the Cleveland Browns?—would be answered.

This game was played out in papers and magazines for the few weeks before the season started—but not as the only sports news because the story of whether Notre Dame could defend its national title of a year ago (it couldn't, going only 4–4–1) was big news at the time. There wasn't the media hype—we can even call it overhype—that there is today. There were no 24-hour sports stations that needed to fill air time. While it was a big deal, it wasn't. For the players it was, as it was for the NFL. The league needed the Eagles to win and win big.

But that didn't happen.

Clearly, the game mattered in Philadelphia. The largest crowd in Eagles history, more than 71,000 people and almost more than double their previous largest crowd, showed up and watched Paul Brown's Browns totally dismantle the Eagles. For four years, Brown had been asking for a Championship Game between the AAFC and NFL champions, but the NFL declined. Why not? What was to be gained? This opening game, which has since been called "the first Super Bowl" and the "most important NFL game to date," showed that while the AAFC overall was much weaker, Cleveland was legitimate.

The Eagles were not only defending NFL champions; they were two-time defending champions. They had done this by bludgeoning teams to death, first by stopping the run defensively. They packed five linemen and two lineback-ers close to the line, daring teams to pass. Because most teams didn't pass much and their passing offense wasn't sophisticated, the strategy had worked. Except it didn't against Brown, who put his four years of scouting to work in hopes of a "championship" game between the two leagues for this inaugural game in the NFL. The Browns did things that had never really been done before, including sending men in motion and using the pass to set up the run. Throughout his career, Brown developed a reputation for his innovations, including the draw play, the pass pocket, game films to study foes, and hiring a full-time staff. He was years ahead of microphones in the helmet when he shuttled plays in with rotating guards.

Part of his full-time staff that day in 1950 was Weeb Ewbank.

All that was missing that day was a loud-mouth quarterback (something Otto Graham never was), a championship on the line (that would come later in the year when the Browns would defeat the Los Angeles Rams for the NFL title), a national love affair involving fans (which would begin in earnest in 1958), and a large television audience (also to come).

STIFF-ARMING GLAM

I majored in photography in my second attempt at college. It's not important right now why I majored in photography, only that I was finally learning. I don't remember much of what I learned now, but I do remember learning about negative space. My father is like negative space, the areas in a photo that we don't normally look at, if I use a simplistic definition. What we typically look at is the positive space, the particulars that draw our eye. For example, in a photo of Alan Ameche scoring the winning touchdown in the 1958 Championship Game, the viewer notices the huge hole for Ameche to run through. He notices the angle of his body, leaning into the hole, his center of gravity toward the goal line so that if he were surprisingly hit or simply fall down, his momentum would carry him across the goal line. He's clearly expecting someone, probably Sam Huff, to whack him. You also notice the great block Lenny Moore is throwing on the left side of the frame. What you only notice through careful scrutiny is the condition of the field—choppy—or the ankle of one of Ameche's linemen that once you notice, you worry that Ameche doesn't trip over it.

In the age of television—and that's what the NFL was becoming by the late '60s—it wasn't enough simply to be good or even great. It seemed you had to have a shtick, a reason for the fan and viewer to remember you. Football had moved from hard-nosed toughness to hard-core entertainment, and while winning helped, it seemed it couldn't be the only thing. The hard hitting remained, but fans needed more. Hard to believe, but football was moving from its beer and steel mill beginnings to glam and Broadway.

That's where Joe Namath comes in. He was the positive space to Dad's negative (actually Dad was a positive force, but in keeping with photography, by definition, he's the negative space); Namath was what you looked at initially, but after checking him out, the opposite also presented itself. Namath was a self-promoting loud mouth who was hip and sexy, the new sports hero, someone who not only threw touchdowns but also showed men the good life. Furthermore, he was a darn good quarterback, a great athlete, and someone who might have been the next "Johnny Unitas"—on the field only—if not for unfortunate injuries. That's hindsight speaking.

In 1969, Joe Namath was everything that Dad wasn't. He was George McGovern to Richard Nixon; he was the Rolling Stones to Peter, Paul, and Mary. He was a wild child in a man's body; Dad was the neighbor who cut his lawn every week whether it needed it or not. Namath represented the newer AFL and the soon-to-be-merged AFL/NFL, the more pass-happy league, while Dad had a foot in both the mill town feel that George Halas was part of and the more scientific, well-choreographed artistry of athleticism that the merger of the two leagues would bring about. Namath was AFL, the rebel league; Dad represented the NFL, a bit stuffy and staid in its ideas and traditions.

****

Namath was born and raised just up the road from Dad in Beaver Falls, Pennsylvania, about 47 miles apart, but other than both being Western Pennsylvanians, there wasn't much in common between them. Namath, nine years younger, was already a legend before he graduated from high school. He was highly sought after and eventually chose Alabama where he played under the legendary Paul "Bear" Bryant and made a name for himself in college, both as a football player and hell raiser, missing the Sugar Bowl his senior year for violating team rules.

Dad was already well established in the NFL. He'd won two championships and three MVPs. He was a perennial pick for the Pro Bowl. In many ways, he'd become the symbol of the NFL. No longer was the league thought of as a beer and brawling league, represented by types like Bobby Layne and Chuck Bednarik. The play on the field had gotten more sophisticated as had the marketing off it.

Namath was the anti-Unitas. Dad simply played the game. When he wasn't playing the game, he was a father and citizen of Baltimore. If he hadn't had a recognizable face and tell-tale gait, he probably could have walked into a lot of cocktail parties and not been recognized. Not so with Namath. He was the symbol of the new era in pro football. He signed a huge contract with the New York Jets of the AFL and immediately abandoned both his Western Pennsylvania roots and his new-found home in Alabama to move to Manhattan. He posed for *Sports Illustrated* on Broadway, he wore fur coats, and he was in panty hose advertisements. That was Namath's personality, but it wasn't Dad's. He was old school through and through, and no matter what was changing around him, he wasn't going to change much, and if he did, it would be because it was the right thing to do, not the popular thing.

Along with Namath came other changes. Bert Bell had been replaced by Pete Rozelle in 1960 as commissioner and with that change came a new feel to the NFL. Gone were the days of Bell, a football man from the beginning who understood the game and directed the league to benefit it. He'd played football in college, coached at Penn, and later owned parts of the Philadelphia Eagles and Pittsburgh Steelers. He was a players commissioner. He used to speak with every team before the start of the season and hand out his home phone number, telling the players if they ever got into trouble or just needed someone to talk to, please call him. And he meant it. I've heard more than one story of an old-timer who called him at home and had a chat, out of season or at night or a weekend. The league offices were near his home in suburban Philadelphia, and he and another man would put together the league's schedule in his kitchen.

Rozelle, never a favorite of my father's, was an advertising man. He was a Californian, a man who seemed to base his life on image and marketing. One of the reasons for Dad's love affair with Baltimore and Baltimore's love for Dad was the fact that he wasn't about image. He wasn't just a façade. There was a sincerity behind Dad's silence and deep stare. What you saw with Dad is what you got. Now, he was smart and savvy enough to know to keep his mouth shut sometimes, but I don't think he did more than the average citizen in presenting a public persona. He worried first and foremost about winning. He didn't care who you were or who did the heavy lifting, as long as that football got in the end zone on offense and didn't get in the end zone on defense.

The merger of the AFL and NFL was going to happen, and an event like Super Bowl III would have happened eventually. The way it works in the NFL, just like in a lot of sports and other endeavors in life like rock music and film, is that nuanced changes were happening before Joe Willie Namath came on the scene. For example, there was Elmo Wright, who came into the NFL in 1971 but was already known for his "high-stepping" ways as he ran into the end zone in college. He also may have been the first player to spike the ball after scoring a touchdown, which he also did in college, and not soon after, the NCAA outlawed spiking the ball. There was also Paul Brown, who is credited with creating taxi squads and brought organization and logistics to practice time. But just because it was going to happen doesn't take away from the magnitude of what happened in Super Bowl III.

The Colts entered the game with the best record in football. They were 15–1 and had done that mostly without Dad. They had the No. 2 scoring team in the NFL and the No. 1–ranked defense. They had four shutouts and four other games in which the opposition was held to fewer than 10 points. The Dallas Cowboys were the top offense in the league and second in defense, but the Colts—maybe luckily—didn't have to play them. The Jets, on the other hand, were 12–3 and while solid, most experts didn't even think they were the best team in the AFL—which most experts felt was decidedly inferior to begin with. The Oakland Raiders had the best record in the AFL, scored the most points, and gave up the second least. The Jets defeated the Raiders in a rematch of the famous "Heidi" game played earlier in November. Both games, and later Super Bowl III, would show, if nothing else, how important television had become to sports.

The Colts were such prohibitive favorites that the betting line on the game opened at 17 points and ended at 19½. Another reason for the points spread was the number of players in the AFL who couldn't cut it or were backups in the NFL. While it's true that the AFL gave chances to some older starts such as George Blanda and opportunities to NFL backups, it's hard now to see that situation without a touch of irony. Dad is one of the great NFL stories of a player being overlooked. Raymond Berry was almost overlooked. It was Ewbank's 1958 championship pregame speech, one of the few he gave in his career, about how most of the Colts were unwanted by other teams and picked up off the proverbial scrap heap, that many credit as one of the reasons the Colts were able to win that day. How quickly people forget that football isn't just a game played on paper with statistics; finally, and ultimately, it gets played on the field, and as a number of Colts have said since Super Bowl III, if they had played the Jets 10 times in 1968, the Colts would have won nine times. It just so happens the one time they didn't win was Super Bowl III.

****

One of the great trivia questions involving pro football is: name the four people who were intimately involved in both the 1958 Championship Game and the 1969 Super Bowl III. Most serious football fans will say Dad and Weeb Ewbank, who coached the Colts in 1958 and the Jets in 1969. Obviously, Ewbank was the winning coach in both. Also, Don Maynard played in both, as a wide receiver for the Giants in '58 and a star wide receiver for the Jets in '69. The final person is Johnny Sample who was a backup in the secondary in '58 and played a starring defensive role in the Super Bowl for the Jets.

Sample was a native of Maryland, having attended Maryland State, now known as Maryland Eastern Shore. Sample is known for lots of things, but most of them, at least in terms of the NFL and its locker room culture, put him on the side of weird. For example, after he retired from football, he became a very good tennis umpire, good enough to call matches at the U.S. Open. Furthermore, he was a black man trying to make it in the NFL, which he did initially as a backup at a time when NFL teams had an unspoken cap on the number of minorities on a team, around seven. They also tended to see blacks as starters, not as backups, but Sample made the Colts in a backup/special teams role, which could only mean one thing: he was very good. If he hadn't been, he wouldn't have made the team. Moore, for example, was a backup just long enough to learn how to play running back, at which point he replaced Buddy Young, another black man. The system wasn't right; that's just the way it was.

Bill Neill knew Sample in a surprising way. Neill's mother-in-law had a maid who came from the Eastern Shore near Pocomoke City, near where Sample was from. He knew that Sample's nickname growing up was "Happy" and so he called him that one day. They had a good laugh about it. Neill saw why he had that nickname: he was a sunshine kind of guy, bright smile, always laughing and kidding around. He was this way in the locker room and on the field. On the surface, everyone liked Happy until there was a problem in the locker room when Sample committed the unpardonable sin as a ballplayer.

Sample stole money from his teammates' wallets in their lockers. He stole from both white and black players. Figuring that it was an inside job, the Colts players and locker room attendants arranged for a sting operation. While both the offensive and defensive players were in meetings, Sample moved from locker to locker in a chair with wheels, the locker area dark because everyone was watching film. One of the attendants—the mythology of this situation has a couple of different people who hid and where they hid exactly—saw Sample rifling through players' personal items. It reached a crisis point when Big Daddy Lipscomb discovered that Sample had stolen from him. He went after Sample in the locker room in front of the rest of the team, and it took three and four teammates to keep Lipscomb from doing bodily harm. The

Colts would eventually cut him, purportedly for dropping a kickoff in a preseason game. There was more to the story obviously, but that was what the Colts announced and the players said to the press. Maybe he did drop one too many kickoffs or didn't rotate correctly into coverage, but there's no question that his teammates couldn't trust him.

The most important aspect of a football relationship for Dad was trust—to do the right thing on a play, to catch the ball when it was thrown to you, to show up on Sunday ready to play, and to treat your teammates right. It didn't matter which one of those you failed at because if you failed at one, you'd failed at all of them. Sample failed at one too many.

****

Where did Dad stand on the Sample issue? I don't know because he never spoke about it, but he was a product of his time. He called black people the "n" word, but it wasn't a word he used regularly or to describe any black man. It was a way he described people who behaved in ways that he didn't approve of. His brother talked about how diverse their childhood neighborhood was growing up in Pittsburgh and how well everyone got along regardless of race.

But that doesn't mean he was forward-thinking about race. On the field, he only cared about one thing: winning. He didn't care who he threw to as long as the person caught the ball. He once told Jim Parker, who wasn't doing a good job on Doug Atkins and complained that he couldn't block him, that if he didn't figure it out, he'd ask Ewbank to find someone who could. Dad wasn't getting on him because he was black; he was getting on him because he wasn't doing his job.

Moore talked about how there were no differences between teammates on the field and in the locker room, but once they left the field, there was separation. The white and black players went different ways. It was because they had to. Not in hindsight, but at the time, whites didn't go to downtown Baltimore even though they could have. At training camp, for example, in Westminster, black players weren't allowed to go just anywhere. They had to stay on campus;

they couldn't go to the one movie theater in town. Across the street from the college campus was a duck pond where Moore would go sit on a bench and talk to himself and God. He understands that's the way it was; he only wished it had been different. Moore wasn't Sample, and Dad knew that.

As for Sample, Dad had him pegged: in 1971, Sample was arrested by the FBI for "cashing checks he knew were stolen." He wasn't accused of stealing the welfare checks, only cashing them. Once a thief always a thief, I guess is how my father would have thought about him.

****

Lost in much of the hindsight in looking at Super Bowl III is that the Jets were pretty good, better than pretty good, actually. Namath is in fact a Hall of Famer. In 1967, one year before the upset of the Colts, Namath became the first quarterback to throw for more than 4,000 yards. He did throw more interceptions than touchdowns in his career, but like Dad, he made his reputation in big games.

The problem wasn't how well the Jets played or how Namath dismantled the Colts' defense; instead, it was how poorly the Colts played. Much has been made of Shula going with Morrall too long or how Morrall missed Jimmy Orr wide open in the end zone for what fans like to think was a sure touchdown at the end of the first half and instead throwing an interception. Experts have gone back and evaluated the game, and what appears to have happened is that the Colts played tight because they were supposed to win. It was also a perfect storm on a football field—luck went the Jets' way from the opening kickoff, it seemed, and didn't go that way for the Colts. I would like to think that if Dad had gotten in the game earlier, his on-field "magic" might have overcome the forces that seemed to be working against the Colts, but we'll never know. That's what Dad thought, too.

What we do know is that the Jets won 16–7. Dad didn't enter the game until Morrall had thrown three interceptions. Maybe Morrall, after having an MVP season, reverted to the mean. Maybe he felt the pressure. His career had been a series of playing for injured quarterbacks and having great years only to lose his job the year after. Maybe that played into the pressure he felt. It's easy to blame Morrall, but Dad never did. It's true that quarterbacks get credit or blame, probably too much so, but in this case it was more than the quarterback. Whenever it seemed the Colts were going to get things going, there was a fumble or a quick whistle nullifying a Jets fumble. One expert looking at the game many years later believed, if not for the poor luck of the Colts, that they should have led at halftime 20–7 instead of being behind 7–0.

But as Dad always said, "The games get played." It's not about matching up statistics; instead it's playing on the field, and on January 12, 1969, the Jets were the better team.

The irony of it all is that Sample was a star—not the MVP, that went to Namath—but he had an interception and played tough defense in keeping Willie Richardson under wraps. What grated both Dad and other Colts was Sample's mouth. While Namath made a guarantee of victory before the game, on the field, he let his passing and running backs do his talking. Sample was another story. He yapped at the Colts' offense the entire game. At one point, he stepped on Matte out of bounds after the play, Matte having run for 58 yards. It was a play Matte still talks about because if the ref had thrown a flag or kicked Sample out of the game, that might have changed momentum. It wasn't called. The official closest to the play—the one who didn't throw a flag—ended up losing a couple of teeth when Matte's face mask made contact with him.

It's the kind of game that was bound to happen at some point. The AFL or a former AFL team was going to win the Super Bowl; it just so happened to be against Dad's team. It doesn't matter which was the better team. It doesn't matter how many times the Colts would have beaten the Jets if they played again because on that day, the Jets won. Interestingly, the Colts played the Jets four more times between 1970 and 1971—obviously not with the exact personnel—and the Colts won all four contests.

Dad, for being a guy who seemed to always look forward, particularly after a loss, this was one loss he never truly put behind him. Most of the blame he put on Shula for not playing him sooner in the game. Dad never liked Shula, and many people say it was because of Super Bowl III. But Dad didn't like Shula before this Super Bowl. Long before this loss, everybody in our house, starting with Dad and ending with Mom, hated Shula. It wasn't a secret. Our feelings for him were so harsh that whenever anyone needed to take a crap, we said, "I'm going to take a Shula." This game just confirmed what Dad thought of him. But looking back at that game, I don't think Shula lost the game because he wanted to get back at Dad. In Shula's mind, he felt he had a better chance staying with Morrall. He was wrong, but there's no question that his career record proves that he could coach. And just like Dad didn't always throw touchdowns, neither did Shula always win every game.

To his credit, Shula learned from this experience. In 1972, when he was coaching the Miami Dolphins to an undefeated season and Super Bowl victory—a former AFL team again winning a Super Bowl—his starting quarterback, Bob Griese, was injured in Game 5 of the regular season and played sparingly in the AFC Championship Game. However, Shula started him over Earl Morrall in the Super Bowl.

Dad must also have learned from the experience because he was getting up in years, particularly as a quarterback and player who had played through some tough injuries. He'd learned by this time—his experience with Colts teams throughout the early and mid-1960s just missing opportunities to win championships—that adding to his two NFL championships was growing shorter. Nonetheless, he would have one more opportunity—1971—in Super Bowl V. At least on the football field, it seemed whenever Dad was faced with a setback, such as a loss to the Jets in Super Bowl III, there was another opportunity to make it right.

CHAPTER 15

Wild Rumors

December 12, 1965
Green Bay Packers 42, Baltimore Colts 27

Dad was out with a season-ending injury. The Colts were leading the Western Division, and if they won this game, they probably would have won the division. By losing, the Colts had to win the next week, which they did, and they needed the Packers to either lose to win the division or tie to force a playoff. The 49ers scored late in that final week to tie the game and create the playoff game in which Tom Matte played quarterback.

What was not as significant at the time, but historically interesting looking back at this Colts game on December 12, was that it was Paul Hornung's swan song in his NFL career. Hornung scored five touchdowns: three rushing, one on a 50-yard pass, and another on a 65-yard pass from Bart Starr. Don Chandler added six extra points, the same kicker who would make the controversial kick in overtime in the Colts' playoff game. The game was close until halftime, and then the Packers scored two touchdowns to take a 35–13 lead. The Colts almost clawed back into the game, scoring twice to make the score 35–27. Late in the fourth quarter, Hornung showed up again, catching the 65-yard pass and putting the game away.

This game was probably Hornung's last great game. It highlighted what a versatile player he was; many experts call him the greatest short-yardage runner in the history of the game. He also could catch passes and block. He occasionally threw a halfback pass. His versatility was such that today there's an NFL award named after him given to the most versatile player in the league for that season. Also, in 1960, Hornung had been the Packers' kicker, setting a record for most points in a season—176—a record that stood the test of time when the length of the season expanded to 14 games and then to 16 until LaDainian Tomlinson bettered it.

The year before, Paul Hornung—the Joe Namath of the late 1950s and early '60s before Namath arrived on the scene—had been league MVP, but it was his being a Joe Namath–type, not his football playing, that would get him in trouble with both Lombardi and commissioner Pete Rozelle. Unlike Dad who was a goodie-two-shoes compared to some other NFL players and their antics, Hornung liked to have a good time. He often violated team rules, resulting in fines from Lombardi. But Lombardi was also smart enough to know that he couldn't control Hornung, and as long as he performed well, Lombardi wasn't too hard on him.

The issue with Pete Rozelle was a different matter. Coming off a 14–1 NFL championship year in 1962, Rozelle discovered that Hornung had been betting on league games, although never against the Packers. Like Dad, who tried to be as honest as possible, Hornung quickly admitted his involvement. He was embarrassed and ashamed. Nonetheless, Rozelle suspended him and Alex Karras for the 1963 season.

Pro football had its roots in the industrial mill towns of the Midwest, but it also had its roots in gambling, particularly the Eastern cities. Art Rooney made money owning horse tracks, and for years, it was rumored that the $500 he used to buy the Steelers came from a racing bet he'd won. He always denied that rumor. The Mara family, who own the New York Giants, was also involved in gambling; Tim Mara, the founder of the Giants, made his start in lower Manhattan as a runner for bookies. Carroll Rosenbloom, who brought the Colts to Baltimore in 1953, had a reputation for gambling, even to the point where some whispered that it was an addiction.

The last thing the NFL needed in the early 1960s, just as the sport was making progress against baseball and college football, was a betting scandal. While the news about Hornung was unfortunate, it didn't become a scandal. Because of the way he handled his situation, Hornung still got elected to the Hall of Fame although it was on his 11th chance. Later in the early 2000s,

Hornung said, "You know what, looking back it just pisses you off. I knew 10 other guys who bet. They didn't get them all in my day. I wasn't going to say anything, naturally. But I knew the guys who were betting. They'd brag about it and talk about it. Even back then, they didn't get everybody who was guilty. There was no use in me causing a stir by saying there were other guys who weren't caught that I knew were gambling. Sure, it was more of a, I don't know, a friendship deal where you'd bet $50 or $100, an insignificant amount. There was nobody betting enough money to throw a game or anything like that. That never happened."

Even years later, maybe a bit angry about missing a season, Hornung understands the importance of integrity in the league. As for the New Orleans Saints players who were suspended during the 2012 season, Hornung agrees: "I never knew of anybody who got paid to take somebody out. That wasn't a part of the game as far as we were concerned. They would look out to really give you that good hit. There's no question. It's a tough game. You go out there, and it's about hitting."

The game on the field is about hitting for the players, but for the fans, it's about cheering and winning. But what actually is happening, both during the game and after, is so much more. Hornung could play hard while betting on the side, not in anyway influencing the outcome of a game. But fans didn't know about this.

Long before a game is played, and long after it's over, there's a back story that changes the game on the field. After the Colts lost Super Bowl III, the repercussions ran deep for the Colts family. Change and adjustment were there, but only if you were looking for it and knew where to look.

WILD RUMORS

The Colts lost Super Bowl III, and while it was beyond surprising, it had implications far beyond simply embarrassment. It's not that the loss added one more straw onto the back of Don Shula. The newspapers in Baltimore were growing tired of Rosenbloom, and Rosenbloom had begun wondering if he wanted to remain as owner of the Colts. Implications weren't limited to management; many of the Colts had played the game expecting to win, and winning meant getting a bigger share of money than losing. While the team may have been overconfident or played tight because of the line, Tom Matte had already bought a house using his expected winner's share as the down payment. He wasn't the only one, either.

There's no question that pro sports have changed since Dad played. The NFL has 32 teams now rather than 12, the season is longer, and the equipment is more technologically advanced. The game seems to have moved—though not entirely—from a player-centered sport to a coach-centered one. There are still marquee players—Peyton Manning immediately comes to mind—but not as many as when Dad was in his prime. The sport seems more individual focused, be it coaches or players, and less team focused. Love affairs between teams and cities last only as long as the team is winning. Probably what has most led to this change is free agency. Players don't stay with teams for a career. Dad played for the Colts for 17 years. It might even be argued that his moving to San Diego was because of a change of ownership. If Dad had had his way, he would have thrown his last pass in Baltimore and moved into the Colts' front office. But even Dad's life had things go ways that were out of his control.

Seventeen years in one city is still a long time. Few players do that today. Few players play that long. They don't have to. The money has gotten better. But the game and playing it is about more than money. There's a rush that only the sport at this level can supply. Super Bowls and the hoopla surrounding winning have added to this rush.

Some things haven't changed at all. Regardless of money, it takes a certain kind of athlete to play football. Not only does a football player need to be athletic, he must also have a high threshold for physical pain, both short and long term. There is something in the makeup of a football player that shapes his persona, maybe even his character. Because of the toughness, there remains an underbelly that hasn't changed regardless of more money, better medical treatments, or more acceptance of race. A silent code exists between players, probably because fans and reporters haven't been through the grind of training camp, preseason, regular season games, and postseason games and all the pain that entails. Even though most fans know there's more to football than what happens on Sunday afternoons between opening kickoffs and the final whistle, I don't think most fans understand the pain endured during the week, the waking up and taking at least 15 minutes before taking your first step, or the lying to doctors and trainers about the stars floating around your eyes because if you tell the truth, you're done for the day, and being done for the day might mean you're done for good.

That's the piece of being a football player that changes what the game means to you, and how you interact with it. Sometimes football players act toward their sport as if it's an evil stepmother. Nonetheless, they wouldn't do anything else. If you don't understand that aspect of being a player, you ultimately won't get any aspect of them. That's how football players think.

I know. I've been around them all my life.

****

In my dad's aborted autobiography—he wrote only one chapter on an antiquated Underwood typewriter in 1995 covering the 1958 Championship Game—he spent the last three pages discussing whether or not that game had been thrown, as in had the Colts gone for a game-winning touchdown in overtime instead of a field goal because Rosenbloom had placed a large bet on the Colts beating the spread. Even I find it interesting that my father spent so much time in that chapter discussing a vaguely held perception by a few people closely connected to football back in the late 1950s, and that he ended his first chapter discussing gambling when he could have been discussing so many other things, like the changing of the game and how television would make the game a different animal than it currently was in 1958.

My father wasn't much of a gambler, and in many ways he was a prude, not only about sex but also about what went on with football teams outside the locker room. The Colts, for example, were famous for having mandatory in-season weigh-ins on Friday afternoons, sometimes as much as a $100 fine riding on linemen making weight. After weighing in and making the con-tracted weight, the team almost in its entirety retired to either a bar about a mile from Memorial Stadium or Bill Pellington's restaurant, the Iron Horse. Dad always went. He'd stay for a beer, maybe two, and then go home. He had a family to see to, but so did a lot of the other players. I think he went home, more often than not because he was the quarterback and needed to keep professional distance from his teammates so that when they screwed up, he could drop the hammer. He also knew he couldn't be around trouble, if that trouble was to become public. He also left because Dad was an introvert. Too much time with too many people got to him. I'm not talking about time on the field with 60,000 fans. That didn't faze him. He didn't know them person-ally. Instead, with his teammates, it was the small talk and the camaraderie: he wasn't comfortable with it regardless of how it may have seemed to outsiders and strangers. He liked to be alone or with a few friends, generally friends who had nothing to do with football.

There's the famous story about Dad after he was traded to San Diego and walking into a darkened training room in which some players were smoking marijuana. He was offered a toke but turned it down. This story has been offered as evidence of why he retired; he wasn't part of that team and the players were more interested in having a good time than winning. That may have been true, but the truth is that San Diego was part of three different cultures, maybe four, that my father didn't understand: the AFL—a rebel league; California—the Left Coast; and a younger generation—the "wild '60s." San Diego also wasn't Baltimore. That was important, too. He said the game had changed—it had to some degree, and he'd been a reason for that change—and that was why he was getting out. That's an explanation, not a reason. The reason was pretty simple: it was time. He could no longer be a great quarterback, but learning that lesson and understanding it didn't come easily to someone who had been a star.

As for the idea of gambling on a game, Dad wasn't so naïve that he knew it couldn't happen. He played with the likes of Bobby Layne, who was a notori-ous wild man but one of many. He played with Jimmy Orr who caught three touchdown passes in a regular season game and didn't remember it after the game because he was either still drunk or just entering the early stages of being hungover. When Orr was told in the locker room the kind of game he had, he shrugged. But Dad didn't care because Orr ran his routes and caught the balls thrown to him. Dad also competed against Hornung, but the Colts lost twice to the Packers in 1963. Dad did card shows and appearances with Mickey Mantle. He once told me the story of Mantle putting mirrors on the top of his shoes so he could look up women's dresses in restaurants and bars. Dad understood the "boyish"—immature really—behavior of some of his teammates and contemporaries. That didn't mean he participated. But he didn't stop it, either. Even still, he was a man's man even if he didn't participate fully in the "boys will be boys" behavior.

Dad easily would have believed that Rosenbloom bet on the game. There's no question that Rosenbloom gambled and gambled a lot. There were, and still are, persistent rumors that Rosenbloom bet on pro football. A story or two floats out there about people he worked closely with overhearing phone conversations about betting on his Colts and even asking for advice about the Colts' chances on a given day.

Regardless of whether or not he bet, there's a problem with the idea that Rosenbloom unduly and illegally influenced games. Rumors float about his game decisions, plays that were called, and some plays that should have been called but weren't. If Dad was alive, he'd say, "Hogwash" or something worse. Rosenbloom couldn't have influenced decisions on the field because Dad was the one calling plays. Dad may be a lot of things, particularly a lot of complicated things, but one thing he never compromised on was winning. That was what drove him, not fame or money or celebrity. Winning was the only priority.

The other thing Dad didn't do real well with was authority. He got along with Ewbank because Ewbank didn't try to run Dad's show: the Colts' offense. He liked Rosenbloom, and he didn't tell Rosenbloom how to run the team, but he surely wasn't going to let Rosenbloom tell him whether to go for a touchdown or field goal.

If you think this is just a son defending a dad, even protesting too much like Dad did in that unpublished first chapter, others have said the same thing. Art Modell, once owner of the Cleveland Browns and the Ravens, doubted the rumor to his deathbed, "It was just a wild rumor." But more importantly, Modell, someone my dad had mixed emotions about, said, "Carroll would never have influenced a coach or anyone else, especially with Unitas as quarterback." Steve Rosenbloom, Carroll's son, added, "Unitas ran his own show. Half the time he didn't use the plays called in from the sideline." Clearly, Dad wasn't going to use a play called by Carroll Rosenbloom.

****

Many years after Super Bowl III, Dad and I were in the green room before the filming of an episode of *Coach*, a TV series that included Bubba Smith, a teammate of Dad's who played with him in Super Bowl III. Smith was one of the greatest college players ever, having led Michigan State to a 9–0–1 season, including a 10–10 tie against Notre Dame in 1966, his last college game. He became the No. 1 pick overall in the 1967 NFL Draft. He was a man-child, a freak of nature, but he didn't have the kind of pro career that many expected. He was good, but not great. Twice he was an All-Star. After his NFL career, he made a much bigger name for himself as an actor, particularly in beer commercials and bad cop movie spoofs. Even as an actor, he was still large, big in that way only sitting in the green room reveals.

That night in the green room, we were waiting as only one can do in show business, unsure when we'd be called to do our scene. We were bullshitting, not unlike what football players do when they're wasting time. Not unlike what these men, Dad included, had done in a locker room before and after practices. Storytelling. Dick Butkus was also there. Al Michaels, now lead announcer for NBC's *Sunday Night Football*, was in the room, too. Dad was telling stories about hanging around Mickey Mantle. There were other stories too, about what, I don't remember because it was simply passing time.

Until Bubba quietly spoke. "You know, I bet on Super Bowl III. Put

Dad played quarterback and defensive back for the University of Louisville. The University has since retired his No. 16, and a bronze statue is erected at one end of Papa John's Stadium.

In the 1960s, Dad was spokesperson for a variety of
companies and products, including Baltimore Federal
Savings Bank, Royal Crown Cola, Crown Central
Petroleum, and Speidel Watchband.

Johnny Unitas (19) takes off for a second-quarter gain against the Washington Redskins on December 1, 1963. *(AP Photo/John Rous)*

Johnny Unitas confers with Coach Don Shula on the sideline while down 20-17 in the final minutes of the game on September 26, 1965, at County Stadium in Milwaukee against the Green Bay Packers. Tom Matte fumbled on the Packers' 23-yard line, and the Packers recovered to hang on for the victory. *(AP Photo)*

A mid-1960s family photo with Mom (Dorothy), Dad, John Jr. (front), Robert (behind John Jr.), Christopher (middle), and Janice in the living room of our house in Lutherville, Maryland.

Dad, John Jr. (behind Dad over his left shoulder), and brothers Robert (to Dad's left) and Christopher (in front of Dad) shooting hoops. (Jos. C. Unitas)

Dad was the 1965 Honorary Chairman of the March of Dimes, pictured here with host parents and their daughter and Maryland Governor (and later vice president) Spiro T. Agnew.

Dad presenting the 1997 Johnny Unitas Golden Arm Award to Peyton Manning.

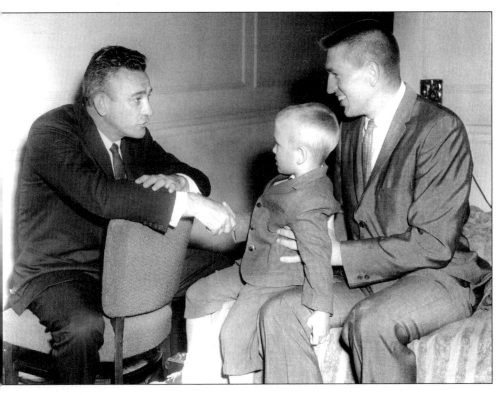

Dad (right) introduced me to Charles Albert Conerly Jr. (left), the quarterback for the New York Giants from 1948 to 1961.

Johnny Unitas (second from left) met President Richard M. Nixon (center) at the White House with administrative staff.

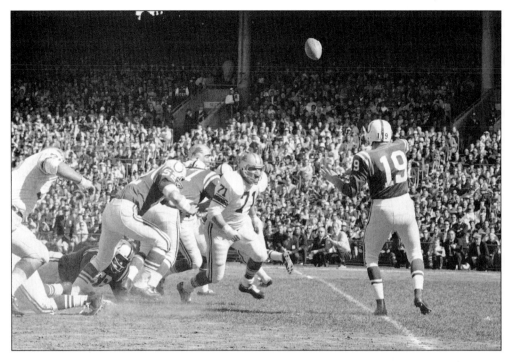

Johnny Unitas (19) passes to Raymond Berry for a touchdown in the first quarter against the Detroit Lions on November 19, 1967, in Memorial Stadium. *(AP Photo/SS)*

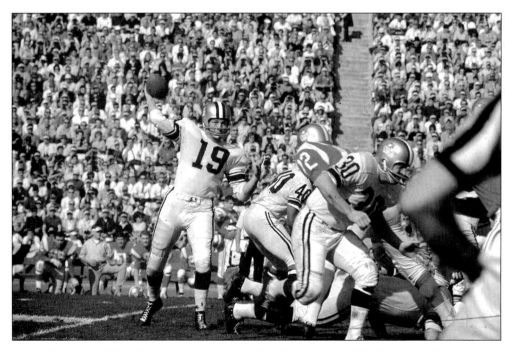

Johnny Unitas of the West All-Stars passes against the East All-Stars in the NFL Pro Bowl on January 21, 1968, at the Los Angeles Memorial Coliseum in Los Angeles, California. The West defeated the East 38–20. His selection, based on his performance in the 1967 season, marked the last of his 10 Pro Bowl appearances. *(AP Photo/NFL Photos)*

John Unitas completed 3-of-9 passes for 88 yards and a touchdown in the Colts' 16–13 win over the Dallas Cowboys in Super Bowl V on January 17, 1971, at the Orange Bowl in Miami, Florida. *(AP Photo/NFL Photos)*

Dad was photographed in his trophy room in Baldwin, Maryland, for a Transamerica promotion.

money down on us [the Colts] and a bit less on the Jets. Just covering myself, you know."

I was stunned. Speechless might be a better word. My father's eyes ballooned to a 500-watt bulb. Bubba had said it so nonchalantly, as if he were talking about the weather or the rising cost of gas. Dad stared at Bubba with those glaring eyes, the same ones he burned into a teammate. It was also the look he'd given me many times, and I knew how to react, but I wasn't sure Bubba would. I knew what that look meant; I was prepared for the worse. Dad said, after a long pause, "Bubba, are you fucking kidding me?" Then one of the show's assistants stuck his head in the room and the conversation ended as quickly as it started.

Considering how crazy and chaotic Dad's and my days were back then when we went to these kinds of events, we never spoke about it afterward. But I remember looking over at Dad at that moment, and he was quickly rather nonplused about Bubba's comment. Football players are "gamblers" by nature; they believe they can win at anything. To make it as far as the NFL, a player has to have supreme confidence in himself, and many, unlike my father, publicly showed that. Some, like Bubba, put something tangible on his talent, but also covered himself by betting on the Jets because that was prudent, at least in his eyes. I don't know if Dad wasn't surprised—by this point in his life, sometime in the 1990s, nothing that happened with his teammates could surprise him. As with everything else that seemed big and pressure-filled and controversial, Dad didn't let on about his thoughts, not immediately or publicly. It was probably a mixed bag of reactions.

****

It's easy to see that Dad and Baltimore were made for each other. While it seems that Baltimore and Pittsburgh are competing sports towns that don't get along—at least not recently as seen in the rivalry between the Ravens and Steelers—they are two cities that have much in common, maybe the most important being they respect working-class, down-to-earth people. That's

Dad. I never asked him why he didn't move back to Pittsburgh, but by the time he retired, he had been in Baltimore more than 18 years and all five of his children were growing up here. It was a glove that fit, so I guess he saw no reason to take it off.

On the other hand, the "marriage" between Rosenbloom and Baltimore and the marriage between Shula and Rosenbloom weren't forgone conclusions. When the Colts returned to the NFL in 1953, it was commissioner Bell who asked Rosenbloom to become an owner. Unlike in today's sports world in which people are clamoring to own franchises, that wasn't the case in the early '50s. While Rosenbloom had been born in Baltimore, he'd long fled it, moving to Margate, New Jersey, and headquartering his non-football ventures in New York City, even though he'd made his millions in Virginia. When he'd hired Shula after the 1962 season, he stated in the *Sun* that he expected Shula to win a championship the next year. That's how good he thought his Colts were. Obviously, Shula didn't win in 1963, lost the championship badly in 1964 to Cleveland (the last Cleveland championship to date), lost a difficult playoff game in 1965 involving the controversial Don Chandler field goal, and then was left out of the playoffs in 1967 with the second best record in the NFL. I've been over this before, but it didn't change the fact that the love affair between Rosenbloom and Baltimore, particularly the newspapers and their reporters, was ebbing. Rosenbloom expected the team's performance, Shula, and championships to keep the papers at bay.

When he lost Super Bowl III, Rosenbloom found his excuse. Shula survived one more year, not a good year when the team finishes 8–5–1 and out of the playoffs. The Miami Dolphins were looking for a coach, and more than likely Shula was looking to get out. He has acknowledged that his relationship was never the same with Rosenbloom after the Jets loss. So it seemed a good deal for everyone, particularly since the Dolphins were making Shula general manager and giving him a piece of ownership of the team. Shula did what probably anyone would have done: he took the deal from the Dolphins.

There was one problem: he was still under contract with the Colts. Later,

Pete Rozelle would agree that it was a problem, granting Rosenbloom and the Colts a draft choice as compensation.

✸✸✸✸

There are two major issues with injuries and football, and those two issues occur after a player accepts that he will be hurt, probably badly, at some point in his career. The first issue—the one my father campaigned hard for after he retired—is what the injuries do to you long after you've finished playing. My father was a billboard for that. He's not even the best example, but he's one example I saw almost daily struggling to walk and hold a golf club in his retirement from football. While he was always bowlegged, he didn't always walk with a limp. Cataloguing my father's injuries would take a diagram of a skeleton and arrows to the many places he injured: ribs, ankles, feet, knees, Achilles, nose, head, elbow, and particularly his hands. He probably broke every knuckle on his right hand. By the time he was 50, just 10 years out of the league, his hand looked like gnarled oak tree roots. He could still look you in the eye, and he did, but the idea of a firm handshake was gone. He sometimes shook hands with his left hand, which was not in much better shape but at least more functioning.

His right hand posed a big problem. One way for Dad to get a job was as a spokesperson for a product, and this often included playing in golf outings. He could also make extra money appearing and playing at celebrity tournaments. But with his right hand gnarled and his elbow permanently injured from the 1968 season, Dad couldn't grip the club. The limp could be dealt with by using a cart.

I don't remember much about Dad's playing days, but it was through watching and playing golf with him that I saw his incredible competitiveness. For anyone who says Dad wasn't a great athlete and couldn't play in the NFL today because he wasn't strong enough or didn't run fast enough, you need only see him play golf. Without formal lessons and despite not picking up a club until adulthood, he made himself into a pretty good golfer. Regardless of how good he really was, he didn't like to lose, to me or J.C., his grandson, or a foursome of strangers at a business outing.

By around 60, sometime in the early 1990s, it looked like his golfing days might be over. Instead, a friend suggested that he Velcro his hand in place to the club, tearing some Velcro off a worn out golf glove and wrapping it around Dad's hand once he placed it on the club grip. It worked, and Dad went to JR's Shoe Repair in Timonium to see Johnny Sauers, the proprietor, near his house to figure out how to make this glove so it wasn't so jerry-rigged. He did, and Dad continued to play golf until his death.

Not all players were so fortunate to escape the NFL with only a gimp and a bad hand (although Dad had lots of other small aches and pains that he ignored and didn't talk about). The last of three times Dad was on the cover of *Sports Illustrated* was about a year before his death; he posed for an article about retired players filing lawsuits to improve health benefits for retired players. He was advocating because he knew it was the right thing to do. The game exacted a price, sometimes that price took years to learn about, and he, along with many others, needed help. He filed a lawsuit against the NFL to get workers' compensation for the disabilities he experienced because of the beating he took while playing. His toughness as a player had come back to haunt him.

But that was the problem: if he hadn't been tough, he might not have made or stayed in the league, and instead of being a famous NFL quarterback (which comes with a lot of nice perks, but also a lot of morning aches and pains), he might have ended up being a carpenter or truck driver, maybe a P.E. teacher.

I'm not 100 percent sure what Dad would say about the recent pay-for-big-hits scandal in New Orleans, but I do know that he spent the last 10 years of his life working tirelessly to deal with the post-football-career health of players. He watched John Mackey deteriorate—as I saw first hand at Dad's funeral—into a shell of his former self. Mackey wasn't and isn't the only one.

But in the late 1960s and into the early 1970s, Dad wasn't yet worried about post-career injuries and whether he'd be able to grip a golf club. Instead, he was worried about the winding down of his career, not a phrase he would have ever used. In his mind, he was a starting quarterback, and then one day he'd be retired. He was in his late thirties, not a young man anymore, with a fifth child, Kenneth, born in January 1969 just before the loss in Super Bowl III to the Jets.

I was in high school. My older sister, Janice, was thinking about college. Dad wasn't just a superstar quarterback who had to deal with football issues off the field, whether they be his declining skills, his relationship with coach Don Shula, or if Rosenbloom could get a new stadium built that he felt the Colts so desperately needed to stay competitive. Dad also had non-football issues with his family. Today, it sounds funny to call problems and troubles swirling around his family "non-football issues," but that's what our lives seemed like at the time. Everyone knew and appreciated Dad for his football ability as if that's all he had on his plate. Sometimes even Dad treated his life that way, too. Maybe he was a product of his time, more a 1950s dad—a man who provided but wasn't around a lot—than a 1960s dad—a man more intimately involved in his children's lives. Maybe he was more involved than I remember. Or maybe, just maybe, while Dad knew how to make the right calls all the time on the field, he didn't when it came to his wife and children. Maybe he had great football skills but not great parenting skills. Maybe he didn't really have any parenting skills at all.

Maybe that's the underbelly of the NFL life that most fans don't see. Yes, there are injuries and gambling and politics that involve coaches and owners and players, but there are also the families.

Although it would take some time to truly surface, the Unitas family wasn't doing well. The family structure was cracked, the foundation weak. Just as the NFL was changing, whether for better or worse, so was my family, and clearly it wasn't for the better.

No matter the reason, life at home wasn't good. As his football career suffered ups and downs, so did his home life. Football was going to end; it does for everyone. Being a father would go on, and for the first time, Dad wasn't All-Pro at something. He wasn't even behaving like a starter or a backup. Instead, he was doing the job of father like someone who needed to be cut.

CHAPTER 16

Football Wise, Business Stupid

February 4, 2007
Indianapolis Colts 29, Chicago Bears 17

The first Super Bowl in January 1967 wasn't even sold out. The Green Bay Packers were expected to win, and they did, easily. When the expected happens, there's not much news or entertainment in it. It wasn't until the third world championship between the AFL and NFL that the game was called the "Super Bowl." Even something as grandiose and culturally important as the Super Bowl took time to become important. Namath after Super Bowl III didn't become bigger than the sport or the game. He was already big, at least in New York, and he was in the long line of New York athletes who Americans have been fascinated with, including Babe Ruth, Lou Gehrig, Joe DiMaggio, Mickey Mantle, Frank Gifford, and Pele (of the New York Cosmos). Today, think about Rex Ryan, who's not even a player but a coach whose every move is monitored by the media it seems, particularly in the media capital of the world, New York.

Super Bowl XLI in Miami was the first in a long time to be played in rainy conditions. On paper, Chicago seemed to be the better team. They had the best record of the two at 13–3. It was a sloppy game, Chicago going out to an early lead. Manning led the Colts in their first Super Bowl since the team left Baltimore in 1984 back from an early deficit to win 29–17. He was named MVP of the game, completing 25-of-38 passes for 247 yards and one touchdown.

No question, by 2007 the Super Bowl was the biggest event in North America. Most Americans would like to say it's the biggest event in the world, but World Cup soccer every four years is bigger. The Olympics are bigger. The biggest part of the 2007 Super Bowl was Peyton Manning, who was named MVP of the game, and he used the exposure to take huge leaps into the world of marketing and commercials. While playing football is an important part of how he makes money, doing commercials is not far behind. Granted, he needed football to open up the off-field opportunities, but once they opened, he waltzed on stage to the tune of millions of dollars a year. In 2013, six years after winning a Super Bowl, he made $18 million from his football contract and $13 million as a pitchman. The Colts win of 2007 was different in that the country took to Peyton Manning so much that he became ubiquitous on television on weekends, hawking televisions, cable services, pizza, and cell phones.

It seemed Manning was going to be big—larger than life—but it took time. It took more time to become a spokesperson than a great football player. He made the Pro Bowl in his second and third seasons, not necessarily a surprise to knowledgeable football people. Manning is from a "royal" football family. His father, Archie, a friend of my father's, played college football at the University of Mississippi, married one of the cheerleaders, was the second pick of the 1971 draft, and produced three boys, two of whom won the Johnny Unitas Golden Arm Award, have starred in the NFL as quarterbacks, and are probably both in line for the Hall of Fame. Because of his college career, finishing second in the Heisman voting and winning Dad's Golden Arm Award, Peyton was expected to dominate the NFL and win championships, but that didn't happen. He often dominated the regular season, but he got labeled for not winning the big one. He didn't win his only Super Bowl until his ninth season, and maybe it took that upsetting of expectations to make him feel like an "everyday Joe." He was supposed to be great right off the bat and he wasn't. He had to struggle. Once he got his championship, his aw-shucks smile and slight Southern accent made him seem wholesome. He might have been born with a golden arm, but that wasn't enough. He needed what Dad had in spades—perseverance.

FOOTBALL WISE, BUSINESS STUPID

If the request to go on *The Ed Sullivan Show* in 1958 was possibly Dad's first non-football-related business request, something almost resembling an endorsement, it wasn't his last. It would be easy today to say he was crazy not to take that $700 to stand up and be recognized because $700 was a lot of money in those days, particularly for a man in a job that didn't have the longest career span (see George Shaw's career and how quickly that turned) with a growing family. Here was a chance for Dad, basically unknown, to gain recognition in New York City, the media capital of the world. In 1958, star athletes, even baseball players, didn't have the same advertising cache that some athletes do today, and athletes like Dad who were not well known had no cache. It was a great opportunity, one that Dad couldn't expect to be available again.

But he didn't take the opportunity. Instead, he wanted to be with his teammates at such a monumental moment (as the experience at the airport would prove because there's no way to replicate that, not even hearing about it or watching it on TV). Publicity just wasn't on Dad's radar. I don't know why, but unlike Namath or Hornung who seemed to have a knack for being in the papers and on most fans' minds as much for non-football issues, Dad wasn't that way. He played football. It was the end in itself. It didn't exist, not even as a thought, as a vehicle to something else. There were superstars in 1958: President Eisenhower, Mickey Mantle, Elvis Presley, and Cary Grant, to name a few, and there had always been superstars going back to the Greeks, but while children dreamed of having lives like Willie Mays, what they were really dreaming about was hitting home runs like he did or running down fly balls in deep center field at the Polo Grounds with his grace and ease. Young boys wanted to run like Frank Gifford or pass like Otto Graham or be tough like Chuck Bednarik, but in many ways, fans had no way of knowing what Graham's or Mays' life was like off the field. Dad wanted to play pro football; it had been his stated goal since sixth grade. Whatever else that meant, he didn't know until he made it. He did know it meant not driving a truck or doing carpentry.

There's no question that great athletes were and are treated differently, most of it good and some of it bad. It's easy today to imagine that athletes have always been wealthy far beyond the average football fan. It's not true. Also, endorsements haven't always been there. Dad had individual opportunities as *The Ed Sullivan Show* points out, but they were generally one-shot deals and tied to specific situations, like winning a championship in an overtime game in New York City, media capital of the world. The next year when Dad and the Colts won another championship, he wasn't given the same opportunity.

****

After Dad's rookie season, a good one once he took over the starting role, he still had to work in the off-season. He got a job with a cardboard company, working as a sales rep and assisting a full-time salesman. They traveled the mid-Atlantic region, calling on any kind of company that used cardboard boxes. A lot of his work was in the Harbor area when the Inner Harbor wasn't hotels and bars; instead, it was a working port. One product that needed lots of boxes was the fruit business. Fruit would be off-loaded from ships and packed in boxes to be trucked around Baltimore and Maryland. Dad would accompany Jack Marsch to the docks, meeting with guys who were Italian, strong, working class, and huge football fans.

Dad understood his role. He wasn't an expert in the shipping industry, or in fruits, or in boxes. While he hadn't reached the fame that would come a year later, he was a recognizable name in the Baltimore area. His job, when he and Marsch entered an office or shook hands on the piers, was to be "Johnny Unitas, Colts quarterback." Dad would simply introduce himself as "John Unitas," no mention of being a quarterback or the Colts. It was Marsch who would mention that he was a rising star. Dad didn't mind that he did, but he wasn't going to do it himself. Later, he would be Johnny U, nothing else needing to be said. This kind of role would remain with Dad throughout the rest of his life. He was there as himself, not as some hotshot salesman or expert. He was okay with that.

As Marsch has told me, Dad was a regular guy. Take him out of a football uniform and off the field, and he could have been a regular Joe trying to get ahead in life. Marsch enjoyed spending time with Dad, chatting the many hours away as they drove around the Baltimore area calling on customers. To this day, he doesn't remember conversations about football. Dad would talk football if customers brought it up, but it wasn't something he forced on them. Marsch usually did that for him only because he understood that Dad's position might help make a sale or increase the amount of an order.

They made a number of sales calls in the area, pushing their product. As with any new account, they had to convince the new customer there was a reason to buy their boxes. Sometimes they made a sale, sometimes they didn't, but generally, the potential customer got to talk a little football, shake hands with a starting NFL quarterback, and feel as if he'd made a connection to someone important who was in the sports section on a regular basis. It wasn't always successful. Marsch's company was interested in breaking into the apple business, which was big at that time in the Shenandoah Valley west of Washington, D.C. But that rarely happened in the Shenandoah. Marsch wasn't particularly confident to start with, but whenever he introduced Dad, not only had most of these apple farmers never heard of him, they hadn't heard of the NFL. He was embarrassed for Dad, but Dad shrugged it off. More than anything, he knew these kinds of people—not apple growers per se—but people who were working hard to make ends meet, didn't have time for fun and games. They didn't have time to watch grown men batter each other. They reminded Dad of his own father and his Uncle Leonard. He wasn't entitled to their respect, and it was okay. Dad's job was to guide the Colts to wins, and in that off-season to help sell boxes. It didn't always work out, but he understood that, too.

Until Dad became a household name after the Championship Game, this is what he expected to do every off-season. He and Jack Marsch were simply two young men with growing families trying to get ahead in the world. Marsch still talks about how down to earth and humble Dad was, how he was interested in making money too, and he was willing to do whatever needed to be done to do it. Dad put in the same long hours that Marsch did—nothing highfaluting about Dad. For many of his teammates, they also worked outside of football. Some of them used their names and local fame as liquor salesmen, and some of them simply got more traditional jobs to make ends meet. For example, Artie Donovan became a professional football player only because the Colts offered him $5,500 for his first season, $500 more than he would have made as a New York City cop. Unlike Dad, he didn't see the NFL as the ultimate career spot. Today it's hard to imagine a player turning down any professional sports opportunity because there's a better financial opportunity outside of sports, but pro sports, except possibly baseball, weren't commanding the enormous salaries they are today.

While Dad only did this one season—the 1958 championship opened other opportunities for him—there's no question that Dad enjoyed it and would have done it again if he needed to. Part of the problem was that Dad only worked from January until June. Football came first.

I remember occasional local advertising jobs that Dad had in the 1960s, mainly because they involved the family. There was a TV commercial in which the entire family sang for Mary Sue Candy's. I hated the experience. I was scared of all the people—the cameramen and producers and employees. They were eyeing us, and whenever we made a mistake—and we all did, but probably me more than anyone else—they stared at us, meaning me, it seemed, as if I was some weird animal at the zoo or a strange creature at a fair sideshow. Naturally, I cried and slowed down the production schedule. Crying wasn't something we were supposed to do, particularly in front of Dad; it made us look weak. But I was sobbing in front of more people than just Dad. It seems like the kind of thing kids would find cool, but looking back, it was another example of having to share Dad. I had to share him on the day of filming and then every time the commercial aired.

We also had free soft drinks delivered to the house; a truck arrived and the driver put cases of bottles in the garage. It happened routinely, every couple of weeks. We had a stocked fridge out there, and while I don't know what Dad got for promoting that brand, it was more than a regular supply of stock but not a lot more.

More typical was Dad's arrangement, if you can call it that, with Richard Sammis, Mr. Nobody, the man who gave Dad office space late in his life. When Dad was playing, Sammis was one of the sponsors of the Colts' games, selling cars. Through his arrangement with the team, Sammis got to know Dad. About once a year, Sammis would remind Dad that it was time to trade in his car for a new one, the latest model. Sammis wanted people to know that Dad drove his product; it was a tit-for-tat arrangement as Dad got a free car once a year, and Sammis could brag about John Unitas driving his vehicles. Amazingly, there was no contract or schedule. They worked off their friendship, and in all their years of knowing each other, they honored this organic relationship.

But Dad's first true outside business venture was a bowling alley right up the street from where we lived when I was little. It was called Colt Lanes with a sign that highlighted the horseshoe. But unlike today when athletes, particularly athletes of Dad's stature, who often get paid for their name and if not, don't put money in the venture and are paid from the profits, Dad was more than a name. He invested money. Businessmen came to him because he had money. Colt Lanes didn't last; it probably didn't lose money, but it didn't make money the way his partners, the business minds of the operation, promised.

That was typical of Dad's off-field activities—they seemed like good ideas on paper, but as realities, they generally didn't work out, at least as well as he was promised. While Dad was an incredible quarterback, he wasn't a very good businessman. Unlike football, business wasn't a cut-and-dried activity with immediate returns on effort and execution. A quarterback immediately knows whether his left tackle is blocking or not; a helmet in the back from a defensive lineman causes whiplash and fumbles or passes that flutter like a plastic bag in the wind. That problem is fixed immediately either by getting someone else to play tackle or changing the offense. In business, it takes time to figure out whether money's being made or not, and if not, why not. Dad's problems weren't because he wasn't smart but because he trusted people too much.

Lenny Moore once had a bar. Like Dad and the Golden Arm Restaurant,

Moore had to trust people who worked for him most of time that the work was getting done, that the cash register was being taken care of, and that the people he hired had the same respect for his business that he had for it. But that wasn't always the case. Unlike card shows, where you either show up or you don't and you sign autographs or you don't, running a service business like a bar or restaurant takes trust and presence. If you're not around all the time, then people have opportunities to take advantage of you. The right hand has to know what the left hand is doing.

Moore points out that in his business, he didn't want to be there all the time. Sometimes he couldn't be there because football was his primary obligation, and sometimes he simply didn't want to work that hard. He worked hard during the season. I think it's fair to say the same about Dad. If you're not going to be working all the time, you have to have people you can trust, managers and employees you know will ring money into the till instead of putting it in their pocket.

Dad trusted too much. That was part of his nature. He assumed people knew how to behave. Adults didn't need reminders about obvious and simple things. For example, Dad wasn't big on speeches and motivation. He hated the idea that his teammates needed reminding that whatever game they were playing was a big game and that it mattered. Ewbank wasn't a big speech-giver and Shula was. Ewbank didn't scream and Shula did. That was one reason Dad liked Ewbank and didn't care for Shula. Dad was famous for being the last to speak in the locker room before going onto the field. He usually said the same thing: "Talk's cheap. Let's play football." Short, sweet, and simple.

But in business, not everyone had the same interests as Dad.

****

Peachy Dixon is a throwback. She was born and raised in East Baltimore and currently lives in the house she grew up in and bought from her parents. She became a football fan in the 1950s because she went to Patterson High

School when they had very good teams, and the Colts were quickly becoming the talk of the town. She learned early that if she wanted to be friends with boys, she needed to follow football and be a fan. She became such a fan that she went to Super Bowl V and watched the Colts defeat the Cowboys. She got there by asking 100 friends to each contribute a dollar to pay for her plane ticket.

She got married and had children young. Her life was a struggle. In some ways, it's not hard to see some similarities between her life—mouths to feed and not as much money as she'd have liked—and Dad's when the Steelers cut him. She was working as a secretary at a local car dealership as well as a waitress at a downtown hotel restaurant. One day, a truck carrying a sign that would go on Dad's new restaurant, Johnny Unitas' Golden Arm, came down the street. She said, that's it. There's a sign, the break she needed to move her life ahead, a chance to get out of the clutches of a husband who wasn't getting the job done. On her lunch break, she had a friend drive her to the York Road restaurant, applied for a waitressing job, and got it. The small-town feel of Baltimore revealed itself again. Dixon was going to meet her hero who she'd been following since 1956 and fallen in love with in 1958.

Originally, the restaurant was going to be an upscale dining establishment, the kind of place where people would go and let other people know they'd been there. But sort of like my father's personality, it ended up being something entirely different. It actually became a family-oriented restaurant. It served seafood and steaks and crab cakes and something called Jack Tar Potatoes, a twice-cooked potato stuffed with chives, sour cream, and bacon bits. It was a nice restaurant with good food, reasonably priced but not too fancy, a place where people wanted to go, particularly after games.

Dad opened the restaurant with his teammate, Bobby Boyd, a defensive back on the Colts who had played quarterback for Oklahoma. Boyd was actually considered as a possible quarterback in 1965 when Dad was hurt and Tom Matte became the starter. Dad knew nothing about the restaurant business, a theme that followed him throughout his life. Boyd knew more and with some help managed the back end of the business, and Dad was the front man, the guy who hung out and glad-handed the customers. He was good at it and didn't mind doing it.

As expected, the opening of the Golden Arm was a must-see, must-do event in Baltimore. Opening weekend went better than expected. Except for a small problem. The toilet in the women's bathroom stopped up and overflowed. Peachy was shocked when she heard about it and rushed into the bathroom to be followed by Dad, plunger and mop in hand. Like any employee, she expected Dad to hand her the tools, but he didn't. Instead, he went about the business of plunging and mopping, all the while women were using the other stalls. Dad established early on the kind of place he was going to run and that no one was above doing whatever necessary to be a success. Whether touchdowns or diner satisfaction, he didn't care who got the glory just so long as touchdowns were scored and customers were happy.

Not only did Peachy Dixon get to work at the Golden Arm from its inception, it also became a foundation for making life-long friends. She also got to work for her football idol, Johnny U. However, at the restaurant, he wasn't Johnny U to the employees. He was simply John or Mr. Unitas, their boss, a man who went about his end of the business, always treating both employee and customer with the highest regard. Dixon's adoration for Dad grew larger from working with him. She was young and he was a celebrity, but that didn't mean he didn't treat her or any other employee right. Since the late 1960s Dixon has worked at three or four of the more famous restaurants around town and waited on lots of famous people, but none of them were as famous and nice as Dad. Not that all of them were arrogant, but he was a cut above.

There were lots of Peachy Dixons in Dad's life, both men and women. It wasn't planned. Usually, it was mere coincidence, but when it happens over and over—just like leading lots of late-game comebacks—it's no longer luck or fate. Dad had radar for people who were still grounded in the everyday, people who struggled to make ends meet, people who were thankful for whatever they had. He'd grown up that way, and while most of his adulthood was lived economically above his childhood station, he never forgot who he was and where he came from. It wasn't just that Dad had radar; some people had radar with him. They weren't out to use him or get ahead because of being associated with his name. Peachy, not even someone who would've called Dad a friend, felt touched by him; she was one of many.

Occasionally, because Dixon was a single mother trying to raise two children, she'd bring one or both to the restaurant until either a babysitter or her parents could look after them. Dad generally sat at the end of the bar, holding court, schmoozing with customers. He'd be drinking Arrow beer. When Dixon's children arrived, he'd put one on one knee and the other on the other side, telling them to get "whatever they wanted." At four and five, they would get Shirley Temples with extra orange slices and cherries. To this day, they believe that if they'd asked for lobster, he would have gotten it for them. As they drank Shirley Temples, he would continue to hold court, talking to friends and customers, oftentimes no difference between the two.

****

The restaurant was a success, but it was also the kind of thing that drew time away from his children and my mom. When you have to share your dad because of football, anything beyond that sharing was too much. I understood that he played football and that required travel and hanging out with team-mates and leaving in early July to go to Westminster and being gone for at least six weeks, but did Dad need to go every Monday when he was in town during the season to be at the restaurant? Clearly, he thought so because that's what he did.

All children share their parents, but our sharing was so public. My friends' parents went to work and did what they did; I didn't know about it, and often my friends didn't, either. But what Dad did, everyone knew about and often judged and commented on it. More often than not, the comments were positive, but occasionally they weren't. Janice remembers being harassed more than I was. Maybe I don't want to remember it. Of more interest concerning Janice is how Dad's profession affected her life, particularly in high school. Janice felt that boys in high school were probably in one of two camps if romance was involved: the chance to say they dated Johnny Unitas' daughter, or too afraid of her famous father to even ask her out.

While I didn't seem to have this same trouble as much, I can see where Janice was coming from. According to my first serious girlfriend, Patty Young—who went to Dulaney High School, a public school where I would have gone if I hadn't gone to Calvert Hall—we attended a couple of parties where Dulaney boys made fun of me. They called me "faggot" and "pretty boy." Clearly if they were looking closely at Patty, they would've known I wasn't gay, but I was somewhat of a pretty boy. I dressed nicely, not because Dad was famous but because Dad dressed nicely. Not expensively, but nicely. Like the firm handshake and distinct signature, Dad wanted to make a good first impression by looking nice. He expected us children to do the same. It doesn't really matter why strangers made fun of me; it's important that it was another example of how my life, and my siblings' lives, was affected by Dad's fame. It was another example of sharing him.

****

The unspoken elephant in the room about my dad when it comes to business is that he just wasn't a very good businessman. That doesn't make him a bad man. Being a good businessman doesn't make one a good man. Being a great quarterback doesn't make one a great man or a great father—but as he got older he got better at it. That's what's so hard for people to understand—my father had his faults and weaknesses.

We don't like our heroes to have weaknesses. He was the Everyman who got up and did his job, showing little to no emotion, playing a violent and destructive sport with a body that looked unimposing, letting his actions speak for him. He seemed simple. He played for a city starved for success, a simple place it seemed, that was looking for someone like them, not someone bigger and more mythic, to lead them to wins and championships.

The fans wanted a leader. The fervor of myth-making begins in communal cheerleading. We don't believe we're capable of greatness, so we look for a surrogate, a John Wayne. My dad did. The Duke was his hero. He watched John Wayne movies whenever he could, particularly late at night if he couldn't sleep or when he was recovering from injuries and surgeries. His fans found their John Wayne in him. Because they didn't believe they were capable of doing great things, they hooked their wagons to the Colts, and the Colts hooked their wagons to my dad. By learning from the greatness of one man, maybe we come to understand our own possibilities, our own potential for greatness.

But this myth-making comes with a problem. My father isn't a myth he's not a made-up Greek god. He's human, but it's in his humanity and the possibility for failure (which happened to him more than most people remember or want to remember) that he becomes more human. He becomes someone we can hitch our wagon to, who we can make greater than is realistic or true, but it's in the lies of this man, my father, that we end up closer to truth, to what it means to be alive, to be part of something bigger than ourselves. It's not religion—and my father was a very religious man—but it's close enough. No matter what your spiritual beliefs, for everyone who loves Baltimore or football or a hard-working guy with a crew cut who threw bullets and seemed like your next-door neighbor when he had his equipment off could rally around, then race, socio-economics, and religion: all of it could be damned when watching my father.

In America, we generally like our heroes to be what we aren't—young, strong, rebellious, angry, controversial, loud, bad, everything that's negative that pushes the edges of authority without being too illegal or immoral. This was definitely true in the 1960s. We'd had too many heroes who were straight-laced and had gotten us into two world wars, nuclear bombs, and racism. He became the anti-typical hero, someone we needed at a time when the world around us—through war and politics—seemed to be falling apart. But one thing every hero must do is win. He did that, but not all the time. In business and around his family, it seems he did it much less often. It wasn't because he didn't care or he didn't think it was important. On the contrary, he wanted to be a good businessman, and he clearly wanted to be a great father.

Instead, he was flawed. He believed in a handshake. If he shook hands on an agreement, then that was as good as getting together with lawyers and drawing up contracts. For a man who had a lot of bad things happen to him before he was 22, it's amazing how trusting my father was. On the field, you had to prove your trust. As Matte has said over and over, Dad demanded that you catch the ball. Raymond always did, so Dad trusted that if he threw the ball to him, he'd catch it. During his 12 years on the field, that trust was reinforced over and over. Off the field, particularly in business, Dad also trusted and he got burned repeatedly.

Even the Golden Arm, probably the best business deal Dad ever made and the most successful, didn't have a perfect arc. He expected problems like clogged toilets. Dad wasn't naïve. He expected his employees to work hard, and waitresses like Peachy did, and Dad never forgot her or her integrity. He understood that businesses weren't perfect. He'd grown up in an imperfect house and football games were far from perfect, but there were certainties that he counted on: Leonard, his older brother, Raymond catching the ball, Jim Parker not missing a block, and my mother to take care of the kids and house. He also expected Bobby Boyd to deal honestly with him. They were more than teammates and business partners; they were friends.

In the beginning, their relationship worked, and it worked so well that they worked together on other deals. Part of the reason it worked is because their individual strengths complemented each other. Dad worked the crowd and Boyd knew the back end of the restaurant business, the ins and outs of food ordering and hiring and running a staff efficiently. Even if he wasn't perfect at that, he was better than Dad. While the Golden Arm evolved as a restaurant from high-end fancy place to more family and local neighborhood eatery, Dad was going to get burned again, this time by a guy who was his teammate, a guy he trusted and respected. Locker rooms taught Dad that trust there was profound, and when it was broken—as it was with Johnny Sample—it was devastating. Boyd was no Sample, or so Dad thought.

As his life moved forward, Dad had to look beyond the field, and he thought he'd found the perfect place—restaurants—to exploit his name and charisma, and he'd found the perfect person to do it with, Bobby Boyd. Just as I was going to learn, life seems so much easier in your twenties when you don't know how truly cruel life can be. Dad should have known that already, but his eternal optimism often got in the way.

CHAPTER 17

Winning Is Redemption

January 29, 1995
San Francisco 49ers 49, San Diego Chargers 26

By the end of the 1994 season, it would seem that Steve Young no longer had to live in Joe Montana's shadow. The San Francisco 49ers had gone 13–3 during the regular season and easily advanced to Super Bowl XXIX. Young had another great season, his fourth consecutive, but when you're replacing a legend—and for winning four Super Bowls, Montana was a San Francisco legend on par with Willie Mays and the Grateful Dead—great seasons aren't enough. You have to win the big one. Young hadn't done that yet. Yes, he'd earned two Super Bowl rings already, but that was as Montana's backup.

By Super Bowl XXIX in 1995, Steve Young had played in the NFL for 10 years. This does not include his years in the USFL. Since taking over for Montana as the starter in 1991 and 1992 because Montana got hurt, Young had been the best quarterback in the league. Before the 1993 season, the 49ers traded Montana to the Kansas City Chiefs in a move that looked familiar to NFL fans and looked really familiar to Dad, like the trade Joe Thomas pulled off with San Diego in 1973. With Montana gone, the 49ers were truly Young's team.

In 1991, Montana missed the entire year with an elbow injury, and Young started 11 games, also missing five games with a knee injury. While Young won the first of his six NFL passing titles, the 49ers at 10–6 missed the playoffs for the first time since 1982. In 1992 Montana only played in one game—the team's last of the regular season—and Young led them to a 14–2 record and an NFC championship appearance. But the 49ers lost to the Cowboys 30–20,

201

and now San Francisco fans were no longer whispering—they were scream-ing—that Young couldn't win the "big one" like Montana who seemed to do nothing but win big ones.

After trading away Montana, whether or not Young could win the big one no longer mattered because he was all the 49ers had. There would be no quar-terback controversy. While the 1993 team was not as strong as the 1992 team, it did win the West again and easily defeated the New York Giants in their first playoff game 44–3 in one of the most lopsided and greatest performances a team has shown in the playoffs. But that "can't win the big one" reputation would rear its ugly head once more as Young and the 49ers would lose to the Cowboys in the NFC Championship Game.

So 1994 became make or break for Young, and it wouldn't be decided by how he did in the regular season or even early rounds of the playoffs. Young had proven he could play, having been named first-team All-Pro for the third consecutive year. While Dad was All-Pro five times, he was never named three consecutive years. Again, the 49ers won their division, and again they advanced to the NFC Championship Game to meet the Cowboys for the third consecutive time. If there ever was a big game for Young, this was it. The NFC had established dominance over the AFC, and many considered the NFC Championship Game in the 1990s as the "real" Super Bowl. Young came through, leading San Francisco to a 38–28 win that was even easier than the score indicates.

Redemption was finally at hand for Young. To lose the Super Bowl after finally defeating his nemesis, Dallas, would have cemented his great-but-not-great-enough legacy, proving once and for all that the 49ers shouldn't have traded Montana. Young didn't disappoint, leading the 49ers to an easy win over the clearly inferior Chargers, throwing six touchdowns, including four in the first half.

Young earned Pro Bowls, MVPs, and lots of wins. He was liked by both teammates and fans, but awards and wins, if they're not the right ones, ulti-mately don't matter. He got what he needed—a Super Bowl win, his only one as a starter. His reputation and legacy were intact, and he wouldn't be thought of as Jim Kelly—four losses—or Fran Tarkenton with three. Young had finally earned redemption.

WINNING IS REDEMPTION

Few things about Dad's career, both during and after football, grated at him. If they did bother him, he rarely brought them up. He did have a tendency, however, of talking around something that bothered him, hinting at it without directly mentioning it. I never heard him talk about losing the 1965 playoff game to the Packers or lamenting having the second best record in football in 1967 and not even making the playoffs. Not even a hint. That just wasn't my dad. He did things to the best of his ability, as honestly as he could, and he let the chips fall where they may.

That being said, Super Bowl III bothered him. Yes, the loss bothered him. He didn't like to lose, but he understood that the Jets played an almost perfect game. But what really bothered him most was not getting in the game sooner. Although Dad never said this directly to me because he liked Earl Morrall and had a great deal of respect for him, he believed if he'd gotten into that Jets game sooner, he would have led the Colts back to victory. We'll never know, but what I do know is that he was bothered by not getting the chance. He felt he should have had the chance because Morrall was totally ineffective, having missed a chance to throw a late first-half touchdown to Jimmy Orr who was wide open and inexplicably throwing short and being intercepted. Dad rarely talked about his football career with his friends or me, but if he was going to talk about specific games and moments—and not just the stock funny stories that all athletes seem to have and tell—he talked about Super Bowl III. I would have thought he'd have talked about the 1958 championship or a time when he was injured, but he didn't. With fans he'd tell a story about Doug Atkins or Artie Donovan and how much he ate or Bill Pellington playing five plays with a broken arm. Generally, he discussed nothing about games and strategies except Super Bowl III.

Dad's issue with Super Bowl III wasn't just Morrall; instead, it was three other things: Shula, his injuries and declining skills, and as my sister has said, his believing his own press clippings. My father was a proud man, but part of him, like it seems with most superstar athletes, had a hard time knowing when to say when. He has admitted to some of his friends that his skills were declining in the late 1960s, but it wasn't so much that he thought he couldn't get the job done as it was he didn't really know what else to do.

There was a sea change happening not only with Dad but also with the Colts and Carroll Rosenbloom. My father wasn't going to go quietly.

★★★★

The 1969 season is a definition of a hangover. After dominating in 1968, the Colts went 8–5–1, finishing a distant second to the Los Angeles Rams. They lost their first two games of the season, badly. They lost to the Rams on Opening Day, and given that the Rams would eventually win the division, in hindsight, this wasn't a bad loss. However, Week 2 saw the Colts lose to the Minnesota Vikings, another playoff team in 1969. The problem wasn't losing; it was the margin by which they lost—52–14. The Vikings would also go on to the Super Bowl and represent the NFL in the last one played before the AFL/NFL merger, losing to the Kansas City Chiefs.

A bigger problem for the team was high expectations. Both fans and the Colts' front office expected a playoff season, possibly another trip to the Super Bowl. When that didn't happen, change was on the horizon. After the last game of the season, a win against division winner Los Angeles, Shula didn't sound like a man waiting to jump ship, but it probably couldn't have been stopped. When Rosenbloom hired Shula in 1963, he expected championships and Super Bowls and said as much publicly. So far, the Colts hadn't delivered. Just after hiring Shula, Rosenbloom was quoted in the *Baltimore Sun*, "I thought the Colts should have won the championship this past year [1962], and they will win it next year. If it were just a case of moving up to second in our division I never would have made the move. I think we will win the title, that is why I hired Shula."

But by 1969, there were still no championships, and there was the embarrassment of being the first NFL team to lose in the Super Bowl. That was more than Rosenbloom could stand. People forget that Ewbank stayed out of the players' faces; he didn't scream and yell, and on game day, turned the playing over to them. He was a manager during the week, but come kick off, especially on offense, it was Dad's and the players' show. Not so with Shula.

Shula was quoted in a 2007 article in the *Palm Beach Post* about the dissolving relationship between him and Rosenbloom, "He had his office in New York and he took a lot of heat from his New York buddies [after the loss to the Jets]. Then he would get on the phone and pass that heat on to me. Our relationship was never the same after that game." But like everything connected to the Colts and Rosenbloom, the situation wasn't simple. Joe Robbie, the owner of the Miami Dolphins, approached Shula and offered him more money than the Colts and a chance to have a stake in ownership to come to Florida. He took the deal. Robbie and Rosenbloom feuded about the situation, Rosenbloom crying foul, and later the NFL awarded the Colts a first-round draft choice as compensation because Shula was still under contract. Not only did Rosenbloom accuse Robbie of tampering, but also he claimed he would never speak to him again. In addition, he said he also wouldn't speak to Shula because while Robbie had committed the "crime," Shula had allowed him to.

There had to be more, at least I think so. Maybe Shula wanted a contract like Lombardi got from the Washington Redskins that included a piece of the ownership action, but Shula at that time wasn't Lombardi. Lombardi had won about three quarters of his games and five championships, including two Super Bowls, in nine years. He's also inherited a team that the previous season had been 1–10–1, had little talent, and no real quarterback. Shula had no championships, including losing to the Jets, permanent embarrassment, inherited a team that was a regular playoff contender, and had the best quarterback in the NFL running the show: Dad.

Long before Shula was gone, players beyond Dad were unhappy with Shula. John Mackey, a quiet, levelheaded superstar (who was the first head of the combined NFL-AFL players' union and clearly understood the power of the press and the game's politics) said that Shula had lost his touch with the players, particularly Dad. Mackey used the word "stifle" as in he called too many plays—Ewbank called none—and in doing that took away Dad's on-field "personality." He also said, "Shula thought he was the biggest thing since bubble gum." He wasn't upset that Shula, while a good coach, was gone.

It wouldn't be totally fair to Shula to say that he was the reason the Colts didn't win championships in his years in Baltimore. In his seven years, he won Coach of the Year honors three times and had a winning percentage almost as high as Lombardi's. But the irony of the leaving is that in signing with the Dolphins, he would be coaching a team that would now be in the same division as Baltimore. When the two leagues merged, Rosenbloom and the Colts agreed to move from the NFL (soon to be the NFC) and join the new AFC. Strange and interesting circumstances happened a lot back then in the NFL.

For the "crime" that the Dolphins committed, the Colts got their No. 1 pick in the 1971 draft, taking Don McCauley from North Carolina who had broken O.J. Simpson's single season rushing record. McCauley would spend 11 years with the Colts, playing a role not too dissimilar from the one played by Tom Matte. He played fullback and halfback, rarely started, and ended his career with almost 6,000 yards rushing and 58 touchdowns. He was a throwback, a guy Dad liked and the kind of player Dad both epitomized and needed. McCauley, in a rookie-hazing incident, was asked to approach Dad and introduce himself, "Hello, Mr. Unitas, my name is Don McCauley. I'm really looking forward to meeting your son." Dad gave him that icy stare he was famous for when a lineman missed a block or a receiver dropped a pass. As McCauley said, when he knew Dad had him, he broke out in laughter. Sadly, he wouldn't play long with Dad as things were ready to change in Baltimore, and it wasn't only the coach.

There was unrest in Baltimore. The love affair with the Colts was coming to an end, at least for Rosenbloom. While some of the issues with the Colts— the main one being either improvements at Memorial Stadium or a possible new stadium—were somewhat out in the open, no one believed the Colts would leave town. That was done in baseball because some major league owners felt like there was more money to be made on the West Coast than New York. The NFL had had teams in Los Angeles and San Francisco since the late 1940s. Initially, Rosenbloom and the Colts had problems with the fact that they couldn't use Memorial Stadium until after the Orioles' season ended. Rosenbloom wanted to build his own practice complex in Baltimore County, using the stadium only on game days. But he also wanted improvements with the facility and a 10-year lease while offering to help (loan) the city the finances.

The problems involved were complicated. Even today, it's hard to know what exactly went on between the Colts and city officials. It's fair to say that no one in management was blameless. At the time, the feeling was that football teams didn't move. Players sometimes did. While Dad would be traded in a couple of years, the love affair with Baltimore and its fans would never end for him.

****

When Shula left, Rosenbloom picked his offensive coordinator, Don McCafferty, to become the next head coach. McCafferty was like a dramatic weather change from stormy to sunshine. One of the first things he announced was that Dad would be calling his own plays. Again, Dad remained somewhat quiet when McCafferty was picked, but teammates like Mackey and Matte loved the choice. Dad agreed with them 100 percent, but he wasn't going to be the voice and face of off-field politics. That was best left to others. His place was on the field; he knew that and so did his teammates and McCafferty.

By 1970, no one was left who played or coached with my dad from the 1958 championship team, and McCafferty was now the only player or coach from the 1959 championship team. He'd been hired by Ewbank to help on offense, having coached at Kent State for a number of years and having played for Paul Brown. While the quarterback position seemed to have been born in Western Pennsylvania, coaching football seemed to have its roots in Central Ohio. The pro football Hall of Fame is in Canton, Ohio, and while football didn't start in Ohio, it's at least the cradle. The forerunner to the NFL began in Canton in 1920 and the Canton Bulldogs won two of the early NFL championships. McCafferty was part of that tradition.

Unlike Shula, McCafferty was easy going. He was what has become known as a players' coach. Most people don't have a strict definition, but part of the definition is that the players like the person. Everyone, it seemed, liked McCafferty. There was a tradition after games that on Sunday night the players, coaches, and wives went out to dinner and dancing. Later in the evening, many of the wives went home, and the players retired to someone's house, discussing the game into the wee hours. Dad didn't tend to be part of this, but McCafferty was. He listened to the players discussing what worked and what didn't. It was both about breaking down the game and the camaraderie that comes from sharing stories while drinking beer.

As one player has told me, back then there didn't seem to be this divide between coaches and players, particularly assistant coaches. The skill position offensive starters worked with the coaches to develop a game plan, both before the next game and during the game, suggesting adjustments based on what they were seeing on the field. The players, including my father, loved working with McCafferty. They were glad he was picked as the new head coach, but they were sad that the special relationship they had with him as an assistant would change in his new position.

****

The 1970 season got off to an auspicious start when the owners locked out all veterans from training camp, delaying the opening of camps by about two weeks. It was the first "official" labor action since the start of the league. Nonetheless, just before camp was to open McCafferty told the *Baltimore Sun* that he thought the Colts had the talent to win the whole thing. Now it was the new coach turning up the pressure instead of Rosenbloom, as he had done before the 1963 season. McCafferty did qualify his stance by stating that the Colts needed to avoid injuries. Dad was 36 and in his 15th season, and Earl

Morrall was 36. Jimmy Orr, now Dad's favorite target and coming off a major leg injury from the year before, was 35. None of these guys were young for their age, particularly Dad and Orr. Both had taken a beating over the years. Avoiding injuries to important players wouldn't be easy.

There was much discussion among prognosticators that the dominant Colts of the 1960s were done. The 8–5–1 record of last year and the loss of Shula would be too much to overcome, the experts said. Dad didn't believe that, and the 1970 team would prove to be resilient. They would play to an 11–2–1 record to win the AFC East, the two losses coming to the defending Super Bowl champion Kansas City Chiefs in Week 2 and the Miami Dolphins in Miami in Week 10 to drop to 7–2–1. They would win out the rest of their games.

The week before Miami came to Baltimore and Shula had his homecoming, Dad played his best game of the year in a 27–3 rout of the Boston Patriots (after this season the Boston Patriots changed their name to the New England Patriots). The Colts were a funny team, relying on defense and some luck, but they were playing better each week. That would come to the surface in the Miami game as the Colts won 35–0 even though looking at stats today, it's easy to assume that Miami won the game. The Dolphins gained more than 350 yards in total offense while the Colts had less than 250. Dad only played three quarters because the game was such a blow-out, leaving with the score 28–0 and Morrall taking over. Dad didn't play as well as he had the week before, but he didn't need to. The defense caused four turnovers, and the Colts returned a punt and kickoff for touchdowns. It was, as this team would become known for, a total team victory. It might be a cliché sometimes, but it was true that day and for the team the entire season.

Dad was correct when he had said in the off-season that it wasn't a rebuilding year, it was a transitional year but a transition from the Colts being defined by Dad and his performances to a more well-balanced team between the three areas that make up football: offense, defense, and special teams. For a team that had the second most wins in either league (the Vikings had 12 during the regular season), only one player was named to the Pro Bowl, Tom Matte, and no one was named first-team All-Pro. Only Bubba Smith made any All-Pro team, and he was named second team by the Pro Football Writers' Association. Not that individual awards and honors are always a determining factor in how good a team is, but they can indicate something far greater than Xs and Os, talent, and stars. This 1970 team won but usually won ugly. The days of Dad winning pretty were probably over, but he'd never cared about how he or the team looked as long as it achieved victories. If there was any justice to the regular season, the Colts defeated the Jets twice, and in less than two years since upsetting the Colts, the Jets finished the year at 4–10. The bright candle named Joe Namath had a short wick. What had burned so brightly earlier was now almost dark. Furthermore, the Colts finished ahead of the Shula-led Dolphins, who defeated the Colts later in the season in Miami. But it didn't matter as the Dolphins finished second at 10–4. Shula may not have been Lombardi yet, but his switching teams worked for both organizations as the Dolphins improved from 3–10–1. They also made the playoffs, losing to the Raiders 21–14.

****

By playoff time, I was a full-fledged teenager. What Dad did for a living wasn't some great thing to me. He had his job, and I had my life, which included playing football. I didn't go to the Super Bowl. None of us did, not even my mom. It wasn't something that was discussed. Other than going to a couple of away games when I worked training camp the summer of 1965, the family didn't go to away games. It wasn't unusual; none of us had gone to Super Bowl III.

****

It probably should have been called the "Ugly" Bowl. Eleven turnovers between the two teams. Dad got hurt and left the game in the second quarter. To get to the Super Bowl, instead of the Giants and Packers and 49ers, the Colts faced a new set of foes—the Cincinnati Bengals and Oakland

Raiders. They easily beat the Bengals 17–0 and then the Raiders in the AFC championship 27–17. Playing at home in the AFC championship had an odd ring to it.

The Super Bowl was a weird game. It was the first Super Bowl played on artificial turf, and it was the last one with a local television blackout even though the game was a sell-out. It was also a chance for the Colts to redeem themselves for the loss to the Jets and a chance for the Cowboys to win the "big one." On paper, the Cowboys had seven players who would later be enshrined the Hall of Fame (and that doesn't include coach Tom Landry) while the Colts had only three, including Dad who clearly was not playing like a Hall of Famer at this point in his career.

The Colts managed to win, and given all the important games and situations in the 1960s that hadn't worked in their favor, the odds were with them on this day. From the moment they defeated the Raiders, they treated this game differently than they had two years earlier. Instead of staying in Fort Lauderdale at a hotel, they stayed at a country club that was not 45 minutes away. Furthermore, when the Colts had played the Dolphins in Miami during the regular season—a Colts' loss—they weren't used to the slope and crown of the artificially turfed Orange Bowl. For the Super Bowl, they practiced for the game at a local college that had fields identical to the Super Bowl. The team had learned its lessons from the Jets debacle.

Even with better preparation and attitude, they probably didn't deserve to win, but then again neither did the Cowboys. In another oddity, Chuck Howley, a Cowboys linebacker, was named MVP, the only time a player from the losing team has been given that honor. He's also just one of three linebackers to win the award. Dad was knocked out of the game in the second quarter with a rib injury, having completed 3-of-9 passes for a touchdown and two interceptions. But even the highlight of the day for Dad was weird, as his 75-yard touchdown pass to John Mackey wasn't even thrown to him. Instead, he threw a pass to wide receiver Roy Jefferson that was poorly thrown and glanced off his hand, then glanced off Cowboy defensive back Mel Renfro's hand and into Mackey's. (At that time, the rules stated that a defender had to touch the ball in between two offensive players touching it, and while there was some question at the time whether Renfro touched the ball, it was later confirmed that he did.)

Morrall replaced Dad. It wasn't that big a deal because Morrall had started two games during the regular season (injuries to Dad) and the bigger deal was that Dad started. Jim O'Brien, who would kick the game-winning field goal to secure the 16–13 victory, has always argued that most of the players thought at this point in their careers, Morrall was the better quarterback. McCafferty went with his gut and started Unitas. They'd been together since 1959. There was a sense of trust. The Colts had to come from behind, down 13–6, and needed a fumble in the red zone—on the 1-yard line—by Duane Thomas to keep the Cowboys from going up 20–6 in the third quarter, probably an insurmountable lead given how this game was played. Instead, a mistake by Craig Morton, the starting Cowboys quarterback, led to a last-minute interception and Jim O'Brien's field goal. Before the interception, the ending had the makings of the first Super Bowl to go to overtime, just like the 1958 Championship Game had been the first NFL title game to need OT. But that was not to be as O'Brien, a rookie, delivered with seven seconds left and giving the Colts a victory, Dad's third NFL title, this one 12 years after his last one.

Even in victory, the relationship between the team and city had changed. Only 2,000 fans showed up to cheer the team after their victory, and I only say "only" because more than 30,000 had shown up in 1958. They were a raucous crowd again, but in the television era, it seemed the relationship between a team and its citizens was more distant, probably because of saturation and because the team seemed more distant—that's what television does, put distance between the fan and team. It might have been the weather—it was only 19 degrees at airport—and it may have been that winning was now engrained into the city's psyche. The Orioles had just won their second World Series, and now, for the first time, Baltimore was champs in two different sports.

****

While the game was the final highlight of Dad's football career, it was the start of the downfall of our family. When I say start, I don't mean that Dad and Mom's relationship fell apart with this game. The problems had been in the works for years. As an adult who is married I understand now, but it was on the way home from Miami that Dad talked publicly about what was happening with his private life. Sandy, who would eventually become my stepmother, was a flight attendant on the airlines that the Colts used to go to Miami and back. They had met before this flight. While on the flight back from Miami and Super Bowl V, Dad turned to a friend within the organization, pointed out Sandy, and said, "I'm going to marry that woman." It may have been a secret to me that Dad ran around on Mom, but it wasn't a secret among his teammates and friends.

Part of being a star is that power and fame is an aphrodisiac, and whether or not Mom wanted to admit it, Dad was both a star and susceptible to the wiles of women. Strangers, particularly young star chasers, didn't care that Mom or Dad had five children. Professional athletes, like politicians, are tempted constantly. Dad may have never made a bad play call on the field, but the same can't be said for some of his decisions off the field. Some of the problem was Dad, and some of it was Mom. He wanted to live the life of a star while Mom, not upset that she was Mrs. Johnny Unitas, wanted to stay at home, entertaining in our kitchen and raising the children. Like most marriages that don't make it, irreconcilable issues occur. People grow tired of each other, forget where they started, and now that they're in a new—and better place—forget what got them there. My parents were a team early in their marriage, but they weren't anymore.

My sister had an idea of what was going on. Mom also knew. Reporters who covered the team knew. Teammates knew. The fans, if they knew, didn't care as long as the Colts were winning. But I didn't know. I had no idea. That would make learning about it that much worse. Soon, the fabric that held our family together would rip apart, just as the fabric that held the Colts together would, too.

CHAPTER 18

Home Wrecked

November 10, 1991
Washington Redskins 56, Atlanta Falcons 17

It seemed like that kind of year for the Falcons: they'd had a big win the week before against San Francisco 17–14, a win that would later be a tie-breaker determiner as both teams finished with a 10–6 record. But a week later, it was a different Falcons team, more like the one that had started the season 0–2 and spent most of the season struggling to get to .500. When it was seemingly over the hump, the team was blasted by the Redskins.

Taken from an NFL historical perspective, it would be the first game that Brett Favre threw a regular-season pass. Late in the game, he actually threw four and completed two, and like Dad, his first completion was to the wrong team. So was his second. It wasn't his debut in the NFL; he had appeared briefly in a win against the Rams earlier in the year but didn't throw a pass. After the Redskins game, Favre wouldn't appear again for the Falcons as he and Jerry Glanville didn't see eye to eye. Maybe it would be fairer to say that Glanville never wanted to draft Favre.

Favre would end his career more than 20 years later, leaving the NFL as the all-time leader for quarterbacks in games played, yards thrown, and touchdown passes. Although my dad had ended his career with a lot of those same records, others had surpassed most of them before Favre finished up.

There are lots of similarities between Favre and Dad. They both played for smaller college programs—Favre played at Southern Mississippi—although Favre was a first-round draft pick and signed a $1.4 million contract. Even though he was a second-round pick with a significant contract, he was traded after that uneventful year in Atlanta to Green Bay where he would become a legend. He was beloved there because he seemed to be one of "them," the typical Green Bay fans who, even in the 1990s and 2000s, still had a love affair with their hometown team.

Once Favre was traded, as the cliché goes, the rest is history. He led the Packers to its first NFL championship since Super Bowl II. By the time he'd retired, however, he was not the beloved star quarterback adored and toasted by a city like Dad was with Baltimore. Favre seemed to be out of the same mold as Dad, but he played the end of his career wrong. For example, he left Green Bay on his own to go to the New York Jets, and this after announcing he was retiring. Then he retired again—from the Jets—only to come back to the league and play for the Minnesota Vikings, a divisional and longtime rival of the Packers. Much of his first and second retirements were public fights with the Packers and its leadership. Small towns don't like that kind of thing, even when one of the fighters, while Southern, is a small-town boy.

Before the "retirement" fiascos, Favre's legend had been built around his gun-slinging mentality on the field, his toughness (he set a record for consecutive games played as a quarterback, one record my father never had), and his small-town roots that included not acting like a superstar.

But it wasn't just that Favre retired and left the Packers high and dry. He didn't. Aaron Rodgers was waiting in the wings. Part of the problem was his waffling about retiring or not retiring. Part of the problem was his having a public spat with the Packers franchise. These issues used up much of the social capital he'd built up with his fans and fans around the NFL. He'd received a standing ovation from the Bears' fans in 2006 when he let it be known he was through, only to come back the next year with the Packers. That ovation was from the arch-rival Bear fans, Chicagoans who hate anyone or anything from Green Bay. Their rivalry is older than Dad and goes back to Curly Lambeau and George Halas.

Favre also had his family image take a hit when it was revealed, not for the first time, that he had sent scandalous pictures and texts of himself to a New York Jets female employee as well as possibly two masseuses. His publicity hit was big. Fans tend to be forgiving and will forgive a few off-field mistakes, but Favre didn't realize the need to keep his mouth shut. The media made a big deal out of his behavior, both football-related and non-football related, but Favre also added more than his two cents worth. Maybe the world has changed with social media and the way athletes are covered, but I don't think so. Unlike Dad, who generally kept quiet when a controversy swirled around him, Favre sought out the press. He spoke too much.

Just like Dad got the last laugh with the Steelers when they cut him, as for Favre's disastrous first game and later being traded to the Packers, football-wise he got the last laugh. The Falcons' 1991 starter, Chris Miller, made his only Pro Bowl and finished his career with a 34–58 record as a starter.

HOME WRECKED

I should have been old enough to see what was coming. But I didn't. Instead, I was living my teenage years like—you know—a teenager. Instead of seeing the troubles around the house, I was chasing my own version of it outside my house. That's how I like to think of my high school years, but it wasn't wine, women, and song like I want to mythologize it. I chased one woman, and we caught each other. She was the first girl of my dreams. I went out at nights, either with her or with my friends to the YMCA to play basketball. While I sometimes drank hot beers in the woods behind my house and occasionally smoked cigarettes, I wasn't wild even if I wanted to think I was. In many ways, I was more like my dad than I thought. My long hair that my mom bobby-pinned up in the back before school to get around dress code rules at my high school didn't make me outrageous; it only gave me the sense of being wild.

My dream girl was Patty Young, and we dated throughout high school. I met her through a friend who I played pick-up hoops with at the local middle school. She was the all-American girl—long blonde hair, blue eyes, slender, and social, so much the cheerleader type that she even became a cheerleader for Calvert Hall, my all-boys high school. And like most romances, she remembers the details a lot better than I do.

She had a friend in seventh grade who had written all over her notebook, "I love Johnny. I love Johnny. I love Johnny." Patty asked her friend who "Johnny" was, and she found out that he was an eighth grader who lived a couple neighborhoods over, a bit nicer than where she lived. I was that Johnny. The first time I met Patty, while I was playing basketball and she was with her friend, I knew that she was special, different in a way that attracted me to her, and it wasn't just her looks. Even though she went to a different school, I found reasons to ride my dirt bike over to her house. We'd meet at an elementary school halfway between our houses. She was my first love, and I was hers. Once she announced to her parents that we were boyfriend and girlfriend, they wanted us to hang around her house, where we'd go to the basement and watch TV and kiss. She was the first girl I ever kissed.

By the time I entered ninth grade at Calvert Hall, the big Catholic school on the east side of town, we were doing everything together, and we would remain together until I graduated from high school. We were drawn to each other for the reasons a lot of teenagers are—looks, lust, popularity—and we were also brought together by situations out of our control because her parents were both alcoholics. While I didn't understand superficially what was happening with my parents' marriage, at some deeper level, I must have. We both were hurting, dealing with deep emotional family issues long before we wanted to or were ready.

I generally hung around with four or five guys at Calvert Hall. They played sports, but generally sports that I didn't play. I only played football although I always wanted to be a basketball star. Tim Cashen played lacrosse. Tommy Lekas, a kid who grew up next to Brooks Robinson about five houses away, was into soccer and baseball. Dan "Worm" Worthington, tall and lanky, played basketball. I didn't really hang with anybody from the football team. I've come to understand why I ran around with Tommy and Worm—because they came from dysfunctional families too, severely dysfunctional ones. Just like me.

While my friends played sports, we didn't play on the same teams. I got along with my teammates at Calvert Hall, but I wasn't close with them.

Freshman year I played quarterback on the freshmen team. I had played rec league in seventh and eighth grade. My first position was offensive guard. I pulled a lot, and I was knocking the shit out of everybody. The next year I went to quarterback because I could run the option well. I got recruited by two Catholic schools and decided on Calvert Hall. Little did I know that in picking Calvert Hall, I would have to go to summer school because my grades weren't as strong as they should have been. Before high school, my mother watched a few of my games; my father wasn't around at all. Obviously, she understood the pressures on me if I played quarterback, and she also knew what football physically does to a person. She saw my father struggle to get out of bed every morning during the season. Only after he retired would I see the devastation the game wrought on him. But there comes a point when even a mother's love and backbone can't keep a boy down, particularly one who wants to imitate his father regardless of the costs. She relented about playing quarterback, and I'll never know how much my father's opinion played into that decision. I'd guess not as much as I'd like to think.

My sophomore year, I made varsity. I was the backup quarterback and started at safety. Somewhere about the fourth or fifth game, I went in on offense because the starter and second stringer both got hurt. We were playing Poly, a public school powerhouse. We were deep in our territory in a passing situation. I drifted back to pass when Greg Schaum, a huge defensive lineman, nailed me, his face mask in the middle of my laces of my shoulder pads. More than 230 lbs. landing on top of 160, maybe. I had the breath knocked out of me, and I was too scared to pop right back up. He towered over me and said, "Don't forget. I'll be back." And I believed him. It was moments like this I realized how right my mother was about the game. At that moment, lying on the ground, staring beyond his behemoth body and helmet toward the blue sky, I wondered what I hoped to get out of playing. I was no longer a crybaby—like I'd been as a kid—but I knew I was overmatched. We, as a team, were overmatched, and this was the kind of game that we were going to lose no matter what, and I just had to suck it up. Schaum's future would reinforce how overmatched we were. He went on to play at Michigan State and in the

NFL for two years with Dallas and New England. While his hit may have bruised my sternum and ego a bit, the ego's okay today as nflreference.com has him ranked as the 10,676[th] best player to ever play in the league. Not my father, but an NFL player nonetheless.

Naturally, at Calvert Hall, I played football. I was a quarterback. Why wouldn't I be? That's what my dad was, so that's what I wanted to be. Except I didn't. Whether it was a hit like that from Schaum or not wanting to carry more of the pressure of being a Unitas, I moved over to defense. Although Dad never even put pressure on me to play sports, much less football and even less so quarterback, the shadow was large. My coaches saw it. To their credit, they let me find my own way. Looking back on it, it seems they were more interested in my wellbeing than what position I played or whether playing a particular position would help them win more. That's not something I understood then, but I appreciate it now, and wonder how many coaches today would do that? One of my freshmen coaches remembered Dad coming to my games but often watching them from inside his car because if he got out, everyone wanted a moment from him or an autograph. It wasn't that he didn't want to give them that; it was just during my games, he wanted to be a father, my fan. He also stayed out of getting involved with the coaches. If he talked to them, like after a game, it was always about something other than his games on Sunday or what the coaches should have done that afternoon. This was also true after he retired and had his second family. His sons' St. Paul's coaches tell the same story: that Dad never once threw around his weight as an NFL great to get playing time for his children or offer insights into how their teams were performing.

A couple of friends played football with me freshman and sophomore years, but stopped when they realized they didn't have whatever it took. I'm told I was a pretty good defensive back, good enough to get a few letters and looks from Division I programs. I'll never know whether they were interested in me or my last name because I didn't really pursue that path. As a junior and senior, we were good, beating our arch rival, Loyola, both years. My senior season was better than my junior one. I knew that I didn't want to play college football but even if I wanted to, Dad wasn't around enough to help me with the process. For a man who had jumped through so many hoops to go to college, he didn't offer any advice. I wasn't asking him to use his name and connections to get me a scholarship or tryout. I just wanted a father who would go with his son to visit campuses, maybe relive a moment or two from his collegiate days. Instead, I got a father who was divorced and distant from his kids, a man too self-absorbed to see that I was hurting and so were my siblings.

****

My life may have seemed special from an outsider's perspective, having a father who was a star in the ever-growing NFL, but it wasn't. Besides the burden of being a junior and having his name, an unusual Lithuanian name in a city that felt like a small town, my parents were headed toward divorce. I never talked to either of my parents about what went wrong, but it was a lot of things, most of them the same thing less famous couples deal with: infidelity and distance growing between a couple. It was also much more. Even today, it's complicated to sort through the mess that became my parents' divorce because of the extra layer of the public being a third member of their relationship, like having a nosy aunt prying into what they were doing and what I was up to. Dad wasn't solely ours, no matter how much we wanted him to be.

I was a decent student, although I probably didn't work as hard as I should have, and while I got into trouble, I stayed out of the limelight. Dad didn't like to be embarrassed, and that would have been true no matter what he did for a living, but being a public figure, it was even more important that we—the children—didn't drag his name into the newspaper and public eye. While Dad never talked about having a reputation to uphold, he didn't have to. I knew about it. We all did. That didn't mean we liked it, but we accepted it and lived our lives as best we could. He didn't want perfection; he just didn't want anything too negative.

I was used to Dad not being at home. That had been the way for years. It didn't mean that he was never home, just not much. Because he wasn't around and neither was I—I was either off doing dumb shit in the woods behind our house or playing hoops at the local middle school or riding my dirt bike—I didn't see or pick up on the changes happening between my parents. But Janice did.

Janice is smart, real smart, by far the best student of the five children. It seemed to come easy to her, although growing up in our house wasn't, at least for her. I loved the family atmosphere we had. While Dad read the paper and put his feet up when he was home, my brothers and I fought and wrestled, competing for his attention. According to Janice, he often pitted us against each other, probably like all parents do, even if they don't intend to. We were mean to her; her nickname was "Bananas," but at times we called her "Ugly." "Bananas" was more Dad's nickname. Brothers are probably supposed to be mean to their sisters, but Mom and Dad should've stopped it. Dad didn't. Like the breaking up of my parents' marriage, I was oblivious to what we were doing to Janice.

Mom and Janice became allies in the competition. Janice became one of Mom's confidants. She told her things, probably the way a lot of mothers and daughters do. But because Janice didn't go out a lot and stayed in her room and read and watched television, she also overheard a lot. That's how she found out that Mom and Dad weren't just going through the typical problems that can befall a pro athlete/celebrity marriage.

****

I used to think that Sandy was the only woman Dad ever cheated with. He seemed too much of a prude and far too Catholic to be a womanizer. Sure, women flirted with him, and he returned the favor but in a weird way, men did the same thing, although not in a sexual way. It was the way Dad interacted with people. He talked to men and women on their level, treated them with dignity and respect, and enjoyed their company. His teammates and the reporters who covered the team protected him, kept his secrets. That was not unusual, but Dad wasn't a serial womanizer. It didn't define him nor did he flaunt it. He was constantly confronted with temptation even when Mom was with him.

Friends now tell stories of women coming up to Dad at his table at the Golden Arm and positioning themselves between him and Mom even as Mom sat at his left elbow. Even Mom's scathing stare didn't stop outrageous behavior. Dad wasn't the instigator or even interested. Oftentimes, he even introduced Mom to the woman fawning on him. One time, a younger, attractive woman with large breasts (that she thrust in Dad's face) was talking to him while Mom sat beside him. Mom got up to go to the bathroom, and then this woman sat in Mom's seat. When Mom returned, the woman didn't move; as a matter of fact, she'd moved her seat even closer to Dad. When Mom asked her nicely to get up, the woman was indignant. As usual, that story has circulated, through rumor, as an example of Mom's bitchiness. She put up with a lot. She knew it wasn't Dad, he didn't ask this woman over, but he also didn't ask the woman to get up when Mom returned from the restroom. When I first heard this story, I was shocked that Mom hadn't cold-cocked this woman. She would have, if she could've gotten away with it, but she was Mrs. Johnny U and knew her place. I've also heard stories about parties and events Dad was invited to. If word got out that he was going, certain women in town would decide to go. If they heard about a social event and he wasn't going, they didn't go.

But he wasn't perfect. He could be crude. He was a pro football player, after all, one who had grown up on the tough streets of Pittsburgh. One time he was asked to go over to a woman's house who he vaguely knew—a divorcee—to "sign a football" for her son, at least that's what he was told. When he arrived, he and the woman had some small talk. The woman disappeared into another room, returning with the ball. "Oh, hell," Dad said, "let's cut the shit. If we're going to fuck, then let's fuck." The woman was aghast. Dad caught himself, realizing he was wrong, and quickly signed the ball. He had his needs and many of these were the product of being a star, of listening to what his adoring fans said, and reading what the newspapers said about him. He was no longer the shy kid from Pittsburgh. Instead, he was the face of Baltimore, the Everyman who'd made it. With making it came the spoils.

Or so he thought.

But not my mother. She understood what being married to a star meant. She liked being Mrs. Johnny Unitas. Who wouldn't? But there was more than simply being married to the Johnny Unitas, the Everyman who made good and still acted like he wasn't better than those he'd passed by. There were five children, 15-plus years of married life, their time together before they were married, and her signing Dad's first contract. The list of memories and struggles, like any marriage, is endless. She didn't simply want to be Mrs. Johnny Unitas. She loved my father. She loved the life they had together. She loved her children and felt she should focus her attention on them. She wasn't wrong in that regard, either. Janice, Bobby, Christopher, and I needed attention. Kenneth was the youngest and was probably too young to know or understand what was going on. We were hurting, probably worse than we realized at the time or were willing to admit.

Mom told Janice that her biggest worry about leaving Dad is that she would end up on the street with five children, selling apples and pencils to make sure her kids had enough to eat. She wasn't 40 and not far removed from the struggles of Pittsburgh. Mom worried that Dad was going to find someone else, a woman who was skinnier than her, prettier, not burdened with raising children. But by all appearances, it doesn't seem that Dad had girlfriends, and he didn't even have that many one-night stands.

That is until Mom opened a piece of mail, an official looking envelope, something about it that told Mom to be suspicious, in which Dad was changing the beneficiary of an investment policy from Mom to Sandy, the other woman. That was the main straw that broke her back. If her financial future was going to be jeopardized, then she had to take action. She did.

One Saturday Mom confronted Dad. My parents weren't yellers nor were they the kind who aired their dirty laundry in front of the kids. They were in the living room and Janice happened to be upstairs. All us boys were outside, away, and they probably thought that Janice was gone, too. She had that effect: so quiet that we sometimes forgot that she was there. Mom and Dad didn't have the first or the last pro football marriage to fail.

Marriages with stars generally are of two types: women who marry their men before they become famous and those who get married after their men are stars and famous. Obviously, my parents were the type who got married before fame, and once fame arrives—and it arrived fast for them—there's an adjustment. Regardless of when you get married, in professional sports—all of them—there was, is, and always will be a culture of adultery. It existed in the 1950s and 1960s, and it continues today.

The biggest difference now is how we report on and view our sports heroes. Fans seemed to care less, or maybe the media protected stars' images more before the merger of the NFL and AFL. With Watergate and Vietnam and the sexual revolution and the social unrest of the 1960s, the relationship between teams and their players and the fans changed. Everything is now news, not just what happens on the field. Social media and its growth in the last 10 years have added to the loss of privacy.

But what happens among teammates and what's known and talked about in locker rooms hasn't changed. Teammates spend lots of time together, they travel a lot, and women chase them as much, if not more, than players chase women. Mom knew a lot of this, but in the end, Dad came home to her, to our house. She was the one who got the wife tickets high up in Memorial Stadium on the 50-yard line.

That Saturday, Mom said, "John, I know all about her. I know that you have her in an apartment in the Glenmont Towers. I've heard all the stories. I know you have this girlfriend. Look, you can hurt me all you want, but you're hurting our kids and that's not going to happen. I've heard you're in love for the first time and this is so wonderful. Fine, go live with her. Go find out what she's really all about. Live your life. I'll stay here and continue taking care of the kids. All I ask is you continue paying the mortgage, helping to support us. I can try to find a job." But at this point Kenneth was only two and back then we're talking 1971, a lot of women were just starting to work outside the house. "Go live with her, and see which one you want. If a month from now, six months, two years from now, you decide you want a divorce and marry her, fine. If you decide you want to come back, that's fine too."

Dad responded, "I don't see what your problem is. I should be able to come and go as I please, and you can have the privilege of being Mrs. Johnny Unitas."

In a voice that didn't belie what was about to be said, Mom said, "John, as I told you, you don't hurt our kids and if you're so wonderful, take your footballs and cram them up your ass because good things won't hurt you, will they? I guess I have your decision, and now I have to do what I have to do."

Although that wouldn't happen immediately, Mom would file for divorce. It was bad that Janice had to hear this. Janice has told me—and I believe her—that I'm the one who told Mom about Sandy, that it was more serious than we understood. Mom had always suspected Dad of running around, but there was never one particular woman; now there seemed to be. I found out about Dad and Sandy at Calvert Hall, in the hallways. Some kids were talking about it, and I could tell by their tone that this wasn't teenage boy bullshit. They weren't talking about Dad's performance on the field or a game that should have been won. This wasn't done in that loud, braggadocio way boys have of arguing when they don't really know what they're talking about. Instead, they were whispering, heads bowed and huddled together, and when I approached, they either whispered softer or shut up. Finally, someone told me.

I went to the bathroom in between periods and threw up. I then went to the main office and called my mother, telling her I didn't feel well—I didn't—but not in that physical way like an upset stomach or flu and achy muscles. My head was spinning. My life as I knew it seemed to be falling apart. In the car, Mom knew I wasn't sick. It didn't take long for me to break down, sobbing, and I told her what I'd heard. I don't really remember much, but I do remember she didn't do much. She already knew.

She was willing to live with it if Dad didn't treat the kids wrong. Clearly that was happening. It didn't matter whether or not he meant to do it, Mom wasn't going to allow us, particularly the three younger brothers, to suffer.

And Janice, who was sitting on the stairs, 16 years old, thought, *Umm, I always knew you were an asshole, Dad, but I just didn't know how big a one.*

CHAPTER 19

The End...
But Not Like in the Movies

August 12, 1978
San Diego Chargers 17, Los Angeles Rams 0

The Colts and Dad will never forget George Allen. He was the Los Angeles Rams' head coach in 1967 when the Colts and Rams tied for the best record in football, only to have the first year of no play-in games. Allen was more than just a head coach of a team making the 1967 playoffs. He was a well-established head coach, so well established that in 1968, he was fired by the Rams, only to have 38 of his 40 players hold a press conference stating they would either retire or demand to be traded if he wasn't rehired. He was rehired, receiving a two-year contract, and he led the Rams to winning the Coastal Division and into the playoffs. But Allen's problems with Dan Reeves, the Rams' owner at the time, were never resolved, so when his contract expired after 1970, Allen left for Washington. And it wouldn't be the last time that Allen was involved in contractual weirdness.

Between 1966 and preseason 1978, Allen established himself as one of the best coaches in the NFL. His list of accomplishments is Hall of Fame stuff, and he was inducted in 2002. He never had a losing season. He finished his NFL coaching career with the third highest winning percentage, behind only Lombardi and John Madden. Although he never won the Super Bowl, he got to one, losing to the undefeated 1972 Miami Dolphins, coached by none other than Don Shula, the winningest coach in NFL history.

In 1978, Allen was hired by the Rams—again—after not signing a contract extension with the Washington Redskins. The NFL had changed since 1968, and now players rebelled against his micromanaging ways and hell-bent intensity. He had been an assistant under Halas and was rumored to be the "coach in waiting" when he left the Bears to join the Rams for the 1966 season. He was more like Shula than Ewbank in terms of demeanor; he was also like Halas but not as bombastic and maniacal as even Halas was. He was very much like both Shula and Ewbank in terms of practice preparation and scouting. In the end, most coaching, it seems, comes down to temperament and what attitude a team and owner require and can tolerate at a given moment.

In some ways, Allen was the first "modern" NFL coach who lived at his office and thought that maybe he was bigger than his team or the league.

Coaches get fired for lots of reasons, many of them valid, some not so. Think about Josh McDaniels, a protégé and Bill Belichick wannabe, who was hired by the Denver Broncos. He probably shouldn't have been, but when he was fired, it was because results didn't match up with expectations. College coaches who are a hot item interest pro teams occasionally, but they don't always work out. It's understandable. College football is different from the pro game, particularly in recruiting and how you handle the players.

Allen brought the same maniacal style and attention to detail, to the point of obsessiveness, but in his second stint in Los Angeles, instead of players holding press conferences in support, they ran to the media to complain. He had rules about how to eat in the team dining hall. One player, a budding star linebacker, left camp. Most of the players, however, thought the differences would be resolved. It's not important the details of the San Diego game, not even that it was a loss because preseason is just that, preseason. Legends, like Allen, were no longer getting the benefit of the doubt. Legendary status should have been enough for him, at least enough to get a honeymoon period that lasts longer than two preseason games. But after the listless game against the Chargers, the Rams' owner fired him.

That owner was Carroll Rosenbloom. His general manager was Don Klosterman, the man my dad negotiated his contracts with when they were both with the Colts. Rosenbloom admitted shortly after the firing that he "made a serious error in judgment in believing George Allen could work within our framework."

Sounds a lot like Dad's situation in his last year in Baltimore and his only year in San Diego. The NFL world was changing—for George Allen and for my dad. As the sport got bigger, mainly through television, the players got more power, and what you'd done in the past mattered less and less.

Not only were endings painful, but they could happen in a blink, as Allen learned.

The End...But Not Like in the Movies

As Dad's career wound down, I wasn't paying attention, just like I wasn't paying attention with how things were at home. Football was now something I did as I was playing in high school. Football, at least as it concerned my dad, was something that took him away from us or put extra pressure on us because of who he was and what the Colts meant to Baltimore. I didn't think about how football had given me a pretty good life, one that was exponentially better than the life Dad had lived growing up. At 15, I couldn't have articulated that, but just because I didn't say it out loud or even think about it doesn't mean it didn't hover over me and my siblings. It was a lot to carry, so I dealt with it the best way I knew: I didn't think about it.

It wasn't the only thing happening in my life that I didn't think about but should have. While I didn't overtly know that things weren't good at home between my parents, I understood it on some level. It was an unspoken truth; my sister knew how bad things were in their marriage; I could only sense it. I was involved in girls and cars and sports, and didn't really have time for Dad and his career or marriage. But the real truth is that I never really paid attention to Dad's career while he was playing. Just like most kids don't involve themselves in their parents' careers or lives, I didn't either. Maybe other teenagers and adults involved themselves in Dad's career, but only because they wanted the Colts to win. My house didn't seem different regardless of whether the Colts won or lost.

I remember hearing once from John Elway, I think, that he'd wished he could have played longer so his children could have really seen him play. At

16 watching my father play wasn't a big deal. He was a football player. Tommy Lekas' dad worked at an office and Tommy never went to watch him. My other friends' dads had jobs they went to every day. So what, I thought. What I really wanted from my dad as his career was winding down wasn't more wins or an MVP; instead, I wanted him at home. I wanted him healthy, sitting in his chair in the den reading the newspaper, one slipper on, the other having fallen off between the chair and ottoman. I wanted a scene from *Father Knows Best*. Football may have made for conversation with strangers when they learned I had the same name as my famous dad, but I didn't want to be famous. I wanted a father who would come to my games and pat me on the back whether we won or lost. I wanted a father who could answer my questions about college and what I should think about it. I wanted stability. I wanted a father who knew more about my girlfriend than just her name.

****

When the end comes, it generally comes fast. Not only did Dad's ending come fast and unexpectedly, it also didn't bring him home. He got traded to San Diego. His ending wasn't simple. And his departure from the Colts can ultimately be tied to the ending of the Baltimore Colts franchise and the move to Indianapolis. That's because the same can be said for three other things that were ending: Carroll Rosenbloom as owner, the family atmosphere that had pervaded the team since its inception in 1953, and our family as a nuclear unit. All these events, including Dad's retirement, happened in roughly the same two-year span. All had been simmering beneath the surface for years.

Looking at Dad's career, it was inevitable that he would have to retire. All players have to stop playing, and only some are lucky enough to decide when. Unlike a lot of occupations in which wisdom and experience are the most important aspect of the job, in football, particularly for a quarterback, although wisdom matters, arm strength must be at a certain level and being able to stay on the field matters. Both of these issues were surfacing with Dad. He had long term damage to his right elbow that was affecting his ability to put zip on his passes. The toughness that he'd exhibited throughout his career was now taking a toll on him. The nagging injuries, plus age, were now leading to more severe injuries, such as a torn Achilles tendon that occurred while playing a friendly yet highly competitive game of racquetball with Tom Matte. While he would recover from this injury—in much less time than anyone including his doctors thought possible—and play again, it was simply another example that he was slowing down. He didn't want to admit that.

And if the league merger and television were changing the role of players in the game, making them in many ways the stars of the league—pushing coaches, like Lombardi and Halas, to secondary roles—it had also pushed money to the forefront of the league. Many players were making enough in salary that they didn't need a second job. Soon, some players would be making enough that they didn't need to worry about life after football, except as a way to stay busy. As money improved, so did the conditioning of the players. Training was year round and training camp was a time to polish execution. Gone were the days of using training camp to get back into shape. Dad had made himself an NFL quarterback by combining his talent with sheer will. Will was no longer as important.

Or maybe he didn't want to admit that he had nothing else he wanted to do. He already had experience in working everyday jobs that most people hold: he'd been a salesman for a cardboard box company and done advertising spots. He already owned a restaurant that was popular and seemed to be doing well financially. Perhaps Dad knew he wasn't a very good businessman, as a couple of bankruptcies would later prove. Or just maybe Dad loved football, the camaraderie of teammates, the euphoria of winning a game, and even the aches and pains that accompanied the game. Finally, maybe it was a little bit of all these reasons. Whatever it was, the NFL isn't a league that lets even its superstars decide how they want to go out; it was and still is a cutthroat business that's about winning, and teams will do whatever is necessary to make sure that happens.

While Dad had never been one to lift weights or do conditioning drills and exercises in the off-season, he stayed in shape, playing softball, being part of the Colts' basketball team, hitting a boxing speed bag, and doing curls to keep his arms and shoulders strong. He was a good athlete, maybe even a very good one, but he wasn't an incredible physical specimen. The lack of looks from big-time college programs and new teammates not believing he was "the" Johnny Unitas probably was and is still based on the idea that great athletes need to look like them, like something closer to a mythological Greek god than a everyday guy walking down the street with slumped shoulders and bow legs as if he'd just gotten back from driving cattle across the range. Instead, his greatness came from his calm demeanor, peripheral vision, quick decision-making, toughness, strong arm, and an uncanny ability to see opportunities and call plays that no one expected. As the arm strength abated, he just couldn't make it up with what announcers today call the "intangibles." One day, even they end.

And as they were deteriorating, the league was changing. Not just in style but substance. Adding AFL teams, more of a scoring league, had led the NFL teams to adapt. In addition to teams adapting by building teams around strong-armed quarterbacks (because of what Dad had done in the league in the late 1950s and '60s) and fleet wide receivers, the league itself adapted by changing rules, making it easier for linemen to block—giving the quarterback more time to stay in the pocket—or limiting contact between receiver and defender, making it easier for the receiver to get open. In a somewhat counterintuitive process, these changes should have been working for Dad as his arm strength waned, but now, quarterbacks didn't need to make as many quick decisions in less than 2.5 seconds. As Raymond has told me, quarterbacks today have generally more than four seconds to throw the ball. In the 1960s, it was around 2.5 seconds. Strong arms were perceived to be more important than hard to quantify intangibles like the ones Dad possessed. With more time to make decisions, Dad's greatest strength, reading a defense between the huddle and the snap, was less important.

But maybe Dad's end in Baltimore wouldn't have come like it did if it weren't for changes that had to do with team ownership and front-office leadership. The changes in Dad's arm were real but also possible to counter with other positive qualities. Rule changes were happening at the rate of one or two a year, slowly changing the nature of what mattered. But what happened in the Colts' front office occurred overnight. Literally.

****

Carroll Rosenbloom's career in Baltimore came to an end before Dad's. Maybe if Rosenbloom hadn't left the Colts—got ridden of them is a better way to describe it—Dad's ending would have been a bit more graceful. Maybe. Baltimore sports fans—according to most people I run into, he was always throwing touchdowns and never threw an interception—have mythologized my dad. Rosenbloom's stay has also been elevated and polished. While I thought the world of Mr. Rosenbloom, particularly as a kid, as an adult I see that all that gleamed around him wasn't without makeup.

There's no question he was a very bright man. There's no question that he loved the Baltimore Colts. From the beginning, there are questions whether or not he loved Baltimore itself. He lived in New Jersey and New York City, and when he was in town on Colts business, he tended to stay in hotels. Although he was born and raised in Baltimore and graduated from City College, the high school that gave George Young his start as a coach before becoming a Colts assistant (and later the general manager of the New York Giants), Rosenbloom had his sights set on something bigger than Baltimore. He took over a struggling company of his father's, one his father wanted to liquidate, and made it into a fortune. He was a competitor, and he didn't like losing.

As a players' owner, he had a mixed reputation. He helped Alan Ameche and Gino Marchetti get started in the fast-food business, a proposition that left both wealthy long after their football careers ended. On the other hand, if he didn't like a player, then he didn't help him out. Marchetti, who Rosenbloom co-signed a loan for so he could start his fast-food chain, asked him to induct him into the Pro Football Hall of Fame. Dad loved him, and so did Mom. He always brought a Christmas basket to our house. He delivered it personally some years, hanging around the living room to talk with my parents. It wasn't a token basket, either; it seemed big enough to feed most of the Colts, more than enough for the seven of us. He gave players Thanksgiving turkeys. There were rumors that he promised an end-of-the-season bonus to the 1959 team if they made the playoffs when it looked like they wouldn't. That is either an urban myth or one of those locker room secrets that the players involved have protected.

By the late 1960s, however, the bloom was off. Part of it might have been the change in American culture, particularly Baltimore culture. After winning two championships in 1958 and 1959, the Colts didn't come close enough again until 1968, and that resulted in the embarrassing loss to the Jets. They had been supplanted by the Green Bay Packers as the team of destiny, as the franchise that every other team wanted to emulate. While Dad was a big name, so were Bart Starr and Paul Horning, but there might not have been a bigger star in the game than the Packers' head coach, Vince Lombardi. Baltimore no longer seemed to be the front line of pro sports, at least not to someone like Rosenbloom who spent his adult life trying to do two things: live dangerously on the edge of risk and get away from Baltimore to somewhere more sophisticated.

Furthermore, football was changing. It was no longer a select group of 12 owners and 12 cities. Even without the AFL merger, the NFL had added four teams. With the merger, the NFL grew to 26 teams. It was no longer the league that did its schedule on the commissioner's kitchen table. It was a league dictated by television. Maybe Carroll Rosenbloom was smart enough to see that—and what better place to be for television than Los Angeles.

Maybe it was the Baltimore press that didn't like him and wrote negatively constantly about him, particularly John Steadman, the man my father and I thought about co-writing Dad's autobiography in the mid-1990s. Steadman, while not stylistically a good writer, was an influential one. Maybe it was Rosenbloom seeing the need for a better stadium, something he worked on long before Bob Irsay took over the team and demanded a new stadium. Maybe it was his new wife, who'd spent her adult life in the "entertainment" business, wanting to live on the West Coast. She, like so many other non-natives, saw Baltimore as about as backwater as one could get. Maybe it was trading the Colts for the Rams and getting $4 million tax-free. Maybe it was all of those reasons.

The difference between Rosenbloom and Irsay was a matter of style. Rosenbloom could be very charming; he was handsome and suave. While he got what he wanted—usually—he also made you feel like you were getting what you wanted. Irsay, on the other hand, was a drunk. While he was a savvy businessman, he didn't comport himself in the way the public, particularly the working-class Baltimore public, thought an owner should behave. Rosenbloom may have abandoned Baltimore, but he was born here. He was seemingly different from many natives; he was Jewish, wealthy, and involved in manufacturing. He worked hard and cared passionately but let the team dominate the spotlight. Even though he was born with a silver spoon in his mouth, he worked hard to increase his fortune, he brought pro football here when it appeared no one else was interested, and he helped put Baltimore on the sports map. He won two championships quickly (at least in football years) and kept the team generally in contention. While a native, he also understood Baltimore's inferiority complex when compared to New York or Washington. He was one of us, but also one of us with a chip on his shoulder. We liked that. Dad was that way. Irsay wasn't a native; he didn't understand what it meant to be a native—not that anyone really does except natives who simply know it when they see it, and Irsay wasn't it.

We'll probably never know how and why the exchange of franchises between Rosenbloom and Irsay happened, although Rosenbloom said on more than one occasion that if players and coaches can wear out their welcomes in cities, so can owners. Irsay bought the Rams knowing he was probably going to get the Colts in a trade. Once it happened, it wasn't a good moment for Dad. For the city of Baltimore, it probably didn't matter who owned the team. Irsay may have moved the Colts in the middle of the night in early 1984, but the idea had crossed Rosenbloom's mind much earlier.

For years, the Colts had loyalties to certain towns, two in particular:

Hershey, Pennsylvania, where the team played the second half of the 1952 season because they'd failed in Dallas and before they officially moved to Baltimore; and Westminster, MD, where the Colts had held their summer camps since their beginning in the early '50s. In 1972, just before selling the team, Rosenbloom moved preseason camp to Tampa. It was both an effort to test-drive Tampa as a possible relocation site, and it was to scare the city, particularly city government, into building a new stadium for the team. It wasn't like today—or even 15 years ago—where the negotiations were carried out in the press and the funding was all public. Rosenbloom was going to invest a significant sum of his own money into the stadium, but apparently it wasn't working out. And then it was.

And then it wasn't, and Rosenbloom was gone from Baltimore. Irsay was in as the new Colts owner, along with his loutish behavior—something that drove my father crazy. For it to be the man who was supposed to be one of the faces of the franchise, the owner, drunk and rude all the time was too much. But an even bigger change than the ownership was at general manager with the hiring of Joe Thomas.

Thomas was a good general manager (but not from my father's point of view), and the way he went about doing his business didn't help the public perception of him with his players or fans. He came here after being in charge of player personnel in both Minnesota and Miami, building very good teams and working with both the players and fans. In Baltimore, Thomas didn't seem to be able to work with either. Thomas wasn't the only one who thought that Dad was winding down. At preseason camp in 1969, the camp after losing Super Bowl III to the Jets, the then general manager Harry Holmes mentioned both Dad's injuries and age: "The older guys are dropping by the wayside now. Unitas is the only guy left from that 1958 overtime win over the New York Giants. We're playing with two ancient quarterbacks."

Dad's teammates, including Jim Mutscheller, Lenny Moore, Jimmy Orr, and Raymond Berry, all saw their physical skills declining, but Dad thought he could still play. His position relied less on pure physical skills. There was something else at work too: Dad was "Johnny U," superstar, the face of the team and the city. And while the NFL was not the same league as when he first entered it in 1955, he was one of the faces of the league, too. How to handle a superstar has always been a problem. Babe Ruth wanted to become manager of the Yankees; the Yankee ownership didn't want that. He was traded back to Boston, the Braves this time, and that experiment didn't work out. He batted .181 before retiring about one-third of the way through the season. Michael Jordan retired on his own, only to come out of retirement twice to play again in the NBA, but not for the Chicago Bulls. Instead he played for the Washington Wizards, two years that seemed like a trip to Purgatory, if not Hell. His points were way down and almost every other positive statistic was also down. Interestingly, while the moves helped both the Braves and Wizards in terms of attendance, they didn't help in terms of wins, and both teams finished with losing records.

****

The Colts had a good season in 1971, although Dad only started five games. They finished 10–4 and got to the AFC Championship Game, only to lose 21–0 to the Miami Dolphins, now coached by Don Shula. This is the same Miami team that would go on to Super Bowl VI and lose, but set the stage for the next year when they would finish the season as the only undefeated, untied team in NFL history.

But 1971 didn't start the way Dad hoped. In early April he tore his Achilles tendon playing racquetball, and even before the season started, there were questions whether or not he was the right man to lead the team. Morrall was a year older, but in football "years," because he'd been a backup so many of them, he seemed younger. Morrall was named the starter at the beginning of the season. Dad missed the entire preseason although he was available to play in the final two exhibition games. Morrall started until mid-November when Dad was named the starter and became the No. 1 quarterback for the rest of the season.

While he waited and the Colts won, he said some interesting things to reporters: "Earl [Morrall] is doing a good job. I don't see how Mac [Don McCafferty] can change quarterbacks in midstream. The only thing that matters is that we continue to win. I'm not going to cause trouble. It's hard enough to play the game without creating problems." In a game against the Jets in early November, the Colts played the first game of Dad's career in which he was physically able to play and didn't. It seemed his career was winding down although he didn't see or talk about it that way. Instead, the next week, Dad was named the starter against a very good Miami team. Morrall was ineffective in a couple of his starts, and McCafferty was ready for a change. Dad would start the final five games of the season and the two playoff games. Now that he was fully back from his Achilles injury, Dad could honor the last year of his contract, the 1972 season. He didn't think his skills had diminished enough to retire although he was the first to acknowledge that he'd lost zip on his ball and couldn't throw as deep as he once had. As he said, that's to be expected and he'd made adjustments. In his mind, he was ready for 1972.

And then Rosenbloom pulled off his bizarre sale of the Colts to Irsay, and everything that once seemed normal with the Colts no longer was.

****

Once the sale of the Rams and trade with Irsay was finished and Thomas named general manager, the new leaders in the Baltimore football scene were saying all the right things. From the beginning, Irsay was questioned about whether or not he planned to relocate the team. Both Thomas and McCafferty stated publicly that they were interested in finding a backup quarterback or someone to be the quarterback of the future. Dad would be 39 this season, and while he talked like he could play forever, it wasn't going to happen. The question was whether Dad would see that his skills had diminished and retire with his dignity intact or would he, like my mom and sister predicted, believe his press clippings and overrate himself.

We now all know the answer, and it's generally the answer most great athletes pick. It's easy to sit in the stands or on the couch on Sunday afternoon and see—very clearly—that a player isn't the same player he was just a couple of years ago. Fans around my dad's age watched Willie Mays and Mickey Mantle deteriorate; they watched George Halas and Woody Hayes do the same thing as coaches that Dad was doing as a player. Recently, we've seen it with Joe Montana and LaDainian Tomlinson. It's much harder for the individual to see the end, especially, as in Dad's case, when he didn't want to.

Dad had stated a year earlier in the *Baltimore Sun* when questioned about the Achilles injury that he wasn't close to retiring. He was asked, "Why not?" And he answered that he liked playing football. It was that simple and in one article, the columnist said there wasn't more to read into it because that's the way my dad was. He didn't need the money; he was doing fine with the Golden Arm Restaurant. Plain and simple, he liked football. He always had. Maybe liking something is the same as not knowing what to do in the future, but no matter, Dad wanted to play. His comeback from the Achilles injury at least a month early proved it. He was willing to work extra hard to stay in a game he loved.

****

Clearly, Thomas had a plan to work on quarterback succession from the moment he became general manager. Not to have a plan would have been stupid. Everyone likes plans that make sense except when they affect you. Everyone likes plans about getting the best quarterback. Before Thomas could trade Dad, he first had to prove that he was washed up.

Even with difficult playoff losses and missed games because of injuries earlier in Dad's career, there's no question that 1972 was the worst year of his career. Statistically, he wasn't awful, but he wasn't great. He started the first five games of the season, and the Colts went 1–4. At that point in the season Thomas wanted to go with youth, thinking about next year in particular, and the future in general. He wanted McCafferty to start Marty Domres at quarterback over Dad. McCafferty, who had been with Dad since 1960, refused. It probably had as much to do with not letting the general manager dictate game-day decisions as to loyalty to Dad, but no matter the reason, Mac looked like he was being loyal. Dad always appreciated that. Since Mac wouldn't do what Thomas wanted, he got fired. John Sandusky, another old friend of Dad's and the offensive line coach, took over. They had played together a long time, Sandusky having coached with the Colts since 1959. Because of their long-standing friendship, Dad agreed to do whatever Sandusky asked.

Dad didn't play much after the coaching change. Thomas got his way: there would be a youth movement on the Colts, and Dad wasn't part of it. Before the season was over, he'd already announced he wouldn't be playing for the Colts in 1973. On December 5, against the Buffalo Bills, in the Colts' last home game of the year, Dad made his final appearance as a Colt. The Colts were leading the Bills 28–0 late in the fourth quarter when Domres got "injured." When asked after the game if he was injured, he said he'd hurt his hip, but later in life, Domres admitted that his "injury" was a ruse to get Dad in the final home game although Domres made Sandusky tell Dad to get ready. When told he might go in the game, Dad said, "You're the boss." Earlier in the season, Dad had made it widely known that he wasn't going to be a charity case, that he didn't want a farewell tour, that he wasn't going to be patronized by going into games as a mop-up guy. He was either the starter or he wasn't going to play. He'd clearly softened from that position.

He entered the game, Sandusky only planning to play him one play so he could be replaced by the third-stringer, Jack Mildren. Dad was told this by Sandusky, and the fact a plane had flown over earlier in the game with a "Unitas We Stand" banner trailing it probably didn't hurt. While Dad wasn't big into ceremony, he also knew that this last game as a Colt was about a lot more than just him. He understood big public moments. He didn't have to like them or want to participate in them, but he did what was necessary. He was a part of the fans' lives whether he wanted to be or not. On this day, against a bad Bills team, the fans wanted him. It was as much for them that he went in as for himself.

Once in, he couldn't have asked for a better ending. He threw a pass to Eddie Hinton that ended up being caught because Hinton did a great job snagging a tough ball while two defensive backs ran into each other, ensuring that Dad's final pass ended up being a touchdown. It was a moment that seemingly only Hollywood could have scripted.

It even came with its controversial issue. As Dad was walking off the field, some people saw him raise his finger in a gesture of proclaiming he was No. 1. That's not like anything my dad would do. Instead, he claimed to me that he gave the one-finger salute to Joe Thomas up in the press box, an action I find more believable. Most people don't because they don't want to. They want to see Dad as more than a hero; they see him as a saint, and I can tell you, while I loved my dad, he was no saint. His throwing a football better than anyone else ever has, particularly in pressure-packed situations with violence aimed right at him, doesn't mean he was perfect off the field. He had a surly side. He didn't like to be crossed, and he particularly didn't suffer fools easily, something he saw Thomas as. I don't know what he did, but whether he did it or not, it has only added to his legend.

One aspect of that final touchdown pass that isn't in dispute was the quality of the pass. It wasn't very good. To throw his final touchdown pass as a Colt, Dad needed something he rarely relied on: luck. Even Cameron Snyder, one of Dad's greatest supporters, wrote negatively in the *Baltimore Sun* about the pass, calling it a "wounded duck."

Dad's career seemed to be in the same kind of flight. It wasn't over just yet, but it was wobbling and would need something like luck to keep going.

CHAPTER 20

California Dreamin'

December 28, 1975
Dallas Cowboys 17, Minnesota Vikings 14

Minnesota had a league-best 12–2 regular season record, the MVP in quarterback Fran Tarkenton, who, in many ways was a throwback, a player who did whatever he had to do to win, more like Bobby Layne than Roger Staubach or Terry Bradshaw, his contemporaries. If Dad was the first "modern" quarterback, the type who saw the passing game as timing and execution, not simply what was done when the run wasn't working, then Tarkenton was the "new" quarterback, a player who relied on his feet and scrambling as much as arm strength. He wasn't Joe Namath; instead, he was more like Michael Vick and Robert Griffin III.

But these Vikings weren't just riding on the coattails of their quarterback. They had Chuck Foreman, a running back who had more 1,700 all-purpose yards and a great defense. They were a force. The Cowboys, on the other hand, were the NFC wildcard team, 1975 being the first year that seeding was instituted for the playoffs. The Vikings were coming off consecutive Super Bowl appearances, having lost all of them. Although the Vikings had the best record, the Cowboys were 10–4, recovering from a mediocre 8–6 record the year before.

Again, the NFL was changing, but the new changes were less about how the game was played and more about team dynasties. Gone were the Colts, Packers, and Bears. Now, the two best teams in the NFC during the last five years were the Vikings and Cowboys, two teams that didn't exist when Dad won his first championship. Between 1970 and 1978, either the Vikings or the Cowboys were in the Super Bowl except one year. The best teams in the AFC were a former NFL team, the Pittsburgh Steelers, probably the worst team historically in the NFL before the AFL/NFL merger, and the Miami Dolphins, also a team that didn't exist in 1958. Dad's former coach, Don Shula, coached the Dolphins. Chuck Noll, also a former Colts coach when Dad played there, coached the Steelers, who won their first of four Super Bowls in the 1970s the previous year.

★★★★

Pro football was now firmly established on television. It was the Sunday afternoon religion with nationally shown double-headers scheduled from early September until late December. In 1970 pro football started being shown on Monday nights, and America was introduced to Frank Gifford (as an announcer), Don Meredith (a quarterback as an announcer) and Howard Cosell. Interestingly, how television handled a game hadn't changed that much, only in how much we were watching. In 1939, only one year after television was introduced, the first NFL game was broadcast between the Brooklyn Dodgers and the visiting Philadelphia Eagles, and it wasn't long after that game that the precedent of using a play-by-play announcer and a color man came into use. Color men have historically been coaches or quarterbacks, the two people who need to know what everyone on the field is doing. The playoffs in 1975 followed the formula of using a play-by-play guy and a color man.

It wasn't a difficult game to call. It was one of the last playoff games played outdoors in the old Metropolitan Stadium in Minneapolis. The weather was cold, as it tends to be in late December in Minnesota. It was another element boosting the heavily favored Vikings. With the Vikings leading 14–10 late in the game and Dallas facing a fourth-and-16, Roger Staubach hit Drew Pearson for a first down. Like the 1958 game in which the Giants felt that Gifford had gotten a first down but was denied, replays indicate that Pearson caught the ball out of bounds. That reception set up what some experts have called "the greatest" catch in NFL history. As time was running out, Staubach threw a 50-yard pass to Drew Pearson, and he caught the ball with one hand, winning the game. This play, too, held its own controversy, some people thinking Pearson pushed off—offensive pass interference—to make the catch. At least one Vikings fan thought so as the official who made the touchdown call was hit in the head with a whiskey bottle.

The late game-winning pass came to be known as a Hail Mary pass. The expression, while it had been used off and on for about 50 years in reference to sporting events, hadn't become synonymous with a late, and lucky, bomb thrown for a touchdown to win a game until this game. Staubach would announce to reporters afterward that it was a "Hail Mary pass," playing off his Catholic upbringing.

This playoff game's telecast was called by play-by-play guy Gary Bender. Dad was his partner and color man. I met Bender later when I lived in California. And neither announcer could take credit for labeling Staubach's pass a Hail Mary, only for being there.

It was the kind of game and moment that could lead to an extensive post-football career. It didn't.

CALIFORNIA DREAMIN'

When I think of the mid-1970s, I think of the Mamas and Papas and their song, "California Dreamin'." Like that band, which formed in New York and had all sorts of money and personality conflicts, both my dad and I went to California dreaming that life would get better than it had been in Baltimore. But life isn't a song, and while California proved to be important, and I don't regret going out there, it wasn't the ultimate tonic I hoped for. I can say that today, and still I stayed almost six years. It didn't work for Dad, either. Dad said that by his actions. He was there less than a year. In the end, family turmoil in Baltimore was better than culture shock in California.

****

Leaving town, maybe having given the finger to the Colts management, Dad, as a superstar deserved more than a trade. For someone of Dad's stature, it's assumed there will be a sendoff, an honoring of the man and his achievements. It's important to understand that Dad didn't play football for individual achievements. They meant very little to him. He wasn't completely oblivious to cheering crowds and the effect he had on people, but he would have traded in his social cache for another championship, or at least a chance to enter Super Bowl III against the Jets sooner than late in the second half.

When Brooks Robinson was planning to retire from the Orioles, the team had a Brooks Robinson Day in his honor. This year, the Ravens honored Ray Lewis, clearly the greatest Raven in history, by letting him do his dance one last time at his final home game. For many athletes, they may not get a going-away or going-into-retirement party in their last year, but they get one a year or two later. That never happened with Dad at Memorial Stadium. When Artie Donovan decided to retire, he dressed for his final game, a preseason game in Salem, Virginia, so that he could go through the ritual of having a teammate help him take his jersey off one last time. Because of Dad's relationship to new management, there was no good-bye, not in his final season in Baltimore, not later.

Citizens, both prominent and everyday, saw this as a problem, so a good-bye was organized for the 1973 Preakness. It is strange that Dad was honored at a horse race, no doubt an important race and Baltimore event, but Dad wasn't honored at Memorial Stadium, the site of many of his greatest exploits. Fred Kail, a local sculptor and huge Colts fan, was commissioned to do a bust of Dad. Not only was he a fan, but also he was a friend of both Dad's and many players on the team. He'd gotten his start in the sculpting business by making an early bobble head figurine of an anonymous Colt that was sold from the customer counter at the Colts' main office. The figurine was so popular that various players asked Kail to create bobble heads of themselves for personal gifts, which he did. He hung out with the team, occasionally playing on the Colts' players' softball team and drinking beer with them on Friday afternoons after practice. He was more than an artist, he was a friend.

Kail wasn't sure how to get Dad to sit for a bust, and he didn't want to give away the secret that Dad was going to be honored, so he lied. He told Dad he had a new camera and he needed to try it out. Whether Dad believed this or not is unimportant. He allowed Fred to photograph him with a ruler next to various spots on his face. Now, Kail had the measurements so that he could make the bust. At the Preakness Dad was given his bust; and he was honored. It mattered and he appreciated it, but people around town still talk about how he didn't get a farewell at Memorial Stadium, a place he helped make into the "World's Largest Outdoor Insane Asylum."

****

Dad didn't like confrontation, and after he retired, he did everything he could to avoid it. After he divorced Mom, I avoided it, too. I couldn't deal with my mom and her comments—criticisms really—of my dad. I didn't want my parents divorced, but once it's done, you have to move on. Mom wasn't able to do that. Maybe she didn't want to. She had played her hand, filing the divorce papers (not the other way around) and filed them because she was concerned about her children. It seems like a pretty reasonable response to a man who had a girlfriend in an apartment he was paying for a couple of miles away from our house. The problem is that divorcing Dad came with consequences. Not divorcing him also had consequences. Either way, Mom wasn't going to be happy, and she wasn't.

There's a famous story about Mickey Mantle and his wife, Merlyn. Mantle, a serial womanizer who made no secret about it, had a girlfriend in Georgia who he was essentially living with. His biological family was back in Texas. He supposedly felt bad about the extent of his cheating on his wife, so he suggested divorce, a seemingly reasonable idea except his wife wasn't interested. She knew if she divorced Mickey, then she would no longer be Mrs. Mickey Mantle, and obviously, that was important to her.

However unfair, the opposite happened to Mom, she did divorce Dad, and she was no longer Mrs. Johnny Unitas. While her former role came with its downside, it also came with its upside. Life is a balancing act, and she decided that protecting her children, particularly financially, was more important than retaining the last name. That doesn't mean she liked everything about the decision. She was vocal about not being Mrs. Johnny Unitas, and even more vocal about the "new" Mrs. Johnny Unitas. She called her a stewardess whore, a cradle robber, and bitch. According to Mom, she stole my father away because she gave good blow jobs, something my dad even brought up once.

I got tired of hearing about it. Mom carried the hate and hatred and expressed them to her children. I felt awkward, and I didn't want to know what happened. Every time I called and we talked, it was constant ragging on Dad. I always skirted issues dealing with my father. If I couldn't have them together, I still wanted to love both of them. When Dad and issues about him came up, I changed the subject or ended the conversation.

But I wasn't the only one struggling. I felt sorry for my siblings living at home because they were under constant duress in having to deal with my mom's feelings and thoughts and emotions about my father and what he was doing with his new life without her. Maybe everyone in my family avoided the family turmoil. Maybe that's what dysfunctional families do: avoid the dysfunction, and when you're not sure what the dysfunction is, avoid each other. Without looking too hard, I could have figured out the dysfunction, but I didn't want to. I needed to get away. I went to college at the University of Miami. But that wasn't far enough, not even close, so I moved to California. Part of going to California, in hindsight, was probably to be closer to Dad, who had just finished playing for the Chargers. I wouldn't have admitted that then. But there were lots of things going on then that I didn't admit to, and now I think I can see what was really going on.

I was blaming everyone else for problems that were bigger than me, and even blaming everyone else for issues that may have been mine to deal with. I wasn't the first kid to have his parents divorce, nor was I the first kid to be the son of someone very famous. At the time, I liked to think I was.

****

My mother once said, long before my parents divorced, "I don't want to be around when John can't play football anymore." She didn't mean it literally although that's what happened. Instead, she was wondering about what Dad was going to do when he couldn't play football. It was a good question, and one that Dad spent the rest of his life—about 30 years—trying to answer. Not that his life after football was boring and unrewarding. Football had been his life, his dream since elementary school. Once he attained that dream, football was both his vocation and avocation and remained that way until he retired. He loved everything about playing pro football, even understanding that injuries were part of the deal. He never complained about them, not once that I heard. Sure, he had outside interests like the bowling alley and Golden Arm restaurant, but those were about making money, not pursuits he engaged in because he enjoyed them. He loved playing the game, particularly the Sunday part of the game. He loved his teammates and hanging out in the locker room. He didn't mind the practices and film studies he did at home because both of those made him a better player.

He didn't like to talk football except as a means of making the team better. Once he retired, football didn't seem to be an option. What he may have liked to have done—be in management—disappeared when Rosenbloom traded the Colts to Irsay. While his football playing life may have ended, his life off the field hadn't.

His football career came to a pitiful end. Most sports careers do, particularly when a player holds on because they have nothing else to do. Most pro athletes get cut, but because they're not a big name, in the fans' minds, it's more like they disappear. Dad was too well known simply to disappear. Even if he wanted to, his stature wouldn't have allowed it. Dad played on—soldiered on may be a better word—because of his true love for football, the fact he didn't have a logical exit plan, and he had no idea what to do with his future. Dad once told Raymond, "As long as they're stupid enough to pay me, I'll keep playing." As the son of a famous athlete, my view is different than the fans', particularly at the end of a career. Fans want to remember athletes in their glory years, as heroes, blood dripping down Dad's face after taking another horrific hit from Doug Atkins late in the game. Even with the blood and wobbly knees, he still leads the Colts to another come-from-behind, late fourth-quarter victory. But as we know, that wasn't what happened.

He signed a two-year contract with the San Diego Chargers for $250,000 per year. But even money, which sometimes seemed as much a motivator as playing the sport he loved, couldn't keep him on the field for more than half a year. He didn't sign the contract hoping to prove he was still one of the top quarterbacks. He just wanted to be a good NFL quarterback. He was under the impression that he was going to the Chargers to start, play decent ball, and mentor their young quarterback, Dan Fouts. He was okay with that. He was okay even with maybe giving up his starting spot to Fouts when he was ready. Initially, he understood his role. At least he thought he did.

Part of the problem with going to the Chargers is that they were a former AFL team, and that bygone culture influenced its current one. The AFL was about points and rebelliousness, symbolized by Namath and the Oakland Raiders. Just because the AFL merged with the NFL didn't mean it immediately became like the traditional NFL franchises. Dad, off the field, was conservative, both politically and psychologically. He didn't like change. He didn't like long hair. He supported the Vietnam War because that's what a good American did. He was a Republican. He believed in the authority of coaches. He believed that the game needed to be respected. San Diego, whatever it was, didn't feel like that to Dad. He might as well have been playing a different sport his new world and teammates were so different.

Dad started for four games in 1973, leading the Chargers to only one victory, a 34–7 win over Buffalo in Week 2. In Week 4, after throwing first-half interceptions against the Steelers, Fouts replaced him in the second half and for the rest of the year. While playing for the Chargers was culturally a different experience, it wasn't culture that did Dad in. It was his body. His love for the game hadn't diminished, but his body had. During preseason in 1974, his second year with the Chargers, Dad announced his retirement. On Wednesday, July 24, 1974, Dad told the media, "I hate to quit playing football. I'd like to play another 30 years. Your mind is willing, but your body wears out."

Even as he went out, Dad understood the nuances of the game, "I'm taking up time on the field when it could be used for better purposes for the younger people." While he mentioned his knees as the main reason, it was also his arm. There was nothing left in his right elbow.

He offered to stay that year in San Diego and coach with Tommy Prothro. Instead, he returned back to Baltimore, where his "home" needed tending.

****

The next phase of his life didn't get any easier. The public wants to believe that Dad simply retired and remained the great Johnny U, not throwing passes but having a life easier than the one they struggled through every day. As disappointing as it may be, my dad struggled, too. So did I. So did my siblings. Because we were a dysfunctional family before Dad retired, we remained one afterward.

****

By 1975, I couldn't live with either of my parents. They were divorced, Dad remarried. Mom was bitter about the breakup of her marriage, bitter about the breakup of her family, and bitter about no longer being *the* "Mrs. Johnny Unitas." Instead of dealing with the reality of a broken family, most everyone in the family resorted to running, even hiding. I was the worst of the bunch.

My sister went to college at Mt. St. Mary's, about an hour away in Emmitsburg, Maryland. I wanted to go to college also, but Dad wasn't around to help me figure it out, either the academic or athletic part. That's why I steered away from football in college. My father took me down to Miami, a school that seemed as far away from Baltimore as possible. I liked the beach, and Florida had lots of beaches. I had long hair. My father didn't like that. I wore bell-bottoms, platform shoes, and collared shirt open. No one recognized my father. We walked in and registered for class. I wasn't able to get into the high rises, so I had to live in an off-campus apartment that was still owned by the university, a two-story building—like a Holiday Inn.

I was by myself. It was a difficult situation. Some friends went to college and knew a few people. I didn't know a soul. I thought it was what I wanted, but once I had it, it wasn't. I thought I was free and that I could do what I wanted to do without the fighting and complaining. I shared one room with three guys. One of my roommates was a black guy; another was from Vermont, who drove a Mazda RX-7, and was into oceanography; and my last roommate didn't have a car. Neither did I. My father and I dropped my stuff in the room, and my dad took off. He had retired earlier that summer, and I don't remember why he left, but he didn't stay long. He didn't help me get acclimated. He was, "Here you go, son. Good luck and call me if you need anything." He now had his own life. I expected this, but now that there was chaos at home and newness on the road, I wished he didn't have to go.

It was August and hot. No air conditioning. Once Dad left, that was that, and I was on my own. I rolled into classes, oftentimes stumbled to classes, not sure where they were, and when I did find them, they were in lecture halls of 300 and 400 students. Initially, I was in heaven, with my long hair, flip flops, relative obscurity, and classes that I got to decide to attend or not. A couple of guys I met suggested I try out for the football team. I wasn't interested. What I really wanted to major in was special education. I was taking 18 credits but ended up dropping six of them.

One guy I befriended had a big green Cadillac convertible with lights in the back that were fins. He loved Jack Daniels but wouldn't smoke cigarettes. He said it was bad for him. He loved psychedelic mushrooms because he thought they were healthy. When he ate them, he thought he was even more healthy by eating apples and drinking Jack. He's the one who initially got me into drugs more than marijuana, but it's not like he put a gun to my head and made me. He only made it seem exciting. He didn't just do mushrooms; he knew how to find them. He knew where all the cow patties were, and at 5:00 in the morning we'd go out to pastures around Dade County and pick mushrooms. He showed me what to look for. We'd find them and come back and take them. I don't think I got high off them. He'd take a mushroom and then he'd drink some Jack D, and if he wanted to feel healthy, he'd take a bite of an apple.

Still, I felt I'd gone to another planet. I was raised as a strict Catholic. When my parents divorced, that was when I went off to the other side. There wasn't the discipline. There was so much hate my mother had for my father and I didn't want to be around her or my siblings, so I went out with my buddies and we smoked pot. Now I was doing 'shrooms and not much else.

I wasn't really "there" in Miami. No one was standing over me, making sure I stayed on the straight and narrow. My father was no longer a nearby authority figure, slapping his silver hairbrush. I wouldn't have survived an hour if my father had known what I was doing. My mother, however, had an idea, but she didn't say anything. She figured I'd grow up at some point. I wasn't hurting her. Some of this rebelliousness had started before college—not as bad or as intense—but I was still cutting the grass, doing all those things a son was supposed to do. She loved us being there. Now I wasn't at home, and I didn't feel my father's eyes on me, scaring me into doing right or making me want to do right as I strove for his approval.

Now even Mom wasn't around, and I couldn't be around her because of her bitterness toward Dad and the divorce. She still loved him. I did too, but I was a teenager and ready to get out from under both of them. In my mind, their problems weren't mine. Obviously, considering my performance at Miami, I was a long way from having my act together.

****

Since college wasn't working out, I ran away again and left Miami. Luckily—although it happened a year earlier—Patty, my girlfriend, had moved to California because her father got a transfer to the Bay area. At Miami, I wasn't doing much, mostly not going to class and doing drugs instead. I wasn't a "druggie," but if I didn't do something drastic, I was heading in a bad direction.

Before going to college, I thought I knew what I wanted to do. I had my future planned. I was going to marry Patty, but not just yet, waiting until after she graduated from high school. For my graduation from high school,

Dad gave me a car, a beautiful red Triumph TR6 sports car. That's really all I wanted. Less than a week after getting the car and a couple of days before she left permanently for the West Coast, Patty and I were driving around Loch Raven Reservoir, not too far from my house.

I had a ring in the glove compartment. We had been drinking, driving around the falls, holding hands, talking about us and our future. We'd already had sex. I was happy and sad, happy to be with Patty and sad because she was leaving and so was I. She was heading west and I was going south. I knew at some level that the life I'd been living was ending; the world that I occupied was changing. Even though I hated most of my current life, I was scared. Change and I didn't get along.

We were talking, one of those serious type of discussions. I was driving too fast and not paying attention and couldn't make a turn. Instead, the car slammed into a telephone pole. I was fine, but Patty had to go to the hospital. I don't know how that all happened, only that it did. The next day, Dad and I went to see her, and I gave her the ring, the one that had been in the car the night before. Dad left the room. She and I talked about marriage, and we cried, holding on to each other. I wasn't ready for the responsibility of marriage, but I was ready to get away from both Mom and Dad.

By the time I got to Miami three months later, although Patty and I had stayed in touch, I was chasing anything that wore a skirt. I was more like my dad than I wanted to admit. Loyalty was important, but only that people be loyal to me.

In January of my freshmen year, my friend from Calvert Hall, David Snedden, died. A truck hit him as he ran across 695, drunk and probably on drugs, after being at a club not far from our neighborhood. I flew back from Miami, but the trip, while sad, only reinforced that I needed to get away. I didn't need school. I didn't need Baltimore, either.

I needed Patty even though I hadn't been faithful to her while we were apart. Clearly, Miami wasn't where I needed to be, so I decided to move to California. I flew out there and lived with Patty's family outside of San Francisco. Once Patty turned 18 and graduated, she got her own place. I got my place, a small studio apartment in San Rafael in Marin County. I lived the life of a hippie, growing my hair long, smoking pot, and working for a nursery, dealing with plants and gardening housewives who seemed bored with their lives, particularly their husbands. I was the opposite of everything Dad represented. I needed to establish residency so I could go back to school, which I wanted to do, but I wanted to do it on my own terms. Eventually, I enrolled at the College of Marin (the same school that Robin Williams went to) and majored in photography—just another example of sowing my wild oats, being different, and getting as far from my father as possible.

****

Dad had his restaurant, where he glad-handed diners and played to his fame, and now he was remarried, and he'd become the type of ex-athlete that he probably didn't want to become: he was a color commentator with CBS on weekends. He was on CBS's seventh or eighth broadcasting team out of roughly eight. No longer was he the star playing on the best team. He was a rookie, relegated to the bench almost. It wasn't as bad as when Dad was trying out for the Steelers right after college, but at 40, my father was reinventing himself. He had a new wife and career, but his new life, while full of surprises—three new children—and adventures, induction to the Pro Football Hall of Fame, and failed business attempts, wasn't the same smooth upward trajectory as his football career.

And I was finding that running away didn't make the problems go away.

The 1970s would be a decade in which Dad and I would slowly find ourselves, one mistake at a time. Being away from each other and my family would draw me back home closer to Dad, and a chance to get to know one another all over again.

CHAPTER 21

New Wife, New Life, Bad Business

January 11, 1986
Denver Broncos 23, Cleveland Browns 20

Things looked bleak for Denver and John Elway. They were down a touchdown and on their own 2-yard line late in the fourth quarter. The wind was blowing off Lake Erie, the temperature having plunged from 30 degrees at game time now to zero with the wind chill. Denver was used to the cold, and Elway was making a name for himself in only his fourth season for leading his Broncos to come-from-behind victories in the fourth quarter.

This being the AFC championship, he would cement his reputation a bit, driving the Broncos the 98 yards, ending the drive—now referred to as "The Drive"—with a five-yard touchdown pass to Mark Jackson to tie the score. Almost as an afterthought, the Broncos would win the game in overtime. Nobody talks about the plays in overtime today. Instead, football fans, particularly Bronco enthusiasts, only discuss The Drive, usually with reverence.

****

Elway has lots of weird connections with my dad. He was drafted as the first overall pick of the Colts in 1983. He refused to play for the Colts, demanding to be traded, and he was. Along with Irsay owning the team, Elway's demands are mentioned as one of the reasons that the Colts eventually left Baltimore, a moment that broke my dad's heart. Also, this particular game in 1986 is mentioned as a small reason why the Cleveland Browns would eventually leave their city and move to Baltimore, a move that took my father a while to accept.

Unlike Dad, Elway was considered one of the greatest college quarterbacks of all time. Obviously, he was the first pick in the draft. While his success wasn't assured, it was assumed. He retired from the NFL as the winningest starting quarterback. He finished his career by winning back-to-back Super Bowls, his last one called by some experts the best game of his career. In 2004, exactly five years after retiring, he was elected to the Pro Football Hall of Fame. His myth as Mr. Comeback was somewhat responsible for the building of Invesco Field in Denver, replacing Mile High Stadium. He spent his entire career with the Broncos, not even something Dad could brag about. Before Elway retired, he invested his money in auto dealerships that did very well. He had married a beautiful, athletic swimmer from Stanford. They have four children, two of whom have gone on to play big-time college sports. As he said in an interview, he seemed to have lived a charmed life.

Then it all began to unravel. In 2003 he and his wife, Janet, divorced— a messy public affair that was particularly hard on his children, the issue regularly played out in the papers. Even having seemingly everything a person could want, the scene behind the public façade wasn't always perfect. He's acknowledged this. It's often the fans who have a hard time seeing it. There was going to be no comeback with his marriage. While it was done for reasons that are specific to him, the pain isn't that different from any other divorce. Even fame and money don't erase emotional hurt. Like Dad, he remarried.

****

Even the football story of the AFC championship doesn't have a great ending. Yes, the Broncos came back to defeat Cleveland, scoring the winning touchdown in the end zone where the famed Dog Pound was filled that day with rabid fans. But two weeks later, the Broncos were throttled by the New York Giants 39–20, beginning more than 10 years of Elway developing a reputation that he couldn't win the big one. There's a difference between winning a big game and winning the Super Bowl. He would eventually put that to rest and retire both a local and national hero, only to have problems much closer and more personal come to roost in his own house.

NEW WIFE, NEW LIFE, BAD BUSINESS

One of our family's favorite words is "asshole." It's usually a negative comment, but sometimes, it almost shows grudging admiration. We want to say something nice about someone, but we just can't. Calling them an asshole is about as good as it gets. We don't limit our use of asshole just to people outside the family. We throw it around like candy sometimes, usually ending up in laughter as Janice might say, "Dad can be such an asshole." I might respond, "Real big asshole." Mom might add, "Just like (and she'd name somebody the whole family knew who thought he was our friend but really wasn't) so and so is such an asshole." We rarely define what we mean; as a family, a group that had been through a lot together, we intuitively understand its meaning. Cursing and ripping people come naturally to us. We come by it honestly.

My mother cursed like a sailor; no, worse than any sailor I ever met. She cursed so much that most of the time I didn't even notice. My friends did. Dad didn't have quite the same potty mouth, but he could throw a four-letter word around if he needed to, and when he did, everyone listened, particularly the children. Maybe he didn't seem as bad because Mom was in the gutter so much, but only in private. It was a side of her that the public rarely saw. If the public didn't like her, it was usually because of tone, not words. It was how she talked, with an edge or bitterness. Dad, on the other hand, said so little in public that nobody really had a read of what he was thinking let alone how he thought or said it.

What I now realize is that after football, the years when I was finding myself and everyone in the family was picking up emotional pieces of shrapnel, my dad was an asshole, in every sense that our family meant the word. He left the game and didn't know what direction his life should take. He left the family and started a new life with a new wife. This is what assholes do, that much our family could agree on. We didn't—and still don't—always get along, but we're usually in agreement about people and how they rate.

I'll be the first to admit that I can be a real asshole. I come by it naturally, getting my anger from Mom and my snottiness from Dad. Fans rarely saw Dad's snottiness, his dismissiveness of other people. His unwillingness to confront issues that mattered in his life was part of his being an asshole. Marrying Sandy may have been the biggest asshole move of his life. But once he married, he moved on with her and had kids. Just like on the field, if the Colts lost, there was no time to dwell on the emotions of it. It was time to get ready for the next game. But our family life wasn't a football game; he was just conditioned to treat everything that way. It worked on the field or in a business deal that went south, but for a long time, it didn't work with our family.

Even though all of his first family members were now adults or close to it, except for Kenneth, we couldn't let go of our feelings, our anger, our sense of neglect, even our sense of ownership. We knew Dad first; therefore, he was ours. We suffered through Dad playing football and all that entailed, so why shouldn't we reap the benefits of being Unitas'? But that's not how it worked out. Looking back, while Dad got a new life, unlike in fairy tales, it wasn't perfect, either. I didn't wish that on him (maybe I did early in his new marriage, but not later as Dad and I came to an understanding regarding his circumstances). Moping wasn't going to change anything. Mom and Dad were divorced. No one was going to put Humpty Dumpty back together again. I realized that if I wanted a decent life, a life not filled with self-pity and anger, I had to move on. So I did. Dad did too, and somehow, somewhere, we met in the middle, finding our places for each other.

****

Fans often forget that football players are still people who have quirks and needs and hobbies and things that drive them nuts and things that don't. Part of the problem of being an athlete—and maybe the only way to see this is to live with one—is that a professional athletic career can't go on forever. People have tried. Gordie Howe played hockey for almost 30 years and George Blanda played in both the AFL and NFL for 26 years, starting in 1949 and playing through 1975. He began his career while Dad was still in high school and lasted one year longer. They are the exceptions. My dad wasn't an exception. Once he retired, he was barely 40, just reaching his prime. Instead of fading off into the sunset, he was remarried and had a new family.

He tried his hand at broadcasting. Whether or not it worked depends on your point of view, but it wasn't something he wanted to do. He did it for five years, and obviously it had its moments. Dad was criticized for butchering English, and he wasn't very good. But he didn't really like not being able to speak his mind. While Dad spent his football life keeping as quiet as possible in public, he wasn't afraid to call out a teammate in the locker room or huddle. He did it with few words. In the announcers' booth, instead of few words, he was supposed to talk all the time, whether or not the situation called for it. That definitely wasn't Dad's style. He also wasn't going to call out the players. He might not have known them, the game may have been changing, and what the fans expected to know about both the game and players was growing. Announcing was too public. Pro football was too difficult without a guy who's not on the field making it worse by ripping players.

Sometime around 1977 or 1978, Dad came to San Francisco with Gary Bender while I was living there. Knowing that he was coming, I called him and asked for tickets to the game. It had been about two years since we'd really talked or seen each other. Probably the last real conversation was after my grades from Miami came out, and Dad had seen enough. He wasn't paying for college anymore, so instead of looking inward at the mess I was, I dashed to the West Coast and Patty. Naturally, Patty and I didn't work out. I was looking around, and Patty tells a story—one that I don't remember—about how she bought us the book, *The Joy of Sex*. I laughed. She was ready to really leave Baltimore behind and become part of the counterculture that Dad couldn't deal with in San Diego a couple of years earlier. I liked women; I like them a lot. But reading books about sex, together, was too much. We were growing apart. I was becoming my father, although I didn't know it. Running around on the love of my life and being prudish when it came to sex. No more Patty didn't mean no more women. I was dating a socialite who I took to the game. We had great seats, and after the game, we saw Dad for about 15 minutes.

Since I hadn't seen much of Dad since going off to college, I didn't even know much about his marriage to Sandy and the wedding. They got married in Reno, Nevada. His life, in my mind, was nothing more than a cliché: retired pro athlete running off with a younger woman for a quickie wedding. That was bad, but the fact that Dad got married 15 minutes after his divorce became final was almost too much. So my girlfriend and I spent a lovely afternoon at Candlestick Park watching a game that I didn't really care about. I asked my dad for the tickets more to impress this woman than to see pro football or Dad. But it was a first step. I enjoyed reconnecting with him. The short meeting was probably what a shrink would've ordered if we'd gone the therapy route.

About a year later, Dad again came to the Bay Area, with Sandy. I don't think I'd ever officially met Sandy, and if I had, I didn't remember it. I was no longer dating the woman who went to the 49ers game with me. Instead, I was engaged to a woman who spent a month in Hawaii with me in a rented RV. That is, until she tired of the claustrophobic life of a campground. We were there, spending the trust fund Dad had set up for each of his five children, ours at 21. I spent it all in less than a month. I'm sure Dad intended it for a down payment on a house or at least something substantial and important. To his credit, he never mentioned the money, and I learned my lesson. In that regard, I'm less like my father today. Money doesn't flow through my fingers like sand, here today and gone today.

Dad and Sandy came to see us in San Rafael, north of San Francisco across the Golden Gate Bridge. We lived in a one-bedroom apartment with a balcony where I kept some large plants, including a marijuana plant. Dad wouldn't have known what it was if I'd been smoking it. I hadn't completely renounced my wild days. After a few minutes of idle chit-chat, Sandy and my girlfriend went shopping, as Sandy tried to be the good stepmother. They went to Pier 1 Imports and brought home a circular throw rug and some bags of knick-knacks. While they shopped, Dad and I did about the only thing two men who didn't really know each other and had grown apart could do: we went across the street to the local liquor store and bought a case of Michelob—Dad's favorite—and spent Saturday hanging about the apartment drinking. It was uncomfortable, but not as bad as it could have been. It felt good to be with him; it felt good that he made the time for me. He'd made the effort, and that's all I could ask. I wanted to have a relationship with him. I also wanted to have one with the rest of my family who I'd seen very little of. It wasn't like I only held a grudge against Dad.

His visit probably was the event that made me realize that I was simply wallowing in my own bitterness, and I needed to get home. I needed to patch up relationships where I belonged: Baltimore. In less than a year, I would be home, living with Dad and Sandy, trying to move beyond teenage angst and anger. I had to figure out what to do with myself. I had to become an adult. No more sleeping around and drugs. It was time to get serious, even if I didn't know it that Saturday afternoon as Dad and I made small talk.

****

I'm not sure what Dad could have done in retirement that would have been fulfilling. When he was struggling to catch on in the NFL, even though he worked construction jobs, he thought he might teach school, do something with physical education and be a gym teacher. Now that was out of the question—he was the most famous football player in the world. Before Rosenbloom traded the Colts, Dad and Rosenbloom had agreed to a personal services contract to become the general manager or director of player personnel for the rest of his life in the Colts' front office. Now that couldn't happen. The trading of teams with Irsay voided the contract. Furthermore, it's never been clear to me that there was ever anything more than a handshake between the two of them. If there'd been a contract, I'm sure I'd have run across it at some point. What did it matter? Other Colts, Buddy Young and Lenny Moore, had stuck around with the team for a while in the front office, and Moore, while good at what he did, didn't find the job as fulfilling as he might have liked.

What Dad loved was football and what Dad knew was how to play football. He understood the intricacies and nuances of the game, particularly on the offensive side. But truly to understand offense, you must think and calculate like someone who plays defense. Dad did that. Naturally, it'd seem the post-playing career for Dad would've been as a coach or general manager.

****

So what did Dad do? He did the smartest thing he could have done: he became "Johnny U," man about town. He traded on his name. He tried to establish a position in business by setting up real estate deals in Florida—that fell though because his lawyer absconded with $5 million—and buying a circuit board company outside of Baltimore—which led to bankruptcy. Even if these opportunities had succeeded, his role was still front man as Johnny Unitas, great Baltimore Colt and NFL icon. Everybody thought he had an idea that could make lots of money, only if they had the right backing, and Dad was considered the right backing. The problem was that Dad couldn't figure out who was trustworthy enough to handle his money and which money-making opportunity was legit enough to throw his treasured name behind.

There was nothing wrong with what Dad wanted to do. Lots of athletes have done it, and more will do it in the future. But Dad wasn't prepared. Unlike his after-practice throwing with Raymond, Dad hadn't done anything to help him understand the nuances of business or the subtleties of human nature and how exploitative it can be when dealing with money. School had never been his strong point; school was where he played sports after classes ended.

While he played football, everyone, it seemed, wanted to be on his good side. He thought people dealing with him were on the up and up. It was probably also part of his nature to trust. That's what he did. It had been my mother who watched his backside. She was his pit bull, but she was no longer in the picture. His flank was exposed. The deal in Florida went bad because the man he was dealing with embezzled Dad's money. The circuit board business went bad because there were environmental issues that came up after his investment. He had personally guaranteed money. He owed banks and government entities. The company, National Circuit, after it had been sold by Dad and his investors because of financial problems, remained an on-going concern. Dad worked for them as a "consultant," meaning he schmoozed potential and long-standing customers at golf outings.

While he was good at making decisions on the field, he wasn't similarly talented off the field, particularly when it came to money. He finally came to understand this. He was better off being the glad-hander, making a nice living and leaving the serious financial decisions to those who knew more than he did. The 1970s and '80s were different for athletes. Dad was expected to invest his money and his name. Even as his money disappeared, his name never did. That's the kind of good will he'd built with his fan base and Baltimoreans. Nothing seemed to tarnish his good will. I wish I knew why, but if nothing else, my father was sincere. What you saw was generally what you got. If he had something to say that wasn't productive, he didn't say it. When he did speak, he was always himself.

He made appearances, he went to card shows, and he got occasional sponsorships. But that wasn't enough. Dad wasn't the kind to have too much idle time; he was easily bored. He got jobs as a company rep. He had jobs as vice president in charge of marketing, nothing more than a fancy name for glad-handing. Just like in the late '50s when Dad had worked as a cardboard box salesman when he knew nothing about boxes or shipping or sales but was being brought along because he was Johnny Unitas, he was going to do that again. He looked like a man of the people; he had a life story like a man of the people; he had the aura and ease around others like a man of the people. So, that's what he became: a man of the people. He traded off his name to make a living. He was fine with that. He did more than shake hands; he was paid on commission, but he didn't hesitate to exploit his name or his "myth." He was at least smart in that regard.

But outside of working as a pretty successful sales rep for his circuit-board company, Dad didn't know what he was doing if everything business-wise wasn't laid out for him. He didn't actively pursue sports memorabilia opportunities. If someone called him, he said yes, and took whatever money he was offered. He didn't understand that his name and life had value. Maybe he did understand and couldn't believe it.

****

Outside of business, Dad and I made peace. I tolerated Sandy. Once their children were born, my half-brothers and half-sister, there was no point in making life more miserable than it needed to be. Each of my brothers and sister worked out their own relationship with Dad. Janice only got together with him when he called, inviting her to lunch. It wasn't perfect, but it was better than nothing. At Christmas, all of us went to Dad and Sandy's house, sometimes receiving invitations at the last minute. We learned that was usually Dad's fault; he was supposed to tell us. We were never sure if he forgot or he didn't want to face the confrontations that might come with a phone call asking us to his house. Generally, everyone showed up and made the best of it. Life wasn't perfect, but we were adults now, and I had come to the realization that life wasn't a fairy tale.

My relationship with Dad was what I made it to be, and once I came back to Baltimore in 1980, I knew that I wanted to know him better, for him to be a part of my life, regardless of the logistics and complications that entailed. He seemed to want the same things although he wasn't good at saying that. We tapped dance around each other at times, learning where we could go with each other emotionally and what was off limits. It wasn't a football game with clear rules, but it was a game worth playing and figuring out.

****

Problems didn't exist just with Dad. Mom and I weren't on the same page, either. She carried her bitterness about the divorce and Sandy. That was to be expected. But after I got married and had children, she was still acting as if I was 13 years old. It was too much to listen to the complaining and bitterness and hate she had for Dad and also the advice—directives really—about raising our children and dealing with Dad. Her directness, always one of her strengths, had become overbearing. She didn't like the fact I spent time with Dad. I didn't care. Although she never said it, she pushed me to make a choice: her or Dad. I chose Dad. I didn't come back from California to listen to misery. Dad had a better handle on his life than Mom.

Although Mom forced me to choose, she and Dad maintained a relationship. I wasn't supposed to do things with Dad, but she could. It wasn't like they went on dates, but Dad called her whenever he needed advice. She still received alimony, and he hand-delivered it most every month. She also knew how to manipulate him, particularly for money. Mom was a shopper and often lived outside her means. She sweet-talked him into helping her out with money. Dad gave her more than what the court ordered. It was probably a reflection of Dad's attitude about money—easy come, easy go—and his deep-seated feelings for Mom. I've heard second-hand that they often talked on the phone, laughing and cutting up like high school kids, maybe how they'd been back in Pittsburgh. As much as Dad had a hard time finding himself after football, Mom had an equally hard time figuring out who she was after divorcing Dad. It wasn't always shits and giggles. But it wasn't always bitterness, either.

Mom died about four months before Dad, in May 2002. A few days before she died, she'd called Dad asking for some financial assistance. She needed dental work, about $500 worth. That's what she said anyway. She died before she got it done. One day, not long after her funeral—which Dad attended—he ran into a former Colts teammate who knew about his "arrangement" with Mom, including the most recent request for help. He said how sorry he was for Dad's loss. The teammate knew Mom. As they were shaking hands, the friend said, "Well, I guess you just saved yourself some money." He chuckled. I'm sure Dad did, too.

Janice has always maintained that Mom and Dad never stopped loving each other. I don't know about that, but I do know, as do my siblings, that Dad regretted leaving Mom. He once said in front of all us, "Mom is the only woman I truly love."

Marriage, like football, doesn't always go the way you hope. Nor does one's bank account. But Dad did what he was best at: he moved forward and whatever thoughts he had about what had once been and how he felt about them stayed inside his head.

I was finally home with my own family. Dad and I were ready to move into a more mature relationship, one of adult to adult. I'd grown up, and Dad knew that. That's all I ever really wanted from him: an acknowledgement that I mattered to him. I now knew I did. Knowing that meant our relationship could move in a new and better direction.

CHAPTER 22

A Mom and Pop (Father and Son?) Operation

October 25, 2001
Indianapolis Colts 35, Kansas City Chiefs 28

It was a Thursday night, an NFL game that was one of many in the increasingly lengthy season. At the time, it was two teams fighting for consistency and respectability in a game that didn't seem important. The Colts entered the game 2–3 and struggling. In 2000 they had been a wild card team, losing a heartbreaking first-round playoff game to the Dolphins 23–17. On offense, they were loaded with Peyton Manning at quarterback and third-year running back Edgerrin James from the University of Miami at running back. Manning also had Marvin Harrison at wide receiver. The Chiefs, on the other hand, were 1–5 and going nowhere.

Although the score indicated a close game, it really wasn't. Furthermore, the importance of this game wasn't in a particular play that won or lost the game; instead, it was in a play at the time no one knew was going to be a big deal until well after the game. Late in the fourth quarter, James, coming off back-to-back 1,000-yard seasons, left the game complaining of knee pain. It was his last carry of the game, and as it turned out, his last of the year. He'd gained 102 yards in 27 carries, his 24th 100-yard rushing game of his career, tying the Indianapolis Colts' record.

After the game, James complained of some pain in his knee, but said, "But the pain started going away so I knew it couldn't be too bad and I was able to walk it off." He was wrong. Not only would his third season be over, but the injury would affect his fourth season, as well. He gained less than 1,000 yards in his third and fourth seasons after gaining 1,700 yards the season before his injury. Instead of making the playoffs in 2001, the Colts ended the year 6–10. Instead of moving forward, they regressed. It wasn't solely the issue of missing James, but that played a big part.

****

This is the way of the NFL—injuries and bad luck can undo a season. Even scarier is that an injury can and sometimes does undo a career. In James' case it didn't. After returning to the field the next season, he was productive for at least six more seasons, but not like he was for the first two and a half seasons. Clearly, he wasn't the same player. '

But as the NFL had changed so much, including playing games on Thursday nights, so had it changed in how players were paid. James signed a rookie contract paying him $49 million and later signed a second contract for $30 million. He didn't need to ever worry about how he would finance his post-career life. Financially, he was set.

Being set as a football player doesn't mean that's how that player's life turns out. Today, the public hears a lot about players who signed huge contracts being destitute not long after retiring. That's not the case with James. Like most people, athlete or not, he wanted to do something with his life post football. And he did. With his millions, he started a summer camp for underprivileged kids, hosting more than 100 kids on a piece of property that he owns in Florida.

James is in some ways like an updated version of Dad. Instead of coming from the athletically rich Western Pennsylvania, James comes from a small south-central Florida town, Immokalee, where he was a star. He grew up poor, much poorer than Dad, and while his father is alive, he didn't have much interaction with him. He lacked college scholarship offers because of his lack of academics, but once he got the required ACT scores, he was off to the University of Miami and a stellar college career.

Not letting his knee injury in his third year stop him, James went on to a fine pro career, one that may get him elected to the Pro Football Hall of Fame. It's what he's done since football that makes James stand out: he's found a way not only to survive away from the game, but he's thrived, having invested his two major professional contracts wisely, so that he can do what he wants without money worries.

The game on the field is constantly changing, but what happens to players because of the games—injuries and money—hasn't changed that much. Careers are still too short for most players, and many athletes spend beyond their means once they retire. It seems so easy—to take money made from a football career that is longer than most players—and invest it, but it's not easy. James figured out how to do that. It took Dad a while, and his road to finding his peace outside of football was much rockier, mainly because he brought it on himself.

A MOM AND POP (FATHER AND SON?) OPERATION

The problem with athletes, I think, is that they become accustomed to two things: the camaraderie in the locker room and the sense of routine. Football, in particular, during the season is a weekly routine: games on Sundays, no practice on Monday, going to the Golden Arm Restaurant to glad hand Monday night, watching film on Tuesday nights, practice during the week, usually at the same time every day and then the games on Sunday afternoons, at 2:00 PM if at home and either 1:00 or 4:00 if on the road. Dad lived that life of regularity, and even his off seasons were filled with recuperation from injuries and driving us to school and going to speaking engagements for various Little Leagues and youth sports teams at night. He had built-in friends and his teammates, wonderful perks of playing football because Dad was an introvert. He had people—his coaches—telling him what he needed to work on and practice. He had people he needed, and teammates who needed him. After practice, he'd stop with his teammates for a beer before going home, and while his teammates often stayed late into the evening, he rarely had more than two beers. From July into January, his life was planned to the minute. He liked that. More importantly, he needed that.

Most people would say that retired athletes miss the rush of thousands of people cheering for them, the thrill of winning games that millions are watching on TV, and even the violence and surviving that violence that has always been football, and if the game plays on for another 50 years, will remain part of the game. There's no question that Dad liked all of those things, the thrills and competing with his body as if an NFL game was a come-to-life chess match. Who wouldn't? Being the last man introduced in Memorial Stadium, the "World's Largest Outdoor Insane Asylum," is heady stuff, but while Dad read his press clippings and probably came to believe his larger-than-life image at times, it was the big, heady stuff that Dad seemed to despise. It was the little stuff, the routines that he needed.

But once he retired, those routines were gone. He had to find something else. My mother thought it would be her and their life together. Obviously, that didn't work out. He had a new family and a second chance at being a father. As he hadn't been the greatest father the first time around, he would use his second chance to be better, just as he used his second chance at the NFL with the Colts to make it. Dad, outside the house, was floundering. Television didn't work out. Investing in Florida was a big bust. Selling circuit boards ran into problems, toxic waste problems that had nothing really to do with circuit boards but kept him from being successful.

He made money—he was not obscenely rich but lived a decent life, and somehow it seemed not to live up to his twenties and thirties. I don't mean he wasn't winning NFL championships and Super Bowls—he wasn't, but no player is in his forties and fifties—but he hadn't found a place that worked for him. He had no routine with his first family, and I saw this. I'm not sure what I saw, but I do know that by the time I returned to Baltimore in the early 1980s, he needed something, needed a purpose. He never articulated that, and since my mother wasn't there to give him a swift kick in the ass, I decided I would. It didn't come to me right away, but it did come. And finally, I kicked. To Dad's credit, he took the help willingly.

****

Interestingly, long before I moved back to Maryland and eventually asked to work with Dad, the situation with the family—because of the divorce and remarriage—had gone from bad to non-existent. All of my siblings from the first marriage ignored my father. They never called him on his birthday. They never sent birthday cards. Nothing. They didn't go out of their way to do anything with him. I moved away, but I remained in contact with both my parents, however sporadic it may have been.

When I came back from California, everybody looked at me like an intruder. I was not the prodigal son. I was the opposite. My siblings just didn't like me. I'm not sure they like me today. They always wanted their handout. They always wanted me to give them stuff. That's what they were looking for from my father all the time, and I guess it was my father who started that shit. When my father came around, he always had something to give them because that's what he expected they wanted, whether it was money or presents. He only came around at Christmas.

Even though everyone except Kenneth was older and basically living on their own, we still needed him and wanted him to be in our lives. But he had the second family to raise, so he wasn't focusing on the first family. Janice felt it and has talked about it. You'll hear it from Bobby. You'll hear it from Christopher and from Kenneth especially. I'd been away and had rarely seen Dad, so much of my anger had dissipated. And I wasn't around to hear my mother speak negatively about everything that had to do with my dad. I don't know if she did it intentionally, but it was like she'd polluted my siblings' brains and attitudes. Hence, they reacted the way they did toward Dad. They didn't know any different because that's all they were hearing at home. That's why I got away. If I hadn't, I would have been stuck in the same rut. When I returned, I just didn't want to have to hear the negative side of Dad anymore. I was ready to move on, to let bygones be bygones. It wasn't a conscious decision, and it had been made much easier by my absence. I understand, even today, why my siblings were so angry with me. If I'd been in their shoes, I'd have been angry, too. When I was back, I dealt with my father positively, and my siblings took to ignoring me. I said to them that he was the only father we had, but for a long time, my mother's feelings toward Dad dominated my siblings' attitudes.

****

Getting married changed things. How, I'm not sure. What I do know is that I was now more settled, at least in Dad's eyes. I was no longer traipsing around California working as a nurseryman. I was working legitimate jobs, long hours, and making pretty good money. There was another side to the story also: business and Dad didn't seem to get along. He was good at being around people, glad handing, and I think he wanted to do more than that. At the same time, when he tried to do more, it didn't work out. The exception was the Golden Arm restaurant. But even that was going to turn. I decided Dad and I should become partners. Given his track record, he had no reason to disagree. He didn't.

To understand how we ended up partners, one needs to look at what he'd done since retiring from football. He'd not made money on virtually any investment and lost money on some, and as Lenny Moore said, probably because he didn't have good business sense. He invested his money into a bank, land, and hotel complex in Florida. It wasn't a bad idea, but the problem wasn't the idea, it was with whom he was executing the idea. His selection of business partners always seemed to be the problem:. What he needed was a new partner, one he could trust. I fit the bill.

****

Unitas is a Lithuanian name. Dad's family came to America from Lithuania to work in the mines, and eventually settled in Pittsburgh. Being named Unitas and being born in the 1920s or '30s wasn't anything special. Most people with last names ending in "as" are of Lithuanian descent, names like Druchunas, Ruksenas, Daumantas, and Armonas. Today there are about 750,000 U.S. citizens of Lithuanian descent, with Chicago having the second largest Lithuanian population in the world. Pennsylvania, not surprisingly, has the second most Lithuanian descendents in the United States. There were lots of Lithuanian immigrants in and around Pittsburgh. Some are famous like Dad, Dick Butkus, and more recently, Joe Jurevicius, a wide receiver from Penn State who played in two Super Bowls. Jurevicius also appeared on the cover of *Sports Illustrated* twice, just one time less than Dad. Famous Lithuanian-Americans are not limited to football—in acting, there are Charles Bronson, Sean Penn, and the Three Stooges, and in tennis, Vitas Gerulaitis.

When Mom and Dad named me John Constantine Unitas Jr. my parents were still living in Pittsburgh, and Dad had just finished playing football with the Bloomfield Rams. The NFL seemed a long, long way away. Becoming a starter and eventual superstar seemed impossible. Those things happened, but not right away, so Dad couldn't have known what he was doing when he named me after himself. Neither could my mother. They had no idea, no reason to think that by the time I was a teenager, anytime I said my name, people, and not just in Baltimore, always asked, "Any relation to the quarterback?" I can't blame my father—not that I would want to—for putting an extra burden on me by inheriting his name. It has been a curse at times, but it's been far more of a blessing.

When my first child, who we call J.C., was born on May 27, 1988, the first person I called was Dad. Naturally, he was thrilled. Our relationship had evolved. I was no longer angry, and he now knew how to deal with and speak to me. He listened to what I had to say. He often considered what I said to be important and even good advice. In his own way, he was acknowledging that in many ways I'd achieved what parents want for their children: I'd made it; I'd made something of myself. I'd done this even though I was named Unitas and had put up with lots of issues because my father was famous.

Once he congratulated me, he asked, "So, what's the little bugger's name?"

I told him we'd named him John Constantine Unitas III. There was silence. He wasn't even breathing.

"What the hell are you doing, naming him what I named you?" Dad questioned. I wasn't sure what he meant.

There was a long pause. I didn't know whether to be mad or thrilled because Dad was acknowledging the burden my last name had been on me, the burden of living with excess attention. "Why'd you name him that? Why would you do that to him?"

I said, "You did it to me, so I'll do it to him. I'm proud of the name, Dad. It is what it is."

But just because I understood what I was doing doesn't make it any easier. When J.C. got hired by Under Armour, he said, "Dad, I'm going to have to start using my name, John."

I replied, "Yeah. And I'll tell you what's going to happen to you. People are going to react when you say John Unitas." When you say J.C. Unitas, people don't know shit. Honestly, they don't. All my life, I was either John Unitas Jr. or Johnny Unitas Jr. or even just John Unitas, and there's always a reaction. Always.

"They look at you, they stare at you. 'Any relation? Are you related to Johnny Unitas the great quarterback?' Yeah, it's my father. I'm John, Junior." J.C. sat at our kitchen table, nodding. He knew what he was going to hear. I'd told him such stories before, but never had it really registered with J.C. until now that he was in the corporate world.

I continued the story: "'Wow, your father was absolutely the greatest. I idolized him; he was my hero as a child; he was my father's hero, my grandfather's. We used to have to sit in front of the television and hear stories about your father, forever and ever, how he played, and what he did when he saw my grandfather at a barbeque and how gracious he was and the fact he even happily signed multiple autographs.'"

While listening, J.C. was filling out forms for work. "Son, you're going to hear stuff. You might get away with it sometimes, and after you meet some people and get to know them, you can just ask them, 'Hey, just call me J.C.'" He came home from the first day from work, and he was in a team meeting and everybody went around the circle and introduced himself, and he said, "I'm John Unitas." Every single person in that meeting was surprised, "John Unitas? Really? Related?" "Yeah, I'm his grandson, but you guys call me J.C."

He was getting the picture now of being John Unitas instead of just

J.C. I said, "Son, you're going to have to deal with that. It's something you'll get used to. People'll have comments. There are things they'll want to know. 'My father knew your grandfather and blah, blah, blah.' But you know something, son, it's good because it gets your foot in the door, but then it's up to you to perform or do whatever you have to do. People are going to recognize that. Just remember: you are your own person regardless of your name."

There's a good and bad side to it, and that's one of the reasons my father, when J.C. was born, was so surprised about what we named him.

****

Five years after Dad retired, he was inducted into the Hall of Fame on his first ballot. No surprise there. As the greatest quarterback of the first 75 years of the NFL (and the biggest challenger, Otto Graham, agreed that he was also), it was a foregone conclusion. What's interesting about the Pro Football Hall of Fame induction is how it has changed over the years. Dad represents the old school inductee, a player who was introduced by the coach he credited in many ways with making him who he had become, Frank Gitschier, his quarterback coach at Louisville, the man who saw the talent in him to recruit him.

****

Everybody, it seems, has a story about bumping into Dad after he retired. Bragging in Baltimore about an encounter with Dad is like saying crab cakes are the Mid-Atlantic epicurean religion. No matter who bumped into Dad and no matter the circumstances, the stories follow a basic plot line: Dad gave time and attention to his fan, his demeanor both gracious and humble, listening, nodding, and agreeing, his grayish eyes locked into the face of his fan. Most of the time, it was a fan telling him about a game that he'd played in. He told me on many occasions that the fan had the wrong game or score or was mixing up two different games, but he never corrected them. The fans weren't usually interested in hearing Dad's perspective, either.

Dad understood how important attention to the fans was, particularly when he was a player, but he was no longer playing. After 1984, the city didn't even have a team. Maybe it was the loss of the city's team that made Dad that much more important. He wasn't just a connection to the past, but he was a connection to a team that existed only in people's memories. Instead of fighting that, Dad embraced it. But no matter the situation or how far removed Dad and football were from each other, he had time for football fans.

It wasn't just in Baltimore, either. The story of Burt Lawson and his son is as good as any example about Dad and his connections with strangers, men in particular, who had watched him cowboy strut onto the field with less than 2:00 left in the game and engineer another come-from-behind victory for the Colts. Those black-and-white television images are engrained in the memories of a generation. Lawson had lived in Baltimore in the early '60s, going to home games when he could. He bought his tickets at various bars that had Colt Corrals (the team's fan clubs); it was the only way he could get tickets.

But it wasn't until the 1990s that Lawson met Dad. Lawson represented a company that did business with a company Dad represented. They bumped into each other at business golf outings, Dad playing nine holes with a foursome and then playing another nine with a different foursome. Eventually, Dad would go to Raleigh, where Lawson lived, traveling together to call on customers. It wasn't the sales calls that brought them together emotionally; instead, it was when Dad met Lawson's youngest, Burt Jr., who Lawson was raising as a single parent. As Lawson said, "He always seemed like from the beginning he took an interest in my son because John was raised by his mother." Lawson was raising Burt by himself after Burt's mother simply left one night and never really came back. It was only later that Lawson saw a parallel between their lives, but at the time, Lawson needed and accepted all the help he could get raising Burt Jr. But even with the parallels, Dad's attention to Burt Jr. is extraordinary, going well beyond the standard athlete spending a day at a children's hospital (because it makes for good press and the kids actually get a big thrill out of it, and Dad did his share of visiting children, rarely with press in tow).

Because Lawson travelled and often with Dad, and because they occasionally played in business golf tournaments together, Lawson would bring Burt along with him. Sometimes, Dad played one hole, the same one all day so that he got a little time with each foursome. Sometimes, Burt hung out with Dad at that hole, the two of them waiting for each group to come through. It's the kind of time, in hindsight, I wish I'd had with Dad, but that didn't happen, and if he couldn't spend time with me, he might as well spend time with another child who not only appreciated it then, but still appreciates it today.

There are two neat stories about Dad and the Lawsons that show just how deep Dad's influence is. First, Dad was in Raleigh on business with Burt. The day he arrived, Burt, always happy to see Dad, mentioned that his son was giving a presentation about Dad for a school book report. Dad asked what time Junior was giving the report and then said, "Let's go surprise him." That's what he and Burt did, driving a few minutes out of their way for a sales call and showing up in the middle of Burt's son's report. It was one of those magical moments that couldn't have been scripted. It was the 1958 championship, only this time, it wasn't on TV and few people were watching. When Dad showed up, the school principal, upon learning about what was happening, told Lawson to drag this thing out as long as possible because he wanted to alert the press. A reporter with a photographer eventually showed up, and Dad willingly had some pictures taken.

But the story doesn't end there. Junior is now grown and married, having played golf at The Citadel. Once Dad even called him to wish him luck in an up-coming match. As a way to show both their thanks and love for Dad, Burt Jr. named his son after Dad, Vaughn Unitas Lawson. Burt's wife, who is from Alabama, agreed to all of this. But she got something in return. Vaughn Unitas' nursery is half decorated in Alabama red, while the other half is in Colts blue and white. That's Baltimore Colts colors, including the 1960s kicking horse emblem, like on the helmet of Dad's era.

****

I had been spending more time with Dad, watching his business dealings in particular. There seemed no rhyme or reason to what he was doing, how he was organized, or how he got paid or how much. My biggest concern was that Dad seemed to be taken advantage of. As Mom always told us kids, "Your father doesn't like confrontation. He needs to be told what to do." Dad had a hard time saying no to anyone. That could be a good thing, as it was with the Lawsons, but it could also be bad.

I saw this in his dealings with card shows, for example. Dad was getting paid less than many of the other athletes signing at a show, and he was signing far more autographs. One show he worked with Mickey Mantle, he got $3,000 while Mantle got somewhere in the neighborhood of $15,000. Mantle only agreed to sign one item per customer and would only sign a specific amount of times during the show. Dad, while making significantly less, didn't make those deals. Most of the athletes got paid up front; Dad, if he got everything he agreed to, got paid long after the show. I knew there was a better way.

I had been dropping hints to Dad, wondering aloud what the hell was going on with his deals. It probably started in the late 1980s. As I married and worked multiple jobs and Dad came to love Christine, he saw me in a different light. I was no longer the screwy kid who cut his hand on glass milk bottles or occasionally needed the silver hair brush to the backside. Once J.C. was born, I was definitely a full-blown adult. I knew that if I wasn't direct with Dad about going into business together, it wouldn't happen. Everything Dad did was on a handshake, and while I appreciated his honesty, I could only stand to watch him get used and see his money disappear so many times. Furthermore, other factors were involved. The marriage between athletes and corporations and media had hit the point where there was big money to be made by lots of people. It wasn't just a limited market for the Joe DiMaggio's of the world to sell coffee makers. Most important, I think Dad knew he couldn't live his life with the same approach.

In 1993, while recovering immediately after knee-replacement surgery, Dad had a heart attack in the hospital. He was hardly sewed up in his leg when his chest was opened, and he had heart surgery. I'm no doctor, but given how bad the damage was, if Dad hadn't had the heart attack in a hospital, he probably would've died. He was lucky. I was lucky, and everybody who loved him was lucky. We got him for another nine years, and we also got a different man those nine years. He paid more attention to all members of the family. There was a peace about him and his relationships with those closest to him that seemed both different and better.

So I approached Dad and suggested that we go into business together. I would be his right-hand man, the guy behind the scenes, his "asshole" to use our family's favorite word. I would arrange the deals, collect the money, and most important, say *no* for Dad. He didn't have to. He could continue to be the front man, the guy everybody wanted a piece of. Now, it would cost more, a lot more. The deals worked this way. We got paid half up front and the other half when we showed up at the show. No more signings for just anybody. The promoters had to be legit. Prior, anybody would call him and tell him to show up. I professionalized it. They had to buy photos from an authorized dealer and 500 signatures max. Anything unusual came with an additional cost. For example, if a customer wanted a helmet signed with anything more than "Johnny Unitas"—a No. 19 added to it, for example—that was an additional $25. Dad didn't keep count. I did. I was going to all his shows now; I was his muscle, at least financially. I was also the one who told customers to get lost if they had one ticket and wanted two items signed. The old Dad would have signed both, no problem. So would the new Dad, but now I was sitting next to him, being the bad guy and saying no.

I also upped the amount Dad got paid. No more varying amounts. It was $15,000 a show. Naturally, Dad was worried we were pricing him out of the market. A few organizers balked at first, but they came around. No more Dad paying his way to a show. Now, there were two first-class tickets involved. The whole operation seems cold, and in many ways, it is, but that's how I had to be with Dad if I didn't want him to get stomped on. No more throwing good money at bad people or ideas. Because I was the asshole, Dad kept his reputation.

There were other opportunities as well. He was in a movie *The Runaway*

Bride with Julia Roberts. He was in *Any Given Sunday* with Al Pacino; Dad played the opposing team's coach. He did a Nerf ball ad with Joey. He did a bb gun ad with Kenneth. He appeared on the TV show, *Coach*, in an episode that had to do with Coach's wife selling a pair of Dad's iconic high-top football cleats at a garage sale. After that episode aired—it was one of my favorite sit coms—I wrote a letter to the producers of the show and told them how much I enjoyed this episode. I proposed that Dad come to Los Angeles and present Coach with a new pair of cleats. They loved the idea. The theme of the show was a sports banquet. On the dais were Coach, Jerry Van Dyke, Bubba Smith, Dick Butkus, and Dad. Al Michaels was the emcee of the event.

None of this would have happened unless Dad was a member of SAG, so I signed him up. He may have been a member in the 1970s when he was a TV color man, but his membership had lapsed. Finding these opportunities was part of being his manager/agent. These things he wouldn't have done on his own. He liked all my ideas. I had to make sure they were executed.

Dad had modernized. He'd never had an agent in his life until he and I started Unitas Management Corporation in 1991 and he'd gone Hollywood. While literally he lived in Baltimore, figuratively he had accepted the California "way," stardom with the glittering lights and green rooms and late-night expensive bar scenes drinking with famous other people—a similar lifestyle he'd struggled with when he was traded to the Chargers in 1973. He knew himself well enough that he laughed at the circle he'd traveled. It was where he was meant to be.

This would be his life for the next eight years, and a good eight years it was.

Dad died in September 2002, J.C.'s freshman year in high school, the day before he was supposed to go watch his grandson play his first football game. Instead, J.C. would be deep in grief, his grandfather never getting to see him throw a pass during an official game. Later that same year, J.C. would write a paper for his English class about the time Dad worked with J.C. on his throwing mechanics, making sure that when he threw the ball, he ended the throw with his first finger pointing directly at the target.

After throwing the ball around for a while, grandfather and grandson did what that grandfather loved doing almost as much as throwing touchdowns: he simply got on his tractor, grandson with him, and mowed the grass. He died the same way: no drama, here one moment, and then gone the next. Simple.

And unexpected. Devastating.

And what had once been simmering family issues became a boiling cauldron of messes that I couldn't have predicted even given how bizarre our family was.

The messes were so big and nasty and mysterious—and some even still unresolved—that it would be years before I felt like I could truly mourn my father's death, celebrate his life, and reflect about how he and I were father and son and what all that meant, both the good and bad.

CHAPTER 23

Lawyers, F------ Lawyers

November 14, 1943
Washington Redskins 42, Detroit Lions 20

It was a typical NFL Sunday, no television, and a decidedly biased local crowd of more than 35,000 people almost filling up Griffith Stadium. Although World War II was being fought and baseball season was over, football struggled to find its place. It did well in industrial areas like Detroit and large metropolitan areas. Elsewhere, however, it was mainly a distraction from Saturday's college games and the cold of the winter months before baseball spring training started again. Dad was 11 years old and living in Pittsburgh where the Steelers were in such dire straits that they'd merged with the Philadelphia Eagles and became jointly known as the Steagles. The only way he would have known about this game and what was going on was to read about it in the paper the next day. He probably did. Like most people, either those at the stadium or listening on radio or reading about it the next day, he had no idea the greatness that happened that day on the field. It wasn't a game like the 1958 championship or the Super Bowl today. It seemed like one of many games played that year.

Washington came into the game undefeated at 4–0–1 and left Detroit still undefeated, but not before Sammy Baugh played what may have been the single greatest football game an NFL player has ever played. It's easy in today's world with quarterbacks throwing for more than 500 yards and running backs rushing for nearly 300 yards—both incredible days for a player—to give in to hyperbole, but Baugh deserves his recognition.

First, the Redskins won, and Baugh was the reason. On offense, he threw four touchdown passes and was the first quarterback to throw for at least four in a game. This record would be broken later in the season by Sid Luckman. On defense, he intercepted four passes, a record that still stands today (tied many times, most recently by DeAngelo Hall) for most interceptions in a game. He also had an 81-yard punt.

The Redskins would win only one more game that year before having to win a playoff game against the Giants so they could lose in the Championship Game to the Bears. While this game stands out in Baugh's career, it was part of a trend that he helped establish: the modern throwing quarterback. The game remained geared toward the run, but Baugh cracked the door to the idea that the pass wasn't just something done to occasionally fool the defense. In 10 regular-season games, Baugh would throw for almost 1,800 yards, one of only two quarterbacks to throw for more than 1,000 yards. The other was Luckman who would pass for almost 2,200 yards. In today's world, it's easy to forget that the NFL—and football in general—started as a game that emphasized running. If Dad was the first great passing quarterback, his forefathers include Sammy Baugh and Otto Graham. Quarterbacks weren't yet considered so valuable that they could only play offense. The impressive Baugh led the league in 1943 in completions, interceptions (caught, not thrown), and punting.

****

Sammy Baugh, like Dad, bounced around a bit after he retired in 1952 before finally settling back in Texas on a ranch. According to Baugh's son, ranching was more enjoyable to him than playing football. Baugh died at the age of 94 in 2008. If Jay-Z, the New York City rap artist, hadn't worn Baugh's 1947 throwback jersey in one of his videos, Baugh would have languished in obscurity as he had for the previous 30 years. Although he won many honors after he retired, most football fans didn't really know who he was or how good he was. He was named to both the NFL's 50th Anniversary team (as was Dad) and its 75th Anniversary team. The NFL Network named him the league's all-time most versatile player.

But he had something at his death that I only wished Dad had: peace and dignity. When he died in a nursing home near his ranch, he was properly eulogized in the national media. But it was the locals who knew and understood him best. As Berle Pettit, former editor of the Lubbock paper, wrote about six weeks after Baugh died in an article entitled, "Sammy Baugh's Legacy Went Well Beyond Football Immortality," "Sammy Baugh well may have been the best football player that ever lived. But around here, folks in Fisher County thought of him as a man who took good care of his cattle and revered the land over which they grazed. While the nation's sports pages devoted considerable space to his homage, folks hereabouts were mourning the loss of an ordinary neighbor and an extraordinary friend."

While Dad wasn't a big-league rancher like Baugh—he did like to drive his tractor around his multi-acre home in Baldwin, Maryland, and raised about 10 to 15 beef cattle at a time—he was someone revered by the locals, both for his life on and off the field. The difference between the two is that six weeks after Dad died, his name was in the paper because his family couldn't get along. Instead of resting in peace, his name—and mine—got dragged through the mud.

Holding career records in the NFL and winning championships isn't always enough. It was for Baugh, but not for Dad, not when my stepmother had her own ideas about Dad's legacy and how a family should, in her case, dishonor it.

LAWYERS, F------ LAWYERS

I say "f---" like I drink water. (Later I'll tell the story of Dad and why he doesn't drink water.) In my house, around the dinner table, someone, usually me or my son, calling somebody a c---sucker is like stating the weather outside. I use "sh--" like young people use "like," as filler or just something to say when I don't know what else to say. Dad cussed, too. My mother really had a potty mouth—worse than Dad's. If cursing indicates that I'm limited in my language skills, I plead guilty. But mostly it allows me to be show my anger when nothing else will.

Right after Dad died, I didn't curse much. Then again, I didn't say much at all. Or do much, at least initially. I was angry (and I usually curse when angry), but this was a different kind of anger. It wasn't about control and feeling helpless, about a situation that I felt I could change if only someone would listen. Dad was dead, and he wasn't coming back. It wasn't a question of fairness or readiness or tragedy. His death simply was, and I needed time and space. I eventually would get better, the pain would go away, and my life would normalize with thoughts of Dad and the good memories. That's the way a death works. It hurts, you suffer, and then you get better, slowly.

Except that's not what happened. Why not? One person: Sandy. I can't stand her. Hate is a strong word but I can't think of a better one. I could call her lots of things, including that "c" word, but I won't. I could go on and on. I know it's childish, but most outlandish emotions are. And why am I not allowed to be childish? Nothing brings out the child in a person better than the death of his parents.

But it wasn't Dad's death that had set me off about Sandy. Instead, it was what happened shortly after he died, even before we'd had his funeral, that occupied my thoughts for the next nine months and beyond—dealing with control of Unitas Management Corporation.

****

Grief is tiring. Death is never easy. That was the case when Dad died. I expected grief to hang over my head. My mother had died four months earlier, and while I wasn't as close to her as I had been earlier in my life and not as close as I was to Dad right now, her dying still hurts me deeply, like ghost pain does to someone who has lost a limb. My emotions were constantly leaping from fuzzy to clear and back, the pain a dull throb to a more pronounced stabbing, electric and sharp. I expected most of this although there's no way to prepare for it. But I didn't expect a feud. And I got one, exacerbating my pain and that of my immediate siblings. Dad was gone, but his legacy was now open to interpretation. His name—my name—mattered.

I now had to fight for something that I've worked most of my life for. I'd finally made a life with Dad, and now that he was dead, the tangibles of that life were being yanked from underneath me. With his death, Sandy had her own agenda about how life after Dad should be orchestrated. Before Dad was even cremated, I was fighting to preserve the business relationship Dad and I had together, and by extension, his legacy. I didn't expect his death, nor did I see Sandy making a grab for everything that Dad was involved in. While Dad's legacy and the business we'd created together was only part of my emotions, it became a symbol of the disconnect between me and my siblings and Sandy and our half-siblings. I should have seen the signs that life after Dad was going to be much harder than life with Dad.

Dad and I had only been in "business" for about 11 years, having started Unitas Management Corporation (UMC) in 1991. The Corporation was built on two simple philosophies: Dad wasn't very good at business, and I would manage him so he could focus on being Johnny U. While I don't claim to understand Dad fully, I knew him. I knew what made him tick. He didn't like confrontation. Although everyone thought he was an extrovert, he really wasn't. He was a homebody. He had his ideas about how he should interact with his fans, and no matter what I, or anyone else, suggested, he wasn't going to shortchange them. If they wanted his time, he would give it to them. I knew when to bring up an idea and when to let it go because he'd dug in his heels. When we started UMC, I said to him, "Look, Dad, you keep being you, doing what you're doing, and you let me be the asshole." He understood what I meant. He could say yes, but if a no was needed, then I would do it. Oftentimes I screened business proposals and didn't even let Dad know about them.

Unitas Management was nothing more than a Mom-and-Pop operation, neither of us working full-time at it, which was a-okay with both of us. We both made some money, but it was about so much more: a chance for the two of us to be together, to connect, and especially for me to make up for the time I didn't get to spend with Dad when I was younger. It also gave me the chance to be around his second family, particularly his kids. While we took UMC seriously, Dad wasn't being managed by a J. Walter Thompson–type agency. He knew that and so did I, but he wasn't being told what to do by people who were professionals but almost strangers. In his post-NFL life, one thing Dad tried to do was avoid being dictated to or having people telling him what he *should* do rather than what he wanted to do.

****

In my backyard is a swing, a two-seater with wood slats. It squeaks as it rocks. The chain is rusted. That's where I spent a lot of time immediately after Dad died, letting the chair's swaying numb my feelings. I remembered the cool stuff like Dad and I hanging out with Telly Savalas while filming a TV show. I also remembered the weird stuff, the kinds of things that made Dad a bundle of contradictions. Dad never chewed gum. When he was a kid in Pittsburgh a relative told him one Saturday afternoon that gum was made from dog shit. Dad was never sure why this man told him this, but he thinks it was because he picked a piece of it off the ground. Even when Dad was old enough to know better, he still didn't chew gum. It was one of the few stories he ever repeated to me about his childhood. Weirder still, at least for a world-class athlete, was that Dad never drank water. He drank lots of coffee but he believed water was contaminated by fish. Fish shit in water, he told me. As I swung in the backyard, I thought of fish taking "Shulas" in water, training camp, the 100-degree temperatures, and Dad not drinking water. These funny moments passed quickly and didn't last long enough. I'd remember—briefly— that while Dad didn't drink water, he did chew ice. He saw no contradiction. Then reality would return.

I had a lot on my mind. Although Sandy was organizing the funeral, I was worried that she'd mess it up. She and Dad were on different pages: she loved being Mrs. Johnny Unitas, while he put up with being Johnny U. He shared himself with his adoring public because he had to, but he didn't need the adoration. Sandy did; she wanted and needed a funeral that said, "Look at me." Sandy would get her way, but that didn't mean I had to like it. I also had to keep Unitas Management going. As crass as this may sound, when a celebrity dies, that's when opportunity arises. Fans want keepsakes, mementos that help them stay connected to an era that's now gone. His death hurt the fans, too. Dad and I had talked about that. He understood and was okay with it. I also needed to write a eulogy. But what do you say about a man for whom it seems like everything has already been said?

And I hurt.

That's why the swinging, the creaking of the rusty chain, was an achy balm.

****

I've always been a crier. I cried a lot after hearing Sheila screaming from downstairs at my office and rushing up the stairs to tell me Dad was dead. But crying changed little. The pain was still there. Sandy's handling of the funeral arrangements put us up against each other. I'd assumed the mantle of representing all the siblings from Dad's first marriage. It wasn't something we siblings had discussed or agreed upon, but when the Unitas' are attacked, we circle the wagons, and we circle them tight. He was our father. We'd grown up with him and suffered and been thrilled and adjusted to living in the limelight whether we wanted to or not. And now the spotlight was on us again, briefly, at the funeral and shortly thereafter.

I don't like Sandy. Never have. Never will. I'm sure she doesn't like me. I blame her for my parents' divorce. Even when I look at my parents' marriage rationally and know that it takes two to dance, and Dad had as much a hand in leaving Mom as Sandy did in luring Dad away, I still don't like her. I've put up with her. Once Dad had my half-siblings, who were not too far in age from my own children, and Christine and I had moved into a house in Baldwin, Maryland, almost next door to Dad and Sandy, it made sense to make peace with her. Once Dad and I were in business together, it made even more sense. But it was never a lasting peace. The best I could do was work out a truce. Whatever was between us—and it wasn't just me simmering—has always been there.

It isn't just me that doesn't like her. My siblings don't like her nor do my children. And my wife, who absolutely adored Dad and thought of him as a second father, can't stand Sandy, either. Christine doesn't have the back story of the divorce and the disintegration of our family. By the time I met her in late 1979, my parents had been apart for six years. Christine didn't even know who Dad was or what he meant to Baltimore and pro football until a few months after we started dating.

My first Christmas with Christine—we weren't engaged yet but things were serious—she bent over backward looking for gifts for the children—Joey, Chad, and Paige—because she felt like she knew nothing about them or the family. She didn't know what to expect, and this being her first "important" time with the family, one that was split and dysfunctional, she wanted to present a good impression. She had finally found the kids presents, but she needed something for Sandy. In this store in Ruxton she found an antique Victorian lamp made out of wood. She knew Sandy really liked the color Williamsburg blue and that she had this little room off the master bedroom she used as her office. This lamp, a Victorian woman with an umbrella—her dress was long and blue—was hand-made with a beautiful shade. Her first thought was, *Oh, my God, this is the perfect gift for her.* She bought it, but it had to be special ordered.

It was close to Christmas. She called the shop and was told that it wasn't in yet. She was freaking out because we were going to their house for Christmas. Finally, the gift came in. On Christmas Day, Sandy opened the box, took the lid off—didn't even pull the lamp out of the box—took the tissue paper off and made an off-handed comment, "Isn't that nice?" and put the tissue paper back over it and put the lid on it. That was it for Christine and me. That was the icing on the cake for the rest of my relationship with that woman. I felt like, *Oh, my god, here Christine was killing herself to get this on time and be the right gift, but nothing we first family kids ever did was good enough for Sandy.* If she'd had her way, we wouldn't have ever seen Dad again. She wanted to start a new life, which I can understand, but that didn't mean the old life never happened and no longer existed.

****

I went to the swing to get away, especially from the ringing phone. Everyone was calling: friends, family, some who I hadn't heard from in years, fans, and people I didn't know. They all meant well, making sure the family was okay and that we understood how important Dad had been to them and his community. I even screened calls because I couldn't listen to another story about Dad. I needed to write my eulogy, run my businesses, and console my family. I did take calls that dealt with the issues at hand. It must have been Friday, less than three days after Dad died. On the phone was Charles Tatelbaum, dad's lawyer and executor of his estate. He was calling about UMC.

When Dad and I started UMC, I did a few things besides charge more money for card shows, standard for managing him correctly. I trademarked his name, image, and signature. I connected with experts in the sports management and marketing fields to make sure we were doing our deals legally, protecting Dad to the fullest extent, and preserving his intellectual personal property rights. He and I also set up a corporation with stock and a succession plan if either of us should die. Dad owned 90 percent of the stock, and I owned the rest. We both entered into an assignment agreement. If he died, an insurance policy paid his estate $125,000 so that I could take possession of all his stock. It was a simple and iron-clad agreement that was standard procedure for set-ups like the one Dad and I had.

Tatelbaum asked about UMC. I told him about the agreement. He asked me to fax it to him, which I did later that day. But there was something about his tone that worried me. The issue with Tatelbaum was five-fold: 1. I didn't trust him because he wasn't a guy who made you want to trust him; 2. He hadn't seemed to steer Dad well, legally or financially; 3. Dad was both naïve and too trusting when it came to business matters and the people he associated with; 4. His loyalties were to Sandy; and 5. Tatelbaum is a f---ing lawyer. Although I had no inkling Dad was going to die, I knew that when he did, Sandy and Tatelbaum would come after me and UMC. I had been around Dad enough to know that I couldn't trust people he or Sandy worked with. Dad had gone bankrupt twice and had a business partner in his restaurant sell out his share without even consulting with Dad. Business was not a football field or game with a ref and immediate and obvious results like whether or not the pass had been caught. Underhanded behavior happened all the time, particularly with someone like Dad who felt a handshake was more than enough to seal and ensure a deal. Tatelbaum and Howard Moffett, Dad's accountant and co-executor, were using their positions in dealing with the estate to shove me aside and take control of UMC. As executors of his estate—but not stockholders—they claimed they could vote me out as head of UMC, and so they did. Sandy, who's not very smart, was taking marching orders from Tatelbaum and Moffett. She was not innocent, but she wasn't the instigator. She also wasn't doing much to hold the family, both sets, together. The shaky foundation that Dad had kept alive quickly collapsed. Sandy didn't seem to care.

I got off the phone and over the next few days called my corporate counsel for UMC. He was located in Chicago and couldn't represent me in Maryland. He suggested getting local counsel so I called Bob Bowie, a lawyer in Towson I had worked with in my legal collections and real estate businesses. On September 24, less than two weeks after Dad died, I was in Bowie's office. When I told him that Tatelbaum wanted all UMC's records, he had me clean out all UMC's deposits and put them in escrow with him. I don't remember how much it was, but it wasn't millions or even hundreds of thousands. It was maybe $20,000. They wanted everything…memorabilia and all of the jerseys Dad had signed, but I had maybe two. We didn't stockpile inventory of memorabilia. As orders came in for product, I'd take them to Dad to sign.

That first time I stepped into Bob's conference room, I felt a burden lifted, as if I didn't have to fight this fight by myself. I stared at him, and he stared at me. He asked what the problem was. I began crying. In front of a f---ing lawyer. It was the kind of cry—even for someone who cries a lot—that I hadn't had in a long time, probably since Jillian was born, different tone but same intensity. Even when I cried immediately after Dad died, it wasn't with this same intensity. I was probably crying as much about Dad dying and about a betrayal by a woman who purported to love my dad as much as I did.

Bob had to deal with two aspects of the situation: the taking over of the corporation, the type of situation he had handled many times before; and my emotional state, the sense of utter disillusionment and sadness, a sheer helplessness. It was my emotions that appealed to him. I was a fighter, I aspired to be something without relying on my dad or our name, and yet I worshiped my father. He saw that I was angry with lots of people, including him. At the same time, Christine and I were like two fingers intertwined. She was supposed to be the fiery Latina but instead had a central calm. She was real. He saw a remarkable bond and saw how I cared about my children and how I worked three jobs and how I went into debt to do this battle. Because that's what we had in front of us: a battle, legal on one level, but the bigger and more important battle—a war—was the emotional one waged over who my father belonged to. I could share him, as I've been doing all my life, but Sandy couldn't.

The anger that Bowie saw was with me all the time. My emotions about Dad's death had moved beyond sadness. I was short with Christine and the kids. I answered the phone but I didn't care who was on the other end. I checked my emails. I went through the motions of living. After talking with Bowie, I knew what Tatelbaum, Moffett, and Sandy were doing wasn't good. But I had no idea how bad it was.

****

Behind my house are woods, about four acres of them. Since it was fall, the leaves were changing. Yes, they were a metaphor. My dad's funeral was less than a week behind me, and I was changed. More important, I was lost, emotionally. I got back to my life as best I could. I needed something more than tears and a hug from Christine although they helped, but what I didn't need was an attack from Tatelbaum, Moffett, and Sandy. After that initial phone call from Tatelbaum, the wheels of taking UMC away from me were underway. They claimed as officers of the corporation and executors of the estate that they could oust me as head of UMC. Furthermore, they refused to take the $125,000 from the insurance policy in exchange for the stock. They wanted the stock for sure and the $125,000, as well.

After taking over the corporation, they asked me to return and run the corporation. I was dumbfounded. Shocked. Hurt. Confused. Angry. I said no. No. F--- no! I wanted no part of them; they didn't know how to run the business. But I still had to testify in a deposition about a deal UMC and Dad had with Dreams, Inc., a company that deals with sports memorabilia. There was no death clause in the agreement stating that even once Dad died the agreement was still in place. The company argued otherwise. It was not the stuff I wanted to be thinking about, but it was part of managing a celebrity and his legacy, even after death. While they still owed UMC in excess of $100,000, we didn't get that much. We eventually settled out of court for significantly less. Today, Dreams, Inc., has a death clause in its sports celebrity contracts.

If how great you are as a football player is determined by how many yards you throw or how many touchdowns you score or how many Super Bowls and championships you win, then it makes sense that how serious I was about keeping UMC should be determined by how much money I spent and how long I fought. In the end, I really don't know how much I spent, but it was in the hundreds of thousands of dollars. I know that I was charged more than $175,000 by Bowie. I had four months when I was billed more than $20,000 for legal expenses alone. Two other months, I was billed more than $16,000. In addition, I also had two other law firms representing me, one for me personally, the other for representing UMC in bankruptcy court. Sandy put UMC in bankruptcy for no apparent reason other than to continue their course of crushing me. We weren't sure what Sandy and her lawyers were up to, but we knew that we had a date with a judge in February. I had no idea contesting of the stock agreement and assignment of the stock would cost so much, nor that it involved so much of my time and emotions. There were letters and conference calls and discussions about how the books were kept for UMC. In hindsight, I now realize that it didn't matter what I did or said or how the books were balanced, Tatelbaum and Moffett were determined to break me. This was their MO. I later found out as a tandem they had done the same to other people and their businesses.

****

UMC wasn't about how much money I might make in the future. It was about protecting Dad's legacy. That's why we set up UMC to begin with. I'm a control freak. It comes from the dysfunction of our household while we were growing up. Since I'm controlling, it made sense to make sure that Dad was being treated right and not taken advantage of. I was tired of seeing that happen. Now dead, I really didn't want him to be abused. I don't think Sandy wanted to abuse his name, but she didn't know what she was dealing with. There's a big difference between being Mrs. Johnny Unitas and marketing and promoting Johnny U's image and reputation. It's not as simple as getting a reservation in a restaurant when the maitre d' says there are no tables until you mention "Unitas." That's nice, but that's not business. Both Sandy and I could argue about how much we loved Dad—we both did—but managing his reputation is about dealing with lawyers and market value and crafting contracts that maximize value without limiting the future. It's not emotional.

At one point, Bowie and Tatelbaum scheduled a late October meeting to talk, but at the last minute, Tatelbaum canceled. I have no idea why, but I have to assume that he never planned on meeting. He was hoping I would cave before the meeting, and if he and Bowie were going to meet, then it would be to settle a smooth transition of power for UMC.

In December 2002, both families went to Louisville for the Golden Arm Award presentation. I wasn't happy with Sandy, but I made nice at the presentation. Few people outside the family knew about the legal battle. There was no reason to be obnoxious. I was hoping for people's senses to come back, but Tatelbaum and Moffett played dirty. Tatelbaum was under indictment in Florida for insurance fraud, a scandal dealing with his ex-wife. He liked to attack early and throw lots of money at a problem. He wasn't above intimidation. I didn't trust him, and he didn't trust me. We were at war. But in Louisville, I put on a pleasant face.

****

That's where the woods behind my house came into play. On weekends, I grabbed a chainsaw and headed back there, ready to do battle with fallen and dead trees, cutting them into draggable pieces that I piled in a corner of my yard. I would slug away at nature for hours, working up a powerful sweat, becoming one with the chainsaw and its roar, the blade chewing up tree and bark, shavings piling on the ground like light-colored ant hills. I sawed until my shoulders and forearms burned, and my hands were blistered and calloused. While I was out there, the tree trunks became f---ing lawyers, the whirling saw blade became me. The saw dust was blood. I hacked them into smaller, workable pieces. My physical pain replaced the emotional hurt, and when I came inside because it got too dark or it started to rain, my throbbing muscles and tingling hands helped me forget briefly that my dad was dead and my stepmother, that bitch and her cohorts in crime, had taken my business. If I'd been left to my chainsaw, while I would have always had a hole where my dad had been there for me, the hole would have gotten smaller until it was manageable.

****

Legal issues take on a life of their own, and this situation with UMC certainly did. The legal system wore on me with motions and petitions and filings and research and precedents. What it doesn't rely on, it seems, is common sense. I talked on the phone, sent checks, and listened to scenarios with lawyers, but most of it didn't make sense. I had the stockholders agreement and there was an assignment. This issue was outside the will and Dad's estate. As I chainsawed more trees and cursed at the hussy and the lawyers, the case dragged on, ideas and words running together. I wasn't dealing with my feelings; instead I focused on the wench and watched as our family's relationship with my half-siblings fell apart. No longer did J.C. and Jillian tromp through the woods to hang out with Chad or Paige.

There were so many accusations that I lost track, and to this day I don't remember when things happened, only that they did. But when the moment of truth came, it wasn't exactly how I expected it—it was so simple that it almost wasn't a moment of truth. Actually, it was two moments of truth. The first was me standing in the courtroom, saying nothing as Bowie and Stephen Nolan, the attorney representing Tatelbaum and the estate, argued in front of Judge Thomas Bollinger, a caricature of a circuit court judge. He looked like something out of a John Grisham novel—round-faced and jowled, bald, the kind of man who looks better in a black robe than civilian dress. Bowie told me he was a fair judge, but he mainly dealt with civil issues, not cases like this, steeped in business law. After the hour was up, we left, and I felt so helpless, so lacking control. Every day that passed with Sandy, Tatelbaum, and Moffett running the show at UMC, the worse the books would be. All the relationships I'd developed were falling apart. People in the memorabilia business trusted me; they didn't know who Sandy and her f---ing lawyer and accountant were.

The second moment came a few days later when Bollinger ruled that that two-bit and her sidekicks got to keep the company. I was so stunned when Bowie called me with the news that I didn't say anything. Just like Dad's life didn't always work out in the precise ways and judgments of a football game and season, neither did mine. Maybe as a response to my father, I'd always carried my shoulders high, thrust forward. It's not something I practiced or thought about, but when I was younger—like most teenagers—I wanted to be anything but my father. Now, after he was gone, I became him: my shoulders slumped, and my back bent. My connection to my dad had been taken away by a judge who didn't know simple law. Bowie reassured me that we would win on appeal and that it wouldn't cost more than $10,000. *What was another few thousand dollars*, I thought, not knowing the quagmire I was currently in that was only going to get deeper and swampier and darker.

As I put the phone down, my house empty, I wondered how we—the entire Unitas clan—had gotten here. Less than a year removed from Dad's funeral, with a plane flying overhead proclaiming "Unitas We Stand," we were beyond divided. We were two separate entities. The mortar of our family was dead, his legacy hanging in the balance, and control over his life, something he tried to stay on top of, was gone.

The mess that became this lawsuit had been a long time in the making. While Dad was a great quarterback and leader, his role as father and husband was much more checkered. But even his checkered history as a parent and husband didn't come out of nowhere. As much as fans want to simplify Dad, his life was anything but simple.

But right then, I thought that Bollinger and Sandy, Tatelbaum, and Moffett didn't know who they were f---ing messing with. These chumps would pay for this, somehow. I may not have inherited my dad's ability to throw a football, but I had gotten a few things from him—I could fight and fight against great odds.

CHAPTER 24

Anything but Appealing

November 20, 1977
Chicago Bears 10, Minnesota Vikings 7

Walter Payton was a throwback. He didn't run out of bounds when he could drop his shoulder and crash into a would-be tackler. When he scored a touchdown, he didn't celebrate; instead, he handed the ball to the referee or a teammate. If he was injured, he didn't let people know. He missed one game in a 13-year career and that was because during his rookie year, his coach decided not to play him. He was tough. He played hard and didn't do anything to embarrass the game. He lived by the motto, "never die easy," a philosophy he learned from his college coach at Jackson State, Bob Hill. Hill once played football with Dad, not very long, but he was in Colts training camp in the 1950s and didn't make the team.

That's not the least of the connections between Dad and Payton. They both retired from the NFL with lots of records, and almost all of them would be broken. Interestingly, both retired as career passing leaders. Dad threw for the most touchdowns for a career during the regular season. Although he no longer holds the record, Payton still holds the record for most career touchdown passes by a non-quarterback, eight. Dad threw for 290. But then in 17 seasons, Dad ran for 1,777 yards, easily outdone by Payton who ran more than 16,000 yards in 13 seasons. They both played the game the way it was meant to be played.

****

On November 20, 1977, Payton ran for 275 yards on 40 carries in what was basically a must-win game for the Bears, a 10–7 victory over divisional rival Minnesota. The Bears were 4–5 heading into the game and would finish the year 9–5, tied for first place in the NFC Central. Maybe most impressive in this win was the fact that the Bears threw for a total of 23 yards. In running for 275 yards, Payton broke O.J. Simpson's one-game rushing record of 273 yards. Maybe even more impressive is the fact that 1977 was a year he put the Bears on his back and ran them to the playoffs. He rushed for more than 1,800 yards that season and led the team in total yards. The football world had moved from a run-based offense, like the one the NFL generally used when Dad played early in his career, to a pass-based offense. In many ways, the Bears resembled a team from the 1940s or '50s.

But Payton wasn't always perfect. He had a game his rookie year in which he ran for zero yards. Maybe the possibility of a Hall of Fame career was less of a surprise than Dad's when they were young—Payton had been the fourth overall draft choice while Dad didn't go until the ninth round—both of them worked for what they got. They assumed nothing and took nothing for granted. While Payton had a 1,000-yard rushing season the year before, 1977 was his true arrival, and this particular Vikings game, was his coming-out moment, the same way Dad had the 1958 Championship Game. In a remarkable 13-year career, Payton had only three seasons in which he didn't gain 1,000 yards, his first, last, and a strike-shortened season in which he was on pace to gain 1,000 yards.

Like Dad, Payton was elected to the Hall of Fame on his first ballot.

✱✱✱✱

While Payton is an icon in Chicago, a face for the modern Bears, a symbol of tough, hard-nosed football without all the preening and prancing that seems to dominate the NFL today (think Ray Lewis), he wasn't a perfect human being. He cheated on his wife—a lot—and even had an illegitimate child he refused to acknowledge. His Hall of Fame induction weekend was a nightmare, according to one biography about him, because both his wife and longtime girlfriend were there, and Payton didn't know how to handle the situation. Who would? But he got himself in that mess. Generally, nobody knows how to handle these kinds of situations. Denial is the most common method. It seems that's what Payton did.

As teammate Gary Fencik, a safety on the 1985 championship team and Yale graduate, said, "I think Walter was a very interesting character, and I don't think he was without flaws. None of us are. The challenge is that you want to live up to the image for your family and your kids and anybody who looks at you as a role model. But the reality is you're human and you have foibles."

We all do. That's probably why we like our heroes squeaky clean because we want them better than we are. That's also probably why we like our fathers that way too, because our fathers are our first heroes. My dad was mine.

ANYTHING BUT APPEALING

Less than a month after Dad died and the phone call from Tatelbaum, I got a letter in the mail from Sandy. It was a map of Dulaney Valley Memorial Gardens, the cemetery where Dad is buried. After the funeral, I didn't know what happened to Dad's cremated remains. Until this letter. Sandy had buried Dad in a very "private" event, one that neither I nor any of my siblings was invited to. On the map, she had highlighted in yellow where his burial spot was with a side note, "bench next to lake under tree." At the top she'd written, "This map will show you where your father was put to rest on May 23, 2003." It was signed, "Sandra." (See Appendix.)

The tone was as if she was writing a grocery list. All my siblings got the same map with the same basic note at the top. I knew I shouldn't have expected more, but I remained hopeful that she might do part of the grieving right, at least let us grieve with some dignity. But that was that. I wouldn't visit the site until months later when a *Boston Globe* reporter visited to do a story. He and I went to the cemetery and took a picture of me standing next to the bench, and in doing so, I glanced at the bench. I noticed there were no spaces for the first family's children's names. That comes as no surprise as it was, once again, all about her. Sandy's handling of the situation was typical: she consulted no one in the first family. It was as if we didn't exist, probably because she wished we didn't. I was also tied up with the litigation, meeting with lawyers as we prepared to fight the original ruling, the one that stated—wrongly—that the company was no longer mine.

Besides the burial and UMC fiascos, there were more troubles. There's an adage that says bad luck comes in threes. Mine was higher than that. My life would be better described by a different adage: when it rains, it pours. Next, Tatelbaum and Sandy upped the ante by accusing me of stealing from Dad and of using UMC to pad my pockets. They'd taken the corporation from me. Dad's funeral was barely over, and I was in the midst of a legal fight to save UMC and a moral one to save my honest reputation. I can be an asshole at times, particularly when making deals, but no one who knows me would ever accuse me of being dishonest. It's a long step from tough, even obnoxious, to criminal. I'm not a thief. Stealing from Dad: it was ironic. UMC was the vehicle through which Dad supported his second family. UMC paid for cars, personal credit cards, cell phone plans, and a townhouse in Timonium for Chad and some college friends to use while he was at Towson University in addition to Mom's $3,500 a month alimony. I did charge Chad rent and occasionally he would be late. I would get on him to pay, but Dad found out and told me to back off. So I did.

I had done everything the court decision asked me to. I'd turned over all records and assets to Sandy and her cohorts. I'd also been dealing with bankruptcy because one of the first actions by the new "leadership" of UMC was to declare bankruptcy. Why? I don't know. The corporation had debts of about $75,000 from two different lines of credit, which was fairly standard stuff for a small company. I even had to hire a bankruptcy attorney and behave as if I owned the company. I believed Bowie when he stated uncategorically that eventually a court would rule in my favor. It was important that I separated my personal life from my corporate one. They weren't connected, and there was no telling what Tatelbaum and Moffett might do next or what lies and accusations they'd make up or hint at. Because they focused on destroying me instead of working out new deals and taking advantage of Dad's death to make money, they did very little. And what they did do was all about Sandy and my half-siblings. Instead of working with the agents and companies I'd established relationships with, they got rid of them. They signed a new deal with a sports marketing firm out of Colorado that, as far as I can tell, did nothing over the next three years that my appeals dragged out as I waited for a decision from the Maryland Court of Special Appeals.

****

I was four months past my dad's death, pretty much all chopped out of wood, not quite ready to think the world was normal but at least ready to imagine the day, fairly soon, when it would appear to be. Christine and I had gone to Ocean City, Maryland, for a marlin tournament. It is the kind of place out of season where a lost man can go to find some quiet and his bearings amongst the blinding white sand and flat beaches. We were there in a condo with friends, and maybe for the first time since Dad's death, I was relaxed.

That is, until my cell phone rang with a number I'd never seen before. My phone had rung a lot after Dad's passing, and a lot of the numbers were unknown, fans of his calling to express their condolences. I was used to sharing Dad with the public, and in his death, it felt good to share his memories. Without others, there really are no memories. Memories are what we tell each other about times past to make us feel better. That's exactly what people did who wrote letters and emails or called, even a few who came by my office or home. Not one of them meant anything but something positive by their efforts.

I took this call, not sure who or what it was, but assuming it was another well-wisher. With the lawsuit, I'd learned you can't have too many well-wishers. But it wasn't a well wisher, nor was it anyone even connected to the lawsuit. It wasn't the press. It wasn't a call I expected or even thought I might get. Instead, it was a woman calling from the West Coast. She said her name and said how sorry she was for my loss. I was on the balcony of the condo in the late afternoon with a glass of wine in my other hand. The woman was explaining where she was calling from, and I was only half listening. That is, until she told me she thought she was my half sister, born just after Dad finished his junior year at Louisville, less than six months before he married my mother.

"Excuse me?" I said, my voice now a whisper. Emotions like torrents of rain enveloped me, my life feeling as if I were caught up in a raging river threatening to go over its banks.

She acknowledged this wasn't a good time to call, but she'd written my father a letter in late August, giving details of Dad's purported relationship with her biological birth mother. The birth mother attended the University of Louisville and was Dad's tutor. She was a year older, a senior when all this "happened." She went into specific detail, but I wasn't processing that kind of detail. All I could deal with was the question of what else could go wrong? How much about my father didn't I know? I understood he had a life separate from me, but this was probably something Mom never knew. Part of being quiet, I guess, allowed him to hide. It sounded possible, but I didn't want to believe it, not now, at least.

She said a lot more, but I needed time to process this. There was a ninth Unitas? All I could think about was that this woman was gold digging. Her story sounded too easy. We'd never found a letter from her. Dad had died less than two weeks after she claimed she wrote the letter. Dad's death was national news.

According to the caller, who said she was older than Janice and had been adopted at birth in Lexington, Kentucky, she'd learned as an adult that her biological father was John Unitas. She was ready to know the truth. That's all she said she wanted: the truth. She said she'd called Charles Tatelbaum and he suggested she call me. Hearing his name sent shudders through me. I didn't know at the time that she had called him because she'd read in a newspaper somewhere, or something like that—the details remain hazy—that he was Sandy's lawyer. She wrote the letter and almost immediately Dad died. Only later would I realize that what I thought were conspiracies were nothing more than unusual coincidences. Regardless, I wasn't ready to deal with another problem, no matter what the issue was. Furthermore, I assumed she was some whack-job looking to exploit my father, either for publicity or money. It seemed Sandy was doing enough of both at the time.

Less than a month later, in February 2003, Judge Bollinger would snatch UMC away from me.

To this woman's credit, she was persistent. She contacted Janice, who had the same reaction I did about her. I contacted some of my siblings, and we decided the best thing to do was ignore her. She wasn't going to be ignored. She got in touch with Uncle Leonard. She wanted to do a DNA test, and she needed a male from the family. Initially, Uncle Leonard agreed to meet with her. The mystery woman flew from the West Coast to Florida and met with Uncle Leonard and Anne, his wife, in a McDonald's parking lot. It seemed like a moment out of a bad murder mystery. In the end, Leonard didn't agree to a test. There was too much going on, too much anger and stress, to add this woman to our family's dysfunction. Anne astutely pointed out that there was enough "blood" on the streets of Baltimore already, probably referring to the lawsuit and severed family dynamics.

****

More than two years would pass before I would get UMC back. It had to go to the Maryland Court of Special Appeals. Although Bowie said it wouldn't be expensive, it was. We didn't change our argument—we had an iron-clad agreement for succession, only Bollinger had misread the law. Part of the reason was that he was biased toward the widow, a fairly standard argument in estate law, but this was outside the estate. It was a situation Dad had anticipated, and he didn't want Sandy to have UMC. He wanted me to have it. I had done right by him; and he didn't trust Sandy.

Ironically, as Sandy and her henchmen were accusing me of using UMC for my personal gain, she was doing the same thing. Their biggest marketing decision was working out a deal with Towson University, a local Baltimore area school, to put Dad's name on its stadium. The stadium was to be called Johnny Unitas Stadium, and his image, number, and signature could be used also. Dad had no direct connection to Towson University other than its location. He didn't go there. He never did any work for them. I don't even know if he ever attended a game there. Towson isn't even an NCAA Division I school. It plays in the Football Championship Subdivision. In 2003, when the stadium took on its new name, Towson ended the year 6–6.

There was a reason for the deal. Chad and Paige, two of my half-siblings, went to Towson. Sandy exchanged the naming rights for free tuition. She also demanded that Towson pay her health insurance, which it refused to do. The problem with this, besides being a bad business decision, is that UMC had been put into chapter 11 bankruptcy when it was taken from me. These kind of deals aren't legal. Furthermore, UMC owned a townhouse in Timonium where Chad lived. The new "directors" tried to sell the townhouse, again something they weren't allowed to do. When you're in bankruptcy, you can't sell or encumber any of the assets without the permission of the bankruptcy court. It's the law. Luckily for them, they couldn't sell it.

Once I got UMC back in 2005, almost three years after Bollinger had ruled against me, I called Towson, pointing out that the deal it struck with UMC wasn't legal. Wanting to avoid more lawsuits, both parties agreed that the name would stay as long as Dad's name, anywhere it appeared, came with a registered trademark symbol.

Around the time I was negotiating with Towson, I popped into the student bookstore. Everything with Dad's name on it—souvenir cups and padded seat cushions, for example—were 50 percent off. A mother and daughter—the daughter clearly a student there—came into the store. They browsed a bit, the daughter finally asking the sales clerk, "Who is this Johnny Unitas guy? Did he go to school here?" The clerk didn't have an answer.

My thoughts exactly.

****

Not all was bad concerning my dad after he died. First, I got UMC back although I had to borrow $75,000 from a friend to get the company out of bankruptcy. The ruling, other than being the correct one, was rather non-dramatic. Sandy, Tatelbaum, and Moffett met with me and my lawyers to work out a returning of the items I'd turned over to them. Once I got my computer back, although it was blank of all the information I had on it back in 2002—apparently they had replaced the original hard drive—and the Lexus, I worked to re-establish UMC's reputation, and by default, Dad's. I borrowed the $75,000, and I had hundreds of thousands of dollars in legal bills to pay. I refinanced my house to pay my bills, and the effort was worth it. While UMC won't ever be a huge money maker (not that it ever was), it has helped reduce my debt. More importantly, I now have control over his entire personal property rights, Dad's image, and persona. I know what Dad wanted. In many ways, he'd become a modern athlete: he understood that his likeness and story were worth something. How much, he left that up to me to figure out. Now that he was gone, and the fighting over the company done, I could be with Dad in a figurative sense.

Once I had UMC back on solid footing, I was able to turn my attention to the Johnny Unitas Golden Arm Foundation and Award. Since its beginnings in 1987, both the foundation and award had grown in stature. The first winner of the award was Don McPherson of Syracuse who set a high standard for upcoming winners. Dad, in starting the award, wanted to honor senior quarterbacks who were good football players as well as on target to graduate while staying out of off-the-field trouble. Dad understood how important education is, particularly if someone thinks he's going to use the NFL to get rich. He needed only look at the example of George Shaw's career and how quickly that ended. While Dad didn't grow up in abject poverty, he knew financial struggles, and he wanted to help athletes in need, the way Max Carey, his high school coach, had helped him emotionally.

Originally, the Johnny Unitas Golden Arm Award ceremony was held in Louisville. At the time UMC had a personal services contract with Transamerica for personal appearances and promoting its brand, and as their relationship grew stronger, Transamerica wanted to be involved in the foundation and award. Other than Dad having gone to the University of Louisville (which had little to do with the foundation, award, or presentation ceremony), there wasn't much holding us to that city. After Dad died, and at the urging of some of the award's bigger sponsors, I moved the whole operation to Baltimore. It made more sense. Since 2006, the ceremony has been here, the night before the Heisman is presented in New York. Our winner, announced ahead of time, often comes from Orlando—where ESPN has its multiple award show on Thursday night—to Baltimore and then goes by train on Saturday morning to New York City for the Heisman presentation.

****

I hadn't heard the last from the woman on the West Coast. Since our phone calls in early 2003 and subsequent months, I'd put her behind me. I didn't have the emotional fortitude to confront the situation. When I did think about it, I thought she was simply someone else grasping Dad's coat-tails. Although she'd never mentioned money and nor had anyone else come forward to claim Dad as their father, my dealings with people around Dad when he was alive was enough to make me cautious. Almost everyone who dealt with him wanted something, if nothing more than a moment of his time. Now that he was dead, people still wanted something, except they couldn't get it from him. Instead, they wanted his money or a memory, and they generally wanted one of the children to give it. It's hard to describe because most of the people were only doing what they thought we wanted.

In the case of the caller from the West Coast, I didn't know what she wanted, but I could only imagine that it involved the family. She'd not only spoken to me, but also to Janice. She'd gone so far as to send a photo album of images of Dad and herself and her children to Janice, trying to convince us that she was related. The album had pictures of our family next to ones of hers. In one picture of our family when I was about five, she went so far as to tape her face next to me, Janice, Bobby, and Christopher. It was creepy, but I have to admit that some of the pictures are compelling. She does look a bit like us. Not enough for me to say she's my sister, though.

Now that I've had the time to reflect about this woman, I realize there might be more to her wishes that have nothing to do with me or the other siblings. She has stopped calling and writing us, particularly when we said we weren't interested in figuring out if she was blood related. Now, that I've had time to process Dad's death, and opportunity to think about this "ninth" Unitas—whether she is or isn't—I know that this woman is simply interested in finding out her background. She's curious. Talking with friends who have adopted children, I've been told that this isn't unusual. She's never asked for money or memorabilia. She's only asked that we listen.

It's too bad that her delving into her background happened so close to Dad's death. It's too bad that I had to deal with it, particularly at a time when I wasn't ready or capable emotionally. With time to think about her claims, I know that Dad had a female student tutor at Louisville. I've also heard over the years that she did more than tutor him. She washed and folded his clothes. I know that Mom never visited Dad at Louisville, even though they were married toward the end of his first semester senior year. There are rumors that my grandmother made one trip to the school toward the end of Dad's junior year, in May, right about the time the West Coast woman was born and put up for adoption, according to her story.

Finally, according to her story, Dad, in the end, tried to do the right thing. He offered to marry the woman he purportedly got pregnant. Her family, thinking Dad was "below" her, refused.

****

In late September 2004, Van Brooks, a football player at Loyola High School, was paralyzed during a game his junior year. He was told that he would never walk again. This was a little more than two years after Dad died, and I was still dealing with the legal issues surrounding UMC. Brooks was a safety and wide receiver. Loyola is the arch rival to my alma mater, Calvert Hall, and is located about three miles from where I grew up. His injury and the resulting diagnosis that he would be in a wheelchair for life drew both heavy local media attention and national follow up.

I didn't know Van at the time. I'd only read about his situation in the *Baltimore Sun*. Amazingly, even though he missed most of his junior year in high school, he pledged that he would graduate with his class, in 2006, and he did, rolling in his wheelchair across the stage. Furthermore, he also declared that he would walk again and that he would graduate from college. Hearing about all this, I decided this was the very situation that Dad had set the Johnny Unitas Golden Arm Foundation up for. I contacted his coach at Loyola, a man I knew and said the foundation wanted to give Van $10,000 for his college education. Normally, the foundation gives a one-time $1,000 scholarship to a student-athlete to continue both his education and football playing in college. Van wasn't going to play football ever again, obviously, and his situation warranted additional financial support, given how expensive his recovery was.

One day, with the help of Loyola, I scheduled a meeting with Van and his parents, giving them the letter stating that the foundation would defray tuition costs of $10,000. As expected, they were overwhelmed and appreciative. And as expected, Van followed through on his promise to graduate from college, and received his degree from Towson University, the same place where Dad's name is now on the stadium. The first thing I noticed about Van was the intensity of his eyes. While his friends talk about his sense of humor, I was taken by his intensity sitting in the wheelchair. He was quiet that day. His eyes reminded me a bit of Dad.

This is the kind of story that Dad had a hand in all the time. He was constantly going to children's hospitals and visiting with kids. The press wasn't invited. He did it because he wanted to. I did this because it was in keeping with Dad and his foundation's mission. And there's more to the story. In 2013, nine years after the accident and eight years after the Johnny Unitas Golden Arm Foundation gave Van a small—but significant—gift, he called me. He wanted to thank me and let me know that he'd graduated from college. He wanted me to know that he was still strong and still making progress, and that the foundation was still making a difference. I invited him to the 2013 award ceremony. I hadn't seen him in years, but the intensity was still there as was the smile.

Without saying it, Van's presence at the event was the legacy that Dad had hoped would live on. Now, Dad's legacy isn't winning come-from-behind games with late heroics; instead, his memory is helping young people in small and sometimes noticeable but usually unnoticed ways. As Dad said, "You gain confidence of those around you by preparation. Leadership is having knowledge of what you're doing. I led by example. I've tried to eliminate the words 'I can't.' Instead I say, 'I will, I will try, I will get it done.'"

CHAPTER 25

Nothing Is Forever

October 7, 2012
New Orleans Saints 31, San Diego Chargers 24

If any city today has a love affair with its team like the Colts did in the late 1950s and '60s, it's New Orleans. Like Baltimore, New Orleans doesn't really have a major college football team to call its own—LSU is upstate in Baton Rouge—and even better than the Colts, the Saints don't have to compete for attention with a Major League Baseball franchise. Furthermore, that love affair has been cemented between the city, team, and particularly Drew Brees because of the Saints' Super Bowl victory in Miami in February 2011, six years after Hurricane Katrina and more than 40 years after the Saints arrived in the city as an expansion team.

But Sunday, October 7, was a special day for the Saints and the city as Brees, who had tied Dad's record for consecutive games throwing a touchdown pass at 47 games, was aiming to break the record. The game carried even more implications than simply Brees trying to break the record. The Saints entered the game 0–4 as a team torn apart by a "bounty pool" that resulted in players being suspended. Probably more difficult to overcome were the suspensions of head coach Sean Payton, his assistant coaches, and the general manager. It was a team in disarray. Week 5 rarely is a must-win situation, but it was that day. Playing at home, Brees needed to do more than throw a touchdown pass; he needed to lead his dysfunctional team to a win. If they didn't this game, even with 11 games yet to play, the season would have been essentially over. This for a team that had won the Super Bowl in 2011. While the Saints may have been a sad-sack organization early in their existence—taking 21 years to finally make the playoffs—those days were long over.

The Saints came ready to play, and the record was broken with 2:58 left in the first quarter when Brees threw a 35-yard pass to a wide-open Devery Henderson who caught the ball at the 10, about 10 yards behind the closest defender. Brees had stepped up into a perfectly formed pocket to deliver the strike. It tied the game at 7–7. He wasn't finished, and he ended up throwing three more touchdown passes and leading the Saints to their first win of the season over the Chargers. It wasn't easy, but it was a win, and that's what was needed even more than a record.

Interestingly, Brees threw for 370 yards, and passed the 30,000-yard career passing mark in his 100th game. Philip Rivers in defeat also threw for more than 350 yards. Dad, on the other hand, took more than 200 games to barely throw more than 40,000 yards, which was a record for most career yards when he retired. Football has changed—it's now a passing game that most teams use to set up the run. At the height of Dad's career, it tended to be the other way around.

The game in December 1960, when Dad passed for his 47th consecutive game with a touchdown, he threw for more than 300 yards, only to have the Colts lose late to the Lions. Detroit scored on a 65-yard touchdown pass thrown by none other than Earl Morrall. Dad, during his streak, averaged less than 250 yards per game while Brees averaged about 300. Not to disparage what Brees did, but it was done in a different era under different rules.

As Dad would have told Drew, it was more important to win the game than it was to break the record. Dad's streak came to a halt against the Rams, and the Colts lost a game that pushed them to the brink of elimination from the playoffs. Records meant nothing to Dad and probably the same can be said for Brees, although I don't know because I haven't talked to him. He's scrappy, coming back from injuries, fighting perceptions that he's too small and not strong-armed enough to make it as a big-time NFL quarterback. Not only did Brees break a long-standing record, he did it against the team that drafted him but eventually traded him, opening the door for Phillip Rivers, who has turned into a very solid NFL starter, though he still lacks winning the big one. Furthermore, what Dad would respect about Brees as much as anything is getting the job done right. Records are nice, but winning is great.

I wasn't there. There was no need for me to be. The record's broken, but I don't feel that it is. I know what Dad did and the circumstances surrounding his achievement. I don't mind that his name won't be at the top of this particular record list. Dad's standard isn't one particular win or one particular statistic. I'm not sure what his standard is. All I know is that I don't see a "Johnny U" playing the game right now. Nothing against Brees or any of his peers, but they're not Dad. It will take more. A lot more. As Dan Fouts, who played with Dad in Dad's last season in the NFL, said recently on national radio, nobody was better than Unitas. Fouts added that he was both an All-Pro player and All-Pro person. Dad's touchdown record may be gone, but what he did for the game and what he accomplished hasn't changed.

Anyway, I think it's the last individual record my dad held.

Nothing Is Forever

It's a Sunday morning in early October. Fall hasn't been in the air until recently, and even today, it's one of those days that can't decide what season it is. Cool right now, but the chill is burning off. The leaves are turning, just barely, but the delay may have more to do with the hot summer than anything else. It's football weather, and I'm standing outside Lucas Field in downtown Indianapolis, a field that is doing for this city what Camden Yards and M and T Stadium have done for Baltimore. I'm in town because my daughter, Jillian, maybe Dad's favorite grandchild in his retirement, has taken a job with Andretti Sports Marketing, headquartered here. She needs an apartment. Maybe I can help.

Indianapolis is a nice city, the picture of Middle America. It's flat and orderly and clean. It's predominately white with the feel sometimes that when you're standing on a downtown street corner, you might be in the middle of a movie set from the late 1950s and early 1960s. It's a comfortable-feeling place.

It's also home to the Indianapolis Colts, the team that once was my dad's beloved Baltimore Colts. While Dad had been out of pro football for more than 10 years when the Colts jumped ship in the middle of the night, most of his fans believe that he hated Indianapolis.

That's not true. He didn't hate Indianapolis, nor did he hate the "new" Colts. He was angry, sure, but he didn't hold the city responsible; instead, he held Bob Irsay at fault, and like almost every Baltimorean I've ever met, he had no love lost for the man. There are a few people here in Indianapolis left over from Baltimore, who followed the team here, and they, too, have nothing good to say about Irsay. As much as I think Dad would be okay with a Unitas living in Indianapolis, I've heard from a number of his teammates that this just isn't true. He may never have told me he held the 1984 debacle exclusively against Irsay, Dad seemed too even keeled, a man who didn't tend to hold a grudge, or the type to stay mad at an entire city for too long. His friends begged to differ, pointing out that Jillian can work for whomever wherever, but that doesn't mean that Dad's forgotten the hurt of both Irsay's handling of the end of his career or the Colts fleeing town in the dead of night. There's lots I don't know about Dad and probably never will. There's lots his friends don't know, either.

On a street corner in downtown Indianapolis, on a Sunday morning, the Colts out of town, there's so much more wrong with the picture I'm seeing as I think about my dad, something I do whenever I stand outside a football field, any football field. If he were alive, he would be at Mass; me, I haven't been in years and don't plan on starting. It wouldn't bother me if Jillian went, but she hasn't mentioned it. Lucas Field, at least from the outside, is a beautiful architectural facility, but Dad would have hated it. Not because it's in this particular city, but because it's indoors. Football shouldn't be played indoors. It shouldn't be played on fake grass, indoors or outdoors. While Dad hated the infield of baseball intruding on Memorial Stadium, he preferred that to the technology of the fancy stadiums and fields of today.

In this same indoor stadium, just last Sunday, the Colts won a game in a way that Dad was accustomed to—a last-minute touchdown pass to upset the hated rival Green Bay Packers. Andrew Luck, the No. 1 choice in the 2012 draft, fired a four-yard pass to Reggie Wayne with 35 seconds left. Luck reminds some people of Dad, the way Peyton Manning does, too. All three of them make quick reads as they stand tall in the pocket, and while Luck hasn't played long enough to be seriously mentioned in the same breath as Dad or Manning, he shows striking similarities. Most of those similarities are on the field only. Luck went to Stanford and was a household name long before he'd finished college. Same for Manning. Furthermore, in the Colts' 30–27 win, Luck, in his fourth NFL game, threw 55 passes and completed 31, both numbers higher than any from any game during Dad's career, much less his rookie year. That's how much the game has changed. Having met Luck, I know Dad would have liked him. He is down to earth and not overwhelmed with his celebrity status. The game will continue to change, and some day Luck's rookie season will probably seem statistically underwhelming.

Stats are nice, but quarterbacking is ultimately about leadership, and that's what Luck did in his fourth game. When Dad retired, he had won more games than any other NFL quarterback. That record would be broken, mainly because the NFL season has gotten longer, not because Brett Favre had a better career.

Finally, Luck has another connection to Dad—he was the 2011 winner of the Golden Arm Foundation's Johnny Unitas Award, sponsored by Transamerica and given to the best senior quarterback in the country. Manning won it in 1997.

****

Dad once told me that the secret was creativity. He was talking about football, but he was also talking about so much more. We were sitting on his patio on his farm, the last house he lived in, drinking Michelobs. "Junior," he said, "never let a team get a key on you. Don't let them think that on second-and-2, he's going to throw this." Dad talked so rarely about his playing days that I shut up and listened. These moments—not spending time with

Dad but his telling me about himself—were so rare I was afraid this moment would disappear as fast and unexpectedly as it happened. "One of my favorite memories was we were playing the Green Bay Packers. I don't remember the exact game, and I can see the player—he was a linebacker—across from me when I came to the line. It was fourth-and-1. The game was tight. Another Packers player asked this veteran linebacker, 'What do you think he's going to do?' The guy answered, 'I've been playing against him for seven years and I haven't a clue.'"

That reminded him of a time when he told a Los Angeles newspaper man, "Always do the opposite of expectations. I never wanted to be typed. I wanted to keep the defense off balance. Then I had them where I wanted them." Dad sure did, both on and off the field, with those who didn't know him, and those who did.

✶✶✶✶

Dad's legacy today is tied to his foundation and the Johnny Unitas Golden Arm Award. I will continue to make sure his name lives on, with the hopes that J.C., my son, and Jillian, my daughter, will perpetuate their grandfather's legacy far into the future. All Unitas' seem to be competitive, but we don't have to engage our feisty nature on a field; instead, we can do it in the business meeting or through selling a product. He was forced to deal with fame. He endured public scrutiny—often acting as if he enjoyed it—but it wasn't the life he wanted. When he decided to be an NFL quarterback, that wasn't a big deal. Most of his classmates thought he was shooting low, as adult dreams go, but by 1960, his name and the NFL were big names nationally and only getting bigger.

While the NFL changes, and probably won't be the same game even 10 years from now, there's always room to honor its stars. Unlike baseball or golf or even tennis, in which it seems you can compare stars of one generation to stars of another, football is too different today from 1960 or even 1980 to do that. Instead of looking at stats and wins and championships, I look at influence. The Johnny Unitas Golden Arm Award is influence. It honors a quarterback, but it concerns itself with more than stats and wins. It looks at a player's academics and character. While these facets don't have to be perfect, they must show that a player is not going through the motions of college simply to play football. While being drafted is nice, there's more to the winner of the Johnny Unitas Golden Arm Award than his ESPN analysis ranking. All the winners have had great senior years. I would like to think all of them are committed to being solid citizens.

What I do know is that some of them haven't been drafted or have been drafted late in the NFL draft. Some have had long, illustrious careers, while some were short and probably not even sweet. Others have been big names, high draft choices. Dad's name and legacy as a player and person will live on through the winners, past and future. His name is synonymous with quarterbacking greatness, and as the Golden Arm award gets bigger and more prestigious, Dad will remain a name that matters. I know that he could care less about that, but it matters, to me at least. He's meant a lot to many people, some who never met him or spent just a passing moment with him. But in that moment, both award winners and strangers on the street have made a connection and continue a chain that goes back to the beginning of the NFL and will continue long into the future. It's a chain of excellence, of overcoming incredible odds, and connecting with everyday Joes, transforming a city, showing today's players that it's possible to be great and humble and that we need more people like Dad, playing the game for its intrinsic values and appreciating the wins but loving the thrills of the game regardless of the outcome.

****

My family and I have an unusual name and a father who was more than just a local celebrity. With a name and reputation as large as Dad's, I'm still surprised when people recognize me—I do somewhat look like him—or hear my name, and whenever this happens, particularly here in Baltimore, it always involves a story. "I met your Dad once," and the storyteller will describe some

321

event that I didn't know about. I love hearing these stories. I didn't when I was younger, but with the vantage point of age and distance in years from his playing career, I've come to see that my father didn't simply do what he thought was right with his life and what it had presented. Instead, my father did far better than anyone should have expected. He wanted the best for us whether he knew how to show that or not.

Not long ago, I told an acquaintance about this book, explaining how both emotionally gut-wrenching doing this would be and how important it would be to tell the truth about Dad, no matter where that led me. He told a story about meeting Dad in 1969 in New Orleans when the Colts played the Saints in their third season. He didn't remember much about the game, but he went because his favorite player was Dad. He played for a neighborhood team, like one that Dad had played on in Pittsburgh during World War II. This was connected somehow to his Catholic parish, but not as organized as Pop Warner. The guy had two wishes: to play quarterback and to wear No. 19. He ended up playing right guard—he was one of the bigger players on the team and not coordinated enough for a skilled position—and he wore No. 70, like an offensive lineman should. But he did get the team to agree to using blue and white as their colors and calling themselves the Colts, even though they were in New Orleans.

The Colts game he attended was played on October 19 at Tulane Stadium, a run-down, mostly deserted place built in 1926 and temporary home for the Saints while they waited for the Superdome to be built. Furthermore, Tulane had pulled out of the SEC in 1966 and the quality of football naturally had declined. New Orleans was on its way to becoming a pro football town.

My acquaintance went to the game. He doesn't remember much about it except that afterward, wearing his team jersey, he stood outside the gate near the Colts bus. Few people were there. He figured they were waiting outside the Saints' locker room. All the Colts came out and got on the bus except Dad. *Where was he?* my acquaintance thought, worried that he was going to miss his chance. He didn't even ask any of the other players for their autographs. He wanted only one. Finally, he saw Dad, sort of limping and swaying, his hair short, his legs bowed. Even if hadn't seen his face, he would've known it was Dad by the swagger and the slouched shoulders. He was banged up, as he often was after a game. His body was beginning to break down. But his walk was as much a part of his being as his haircut.

The bus was running. Dad was the last one out of the locker room, and his teammates were waiting, ready to go. My friend thrust his hand with a piece of paper and pen. Dad stopped. He spoke to my friend, only a boy who saw in Dad someone bigger than a football player. He was bigger than life itself. Dad grabbed the paper and wrote his name, neat and exact as always, and then, as only Dad understood, he ruffled the boy's hair. He made that deeper connection.

My friend, a native from New Orleans who loved Dad because of his high tops, his bow-legged gait, and his swagger had gotten the autograph he wanted.

It's the only one he's ever gotten. Once he had Dad's, he had no reason to get anyone else's.

****

I didn't have much choice in who my father was, but I realize that, like my New Orleans acquaintance, I got a pretty good one. I couldn't get another one, but even if I could have, there was no reason. Dad was a great quarterback, but he occasionally threw interceptions; he didn't win every game nor did he always lead the Colts back from the brink of defeat. As a father, he was the same way. He did most things right, and those that he didn't, he tried to make up for them. He wasn't perfect, but then, nobody is. Not me, not my siblings, not my mom. Nobody. It's hard for a myth to live up to the legend in real life. Dad surely didn't.

And that's okay.

EPILOGUE

So much has changed. Baltimore isn't the rust-belt, down-and-dirty industrial city it was in the 1950s. Today, it's cleaner. While steel is still made here, barely hanging on by a thread, in a year or two, steel production may go the way of airplane manufacturing in Baltimore—not happening—or the way pro football went in this town for more than 10 years. But football is back, and the Ravens have won their second Super Bowl. The game played today isn't what Dad played more than 40 years ago. And that's okay. He wouldn't mind it because the football he played in 1958 wasn't the same game that George Halas played when he both played and coached the Chicago Bears in the 1920s. The world changes, some of it slow, subtle, and not even noticed until it's too late. That seems to be the way with pro football. Some of it's changes are swift, overnight even, and that seems to have been the way with Dad and me and the family.

****

Football clearly isn't the same. No longer is the NFL 12 teams, a league competing with Major League Baseball and college football for its place in our hearts. It's now 32 teams and king. It towers over both college football and baseball, but its shadow isn't the same as those two sports. It values the here, the now, the today. The Colts reside in Indianapolis; Baltimore's team is the Ravens, twice Super Bowl champs. Football has changed so much that teams don't even respect their own championships. The New York Giants, one of the venerable franchises in the league, first mention their four Super Bowl wins before mentioning they also won four championships in the pre–Super Bowl era. It's Super Bowls or bust.

Its stars are Tom Brady and Aaron Rodgers, or Joe Flacco and Ray Lewis. A lot of today's 20-year-olds don't know who Gale Sayers and Otto Graham are; they barely know who Joe Montana and Joe Namath are. Here in Baltimore, many young people know who Johnny Unitas is only because they pass his statue on their way into M&T Stadium (no more Memorial Stadium to honor dead war veterans; instead, a stadium name to advertise a bank headquartered out of Buffalo, New York). Maybe their dads or their granddads talk about Dad or maybe they've visited The Sports Legends Museum. All of Dad's individual records are gone. He finished his career with barely more than 40,000 yards, the first quarterback to do that. Today, there are 14 players in front of Dad. Ten years from now, there may be 30 or even more. The NFL has become a passing league, and much of that is due to Dad. The league wants more scoring, showcasing its skill positions. All that's okay. Dad expected his records to fall. He didn't seem to mind when he was alive and they were falling. He didn't care about trophies and awards. He cared about winning, and even more he cared about playing the game right, and always playing it hard. He didn't care about football that much once he retired. Not because it had changed, but because he had moved on to another life.

✳✳✳✳

I read not long ago a comment about how there is a distinction between what's remembered, what's told, and what's true. That's true of Dad's life. Maybe the easiest part of his life is what was true. You can look up his accomplishments. They still jump out at you. Mostly what's been remembered about him is good, myth-making stuff, the kind of things that aren't as true as they can be because they don't fit into the storyline. The storyline is what's been told.

But here's the truth: my dad, as I've said more than once, had his flaws. He threw interceptions and incomplete passes although his fans only remember his greatness. They remember the two-minute comebacks that worked, probably because he always worked hard and never gave less than 100 percent.

He didn't always complete his passes. He didn't always win his games. He didn't always win championships. While he was tough, he missed games because of injury.

Off the field, his life wasn't always pretty or easy. We want our heroes, especially ones with larger-than-life statues outside stadiums, to be better than we are. That's what every son wants of his dad.

Here's another truth: Dad was an average Joe. He grew up one and remained one throughout his life. He just happened to be an average Joe who threw a football really well. Dad didn't change a whole lot in his life. He worked hard from a young age, maybe because his dad died and his family needed him or maybe because that was just the way he was wired. He wasn't a great scholar, but he was a student of what was happening around him. He knew what he liked and what mattered.

Life is tough. Divorce doesn't make it easier. A second family adds to that. So does fame. So does having a unique name. Lots of things were thrown into the pot that became my dad's life, and that had an effect on me. Too bad, I now realize. Everyone has stuff thrown at them. The only difference is that mine, and Dad's—but he chose his profession—were often thrown around in public. Some still are. My life isn't interesting because it's been all that interesting; rather, it's interesting because of who Dad was and what he did on the football field. I'm okay with that now. It's nobody's fault that it's taken me awhile to figure that out, but I'm there and ready to move forward.

Dad didn't change. Instead the world, particularly the NFL, changed around him. He grew, but his core remained constant. And he stayed true to himself and what mattered—giving his best and not worrying what happened once that path was chosen.

★★★★

Just because Dad was an incredible football player didn't make him an incredible businessman or the perfect dad. It has taken me a while to realize this. He did the best he could, and sometimes the family got caught up in wondering why he wasn't the championship dad like he was a championship quarterback. But that's not fair. He wouldn't have been a better father if he'd never made it in the NFL. Maybe he would have been worse. It doesn't matter now. Dad was the father he was, and when he had a chance to father children a second time, he was better at it. Just like when he watched game film and learned from it. While I wasn't always around with his second family, I did live nearby and my children played with my half-siblings. If nothing else, he was around much more. He participated in their lives. I'm glad he did. He loved them. He also loved the first family, and while we didn't always realize it or were too mad to see it, we all eventually found our place and peace with him.

****

A person's legacy is what he passes down. I've done alright for myself, I think. I have Mom and Dad to thank for that. They must have passed down enough of the right stuff or I wouldn't be as happy and strong and proud as I am today. That's the truth. How it gets told is different according to who's telling. All I know is that it takes a while to get used to the idea that Dad is dead, and that I'm okay with how our relationship unfolded. Unlike many of his fans who only remember the good stuff he did on the field, I remember my dad and my mom, both their good and bad. For a long time, I put my father's strengths on the back burner. Now, I don't have to.

Just because my dad is famous doesn't mean I have to be. I don't want to live vicariously through him even though some people continue to put me in that situation. I don't want to live a life where I believe the myth, either of him or my last name. Even if I tried to live up to the level of my dad, I can't. I have to be my own person.

I am who I am. Yes, I went through all this stuff and survived. If I were a Jones or a Smith, no one would care. But I'm a Unitas. I like being John Unitas. I'm proud to be John Unitas. That's who Dad brought me up to be, a man of character, of integrity and values, a man who respects those around him. He didn't live too bad a life, and I don't think I have, either.

THE END

APPENDIX

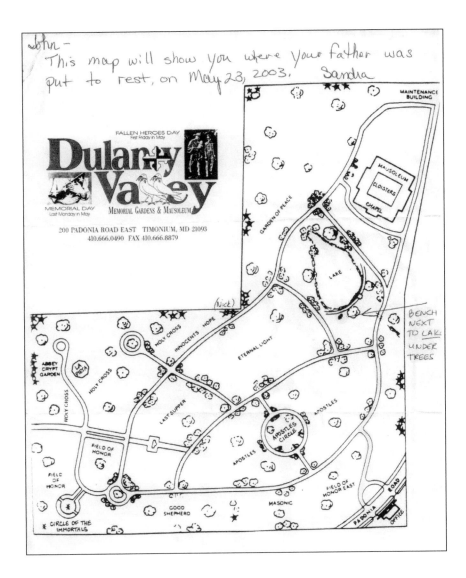

The children of Dad's first family were not invited to his burial. Several weeks later, Sandy sent each of us a map highlighted with the location where he was laid to rest. Mine is pictured above.

November 9, 1972

Mr. Johnny Unitas
c/o The Baltimore Colts
600 North Howard Street
Baltimore, Maryland   21201

Dear Johnny:

Your contribution to football in general and the
Colts in particular has been incalculable, and Judy
and I join with your other millions of fans in feeling
sad that you have decided to resign.

You have our very best wishes both now and in
all your future endeavors.

Sincerely,

Ted

THE WHITE HOUSE

STATEMENT BY THE PRESIDENT

The Thanksgiving Day Salute to Senior Americans is an effort to pay tribute to our older citizens by including them in a special way in our Thanksgiving Day festivities. The first Thanksgiving Day Salute was held in Washington, D. C. in 1964 and has since become an annual event in the Nation's Capital. In 1969, Mrs. Nixon and I participated in this event by hosting a White House Thanksgiving Day dinner for 220 senior Americans.

This year, the Thanksgiving Day Salute to Senior Americans will be observed in all 50 States and in Puerto Rico. As a part of this program, Governors of the 50 States and Puerto Rico and their wives have been invited to host Thanksgiving Day dinners for elderly men and women who are living alone or without families. Many Governors have already responded by issuing proclamations supporting this effort, and many plan to share their holiday festivities with older citizens in their areas. Senators and Congressmen have indicated that they will participate in the Salute by visiting homes for the aging on Thanksgiving Day.

This program was originated by VIP, a nonpartisan, nonprofit organization, composed of prominent Americans and college students and headed by Johnny Unitas, president. Mrs. Mamie Eisenhower is serving as honorary national chairman for the Thanksgiving Day Salute.

This expression of concern for older Americans grows out of a deep respect for the part they have played -- and continue to play -- in the growth and development of our Nation, and in the personal life of each and every one of us. It provides a special way to express to them the appreciation, the admiration and the affection of their countrymen. I therefore call upon all Americans to join in this special tribute, and I sincerely hope that the Thanksgiving Day Salute to Senior Americans will become a national tradition.

#   #   #

Senate

The Senate met at 9 a.m. and was called to order by Hon. HAROLD E. HUGHES, a Senator from the State of Iowa.

PRAYER

The Chaplain, the Reverend Edward L. R. Elson, D.D., offered the following prayer:

Eternal God, who art above all and through all and in all, without whom life has no divine meaning or destiny, but with whom there is light and leading, power for the present and hope for the future, enter our waiting hearts and be near us when we need Thee throughout this day. As Thou didst guide our fathers, be to us a pillar of fire to guide us through the perils and darkness of our age to the haven of hope which is Thy kingdom. We pray now that the words of our mouths and the mediations of our hearts may be acceptable in Thy sight in this place on this day.

In the name of the Master of Life. Amen.

DESIGNATION OF THE ACTING PRESIDENT PRO TEMPORE

The PRESIDING OFFICER. The clerk will please read a communication to the Senate from the President pro tempore (Mr. ELLENDER).

The second assistant legislative clerk read the following letter:

U.S. SENATE,
PRESIDENT PRO TEMPORE,
Washington, D.C., November 11, 1971.
To the Senate:

Being temporarily absent from the Senate on official duties, I appoint Hon. HAROLD E. HUGHES, a Senator from the State of Iowa, to perform the duties of the Chair during my absence.

ALLEN J. ELLENDER,
President pro tempore.

Mr. HUGHES thereupon took the chair as Acting President pro tempore.

THE JOURNAL

Mr. MANSFIELD. Mr. President, I ask unanimous consent that the reading of the Journal of the proceedings of Wednesday, November 10, 1971, be dispensed with.

The ACTING PRESIDENT pro tempore. Without objection, it is so ordered.

COMMITTEE MEETINGS DURING SENATE SESSION

Mr. MANSFIELD. Mr. President, I ask unanimous consent that all committees may be authorized to meet during the session of the Senate today.

The ACTING PRESIDENT pro tempore. Without objection, it is so ordered.

ADJOURNMENT SINE DIE 1971

Mr. SCOTT. Mr. President, I have only one comment to make: I hope we can get out of here by December 1.

If we work hard, I think that we can.

QUORUM CALL

Mr. MANSFIELD. Mr. President, I suggest the absence of a quorum.

The ACTING PRESIDENT pro tempore. The clerk will call the roll.

The second assistant legislative clerk proceeded to call the roll.

Mr. MANSFIELD. Mr. President, I ask unanimous consent that the order for the quorum call be rescinded.

The ACTING PRESIDENT pro tempore. Without objection, it is so ordered.

VACATING OF ORDER FOR RECOGNITION OF SENATOR HARRIS TODAY

Mr. MANSFIELD. Mr. President, I ask unanimous consent that the order granted by the Senate, allowing the distinguished Senator from Oklahoma (Mr. HARRIS) to proceed for 15 minutes today, be vacated.

The ACTING PRESIDENT pro tempore. Without objection, it is so ordered.

HAPPY BIRTHDAY TO THE REPUBLICAN LEADER

Mr. MANSFIELD. Mr. President, it has just come to my attention that my distinguished colleague, the Republican leader in the Senate, the Senator from Pennsylvania (Mr. SCOTT), has a birthday today.

As a friend, as a close associate, and as one who admires and respects the distinguished Senator, I take this occasion to extend to him my heartiest felicitations and best wishes, and to express the hope that he will be in his present position for many years to come—and that means being in the Senate as well.

It is a pleasure to work with Senator SCOTT, an old pro, who is understanding, who always puts his cards on the table, and who has been responsible in large part for the most pleasant and personal relationship and friendship which exists between the two leaders.

I salute you, sir. You have done a great job as a Member of the House and the Senate, as a member of the Armed Forces of our country during the Second World War, and as a man who has represented his State, his country, and this body with distinction and integrity.

Mr. SCOTT. Mr. President, I would not ruin the thoughtful and kind comments of the distinguished majority leader by any reply of mine, other than

to say that I appreciate very much the complimentary words of my good friend, the distinguished Senator from Montana (Mr. MANSFIELD).

I am delighted that we have been and will be able to work closely together on the basis of mutual trust and understanding. There will be no question of that.

I wish that all human relationships were as good as mine with the distinguished majority leader. I thank him very much for his kindness.

As with all birthdays, I regret them sincerely.

Mr. MANSFIELD. The older one gets, the shorter time becomes.

AUTHORIZATION FOR SECRETARY OF THE SENATE TO MAKE TECHNICAL AND CLERICAL CORRECTIONS IN S. 2820

Mr. MANSFIELD. Mr. President, I ask unanimous consent that the Secretary of the Senate be authorized to make technical and clerical corrections in the engrossment of S. 2820, which was passed by the Senate last evening.

The ACTING PRESIDENT pro tempore. Without objection, it is so ordered.

QUORUM CALL

Mr. MANSFIELD. Mr. President, I suggest the absence of a quorum.

The ACTING PRESIDENT pro tempore. The clerk will call the roll.

The second assistant legislative clerk proceeded to call the roll.

Mr. GURNEY. Mr. President, I ask unanimous consent that the order for the quorum call be rescinded.

The ACTING PRESIDENT pro tempore. Without objection, it is so ordered.

ORDER OF BUSINESS

The ACTING PRESIDENT pro tempore. The Senator from Florida is now recognized for a period not to exceed 15 minutes.

THANKSGIVING DAY SALUTE TO SENIOR AMERICANS

Mr. GURNEY. Mr. President, I should like to spend a few minutes this morning to discuss a program which I think is worthy of the highest commendation.

Mr. President, a nonprofit voluntary organization known as VIP, Very Important Patients, whose honorary chairman is Mrs. Dwight Eisenhower, has established a project to encourage visits on Thanksgiving Day by Members of Congress to those of our senior Americans who are unfortunate enough to be institutionalized. They have received the full cooperation of the American Association of Homes for the Aging and that organization is to be commended as well.

S 18139

repay. We owe them a tribute of personal respect, a tangible sign of caring and appreciation.

I commend the sponsors and director of this program and I hope that all Americans will adopt this special way of giving thanks to those who gave us what we have to be thankful for.

THANKSGIVING SALUTE TO SENIOR AMERICANS

Mr. FANNIN. Mr. President, an organization known as VIP—Very Important Patients—has initiated something I believe deserves an expression of congressional approval here on the floor of the Senate.

VIP has established a campaign to encourage Members of Congress to visit institutionalized senior Americans on Thanksgiving Day.

A great lady, Mrs. Dwight David Eisenhower is serving as honorary chairman of this organization. And the president of VIP is Mr. Johnny Unitas, perhaps the greatest football player of all time.

Mr. President, I think that VIP has a fine idea. I can think of no better day on which to personally express our appreciation for the elderly whose work and perseverance have built this Nation into the strongest and most prosperous on earth.

It is most unfortunate that so many Americans have taken the senior citizen for granted and have ignored his needs. It is tragic that in so many cases senior citizens have been shunted aside, removed by their problems from the rest of society.

All too often one sees our senior American, alone and isolated from his family and loved ones, who exists but truly does not live.

And so, Mr. President, while I regret that such a campaign is necessary in today's America, I recognize that it is in fact necessary. I, therefore, commend Very Important Patients organization for what I believe to be a fine effort in establishing what hopefully may become a tradition. Hopefully, all of us, not just Members of Congress but every American, will become more aware of the debt to the generations that have contributed so much to our current well-being.

QUORUM CALL

Mr. MANSFIELD. Mr. President, I suggest the absence of a quorum.

The ACTING PRESIDENT pro tempore. The clerk will call the roll.

The second assistant legislative clerk proceeded to call the roll.

Mr. PERCY. Mr. President, I ask unanimous consent that the order for the quorum call be rescinded.

The ACTING PRESIDENT pro tempore. Without objection, it is so ordered.

ORDER OF BUSINESS

The ACTING PRESIDENT pro tempore. Under the previous order the Senator from Illinois is recognized for not to exceed 15 minutes.

THE SALT TALKS

Mr. PERCY. Mr. President, President Nixon's initiatives in foreign affairs are heartening to those of us who place high priority on attaining a world without war.

In this Administration the foreign policy emphasis is on reducing world tensions by improving U.S. relations with all countries.

As the President himself said in his report on foreign policy of February 25, 1971, he seeks to "build . . . mutual respect with our friends, without dominating them or abandoning them" and he strives for "mutual respect with our adversaries, without compromising our principles or weakening our resolve."

This is a wise policy which requires much patience, understanding, wisdom, and skill to achieve. Yet already the Administration has demonstrated what can be done with a wise policy:

The NATO partnership has been strengthened.

The Indochina war is being deescalated rapidly.

U.S. relations with Eastern Europe are being improved.

A fresh start has been made on the problems of international economic policy.

For almost 16 months the guns at Suez have been silent.

Rapprochement with Mainland China has begun.

A Berlin settlement is being negotiated.

Talks on mutually reducing troop levels in Central Europe are in prospect.

Serious talks on nuclear arms limitations give promise of agreement in the not-too-distant future.

For these reasons I submit that the administration is doing extremely well in foreign affairs and has earned our confidence.

It is in this context that I turn to consider our relations with the Soviet Union, and more particularly the negotiations on strategic arms limitations which will resume in Vienna on November 16, 1971. While it is not known exactly what numbers would be involved in the limitation of offensive and defensive strategic missiles under the terms of the most recent U.S. proposal, it is my understanding that the overall numbers of missiles on both sides would be approximately the same, although the mix would be different.

I believe that the approach of President Nixon in this respect is both realistic and equitable. This Nixon initiative would halt progress on the very systems which are powering the arms race, the anti-ballistic missile and the offensive ballistic missile systems. These are the weapons which today contribute to the possibility of a first-strike capability, with all the horrors for mankind such a capability can entail. As I said last March, the action-reaction cycle of the arms race must be broken. The Nixon initiative would do just that.

The logical starting point in reducing strategic arms is with those weapons which by the nature of their mission or their technical attributes can most readily be employed in a first or preemptive strike. These are the relatively accurate and vulnerable land-based missiles of both sides. To illustrate: From the Soviet viewpoint, reductions in U.S. ICBM's and in the ABM's which defend them would have a stabilizing effect in that the primary targets of a Soviet first-strike would be decreased, the U.S.'s most credible first-strike weapons would be decreased, and the U.S. ABM—which the Soviets see as potentially useful to defend against a Soviet retaliatory strike—would be decreased also.

The same reasoning also holds from the U.S. viewpoint, with the proviso that, for technical reasons, the new and large Soviet ICBM's appear more destabilizing than their ABM. The SS–9's are known to have great payload and accuracy, while the Soviet ABM at this stage of development is evaluated as relatively ineffective.

There would appear to be a significant range of limits which might be agreed to, all consistent with the deliberately ambiguous language of the joint announcement of the two Governments on May 20, 1971. Therefore it is appropriate at this time to examine the possible outcomes of SALT and their implications.

Since the United States is committed to efforts to halt the arms race—and about this there is no question—the most important unknown in any assessment of the negotiations is the ultimate goal of the Soviet Union. We do know that since World War II and especially since the Cuban missile crisis the primary strategic goal of the Soviet Union has been to catch up with the United States in every way, but especially in terms of military power. There has been no reason to believe that this Soviet objective has changed; in fact, recent statements by Leonid Brezhnev reiterate the objective.

Because the Soviet Union has delayed serious discussion of limits on offensive missiles and has unrelentingly continued its deployment of offensive systems, it is assumed by many observers that the U.S.S.R. may be using the SALT talks to make further gains in relative military power. One cannot wish away the fact that the Soviet Union continues to deploy SS–9's and Y-class nuclear submarines.

In contrast, President Nixon's foreign policy initiatives have shown a U.S. willingness to meet any nation halfway in the quest for peace and security. The President is acting in good faith; it also behooves the Soviet Union to act in good faith if it wishes to have an arms limitation treaty acceptable to the U.S. Senate. If the Soviets wish to use the strategic arms limitation talks to achieve an advantage in the power balance, their effort will serve to fuel the arms race, not halt it.

If the Soviet Union takes into consideration the fact that neither side can achieve unilateral advantage from the SALT talks, the new round of talks could culminate in an agreement which would truly be a step toward peace. This would be cause for satisfaction by both countries, but not for complacency or relaxation. While the strategic arms race would be largely halted, we would still live under the shadow of potential nuclear destruction. So even as we seek ways to reach the first accord, we must also

I can think of no single group of persons more deserving of a heartfelt, national expression of thanks. I, personally, am grateful for this opportunity to emphasize the worth of older Americans to our society. Too often, even in these Chambers where the meaningful, cherished elements of American life are daily reflected in the deliberations of my able colleagues, we tend to forget senior citizens and their contributions to this country. We seldom pause to recognize the determination of our elders to continue to be active in a stream of social life, to be integral members of the human race, and to maintain their independence and self-respect. Our failure to demonstrate our affection for our elderly and our concern for their happiness is regrettable. As a nation, we have, in recent years, promoted the elements of a youth culture. We have applauded as virtues the activity, the freshness, the exuberance, and the excitement of youth. We have attributed much of the success of our national endeavors to the drive of a youthful spirit. We have assumed a psychology of youth orientation which is important but which has all but obscured the light of wisdom and the view of experience that older Americans have shed on our country's problems.

The contributions of our parents and our grandparents cannot be measured. Each of our own lives demonstrates the direct influence of today's elderly citizens; more importantly, the very character of this Nation has been formed largely through the efforts of persons who now find themselves in the shadows of American life, watching the fruits of their efforts and ambitions from standpoints of isolation and separation.

Strong, enthusiastic support of the Thanksgiving Day salute to senior Americans can mark a national commitment to give our elders the opportunities to enjoy and to continue to lead useful, happy lives. It can erase from their minds the memories of solitude and mere toleration. Our country does itself a disservice by overlooking the talents of older citizens and by failing to recognize the tremendous debt that is already owed them.

I heartily endorse this Thanksgiving Day salute as an activity of utmost importance, and I urge all Senators to lend their energies and support on this day to convince our older Americans that they are the very foundation of our country's future accomplishments.

Mr. President, I ask unanimous consent to have printed at this point in the RECORD a letter from Miss Carmella La-Spada, national coordinator of the Thanksgiving Day salute to senior Americans and Johnny Unitas, president of the VIP, and also a statement prepared by the distinguished Senator from Hawaii (Mr. FONG).

There being no objection, the material was ordered to be printed in the RECORD, as follows:

THANKSGIVING DAY SALUTE
TO SENIOR AMERICANS,
Washington, D.C.

DEAR SENATOR: This is to thank you for your reply to the VIP invitation requesting your participation in the Thanksgiving Day Salute to Senior Americans.

We are sincerely appreciative of the response from Senators and Congressmen who have enthusiastically agreed to participate by including older Americans in their own holiday festivities or by visiting a home for the aging in their State or District. We hope this "Salute" will become an American tradition.

This tribute is not meant as a token recognition but as a sincere acknowledgement of the debt we owe our older citizens and the affection we have for them. At the same time this annual event, remembering the older Americans amongst us, is symbolic of the continuing care we have for them throughout the year.

On behalf of VIP, we wish to express our gratitude to you. We believe that many more Amercans will have a happy Thanksgiving Day this year because of your concern and your personal efforts.

Wishing you and your family a very happy Thanksgiving, we remain

Sincerely,

JOHNNY UNITAS,
President, VIP.
(MISS) CARMELIA LASPADA,
National Coordinator, Thanksgiving Day Salute to Senior Americans.

STATEMENT OF SENATOR FONG, THANKSGIVING DAY SALUTE TO SENIOR AMERICANS

Mr. FONG. Mr. President, it gives me great pleasure, as ranking Minority Member of the Senate Special Committee on Aging, to add my voice of praise for the "Thanksgiving Day Salute to Senior Americans", sponsored by VIP.

VIP is a voluntary organization, the full name of which is Very Important Patients, and is devoting its efforts to increasing opportunities for enjoyment of life among the elderly who reside in homes for the aging and other institutions caring for older persons, especially the infirm and sick. Led by famous football player, Johnny Unitas, VIP is doing a great work.

When one considers the magnificent contributions which older Americans have made to our Nation, it is only fitting that those among them who are least able to care for themselves should be given special recognition by an organization such as VIP. They are truly Very Important Patients. We should all do all we can to add a bit of joy and pleasure to their lives. That many live most sheltered lives, and are severely restricted in their ability to mingle freely in society, make it most appropriate that we pay the debt our society owes them collectively in every way we can and at every opportunity. That they are wonderful human beings individually doubles our obligation.

In the work of our Special Committee on Aging, we have learned poignantly that many older persons are sorely in need of efforts by their juniors to brighten their lives and reduce their loneliness. The Thanksgiving Day Salute is a worthy innovation in bringing such extra joy into their lives.

Appreciation should also be expressed to the American Association of Homes for the Aged, the national organization of non-profit homes, for its operations with VIP in this endeavor. AAHA thus continues a splendid record, pioneered for decades by religious, fraternal and other organizations, of showing that some one truly cares. We who are more fortunate, of all ages, should emulate their concern for the aged—to whom we owe so much—whenever we can.

Mr. PEARSON. Mr. President, the Thanksgiving Day salute to senior citizens gives all Americans a chance to show their deep appreciation for all the contributions which they have made to this Nation. In this regard, I would like to express my gratitude to Johnny Unitas, the president of the Very Important

Patients program, and to Miss Carmella La Spada, coordinator of the Thanksgiving Day salute, for giving us this opportunity.

Certainly we cannot deny the debt we owe the Nation's elderly. Many of those now retired have lived through two world wars, suffered through the greatest depression in our history, and raised families in a time when there was inadequate supplies of money, food, or clothing.

Yet they also displayed the fortitude and courage to overcome adversity by contributing to an unprecedented advance in all facets of human endeavor, resulting in a society which knows no peer in the quality of life it can offer its members.

Mr. President, we owe these Americans a great debt. Yet now they face a crisis. Many of the Nation's elderly are isolated in nursing homes and retirement centers, far from the society they helped to shape. Many are forced to live a lonely, reclusive existence because of inadequate transportation, lack of funds, or poor health.

The VIP program, with the Thanksgiving Day salute, seeks to bring the plight of the Nation's elderly to the attention of all Americans by arranging for interested persons to visit residents of nursing homes or convalescent centers. The program will help demonstrate to these people how grateful all Americans are for all that we have today. The Thanksgiving Day salute to senior citizens gives us all the opportunity to share our freedom with someone who helped preserve and strengthen it during America's leanest years.

Mr. BIBLE. Mr. President, I should like to add my comments to those of my distinguished colleagues regarding the Thanksgiving Day salute to senior Americans.

Thanksgiving Day is one of the oldest traditions of our American heritage, a tradition which is still meaningful to all Americans because we, as individuals, and as a nation, have much to be thankful for. The original Thanksgiving Day, as our history books remind us, was an expression of thanks and gratitude on the part of our Pilgrim Fathers for the bounty of their new home and the friendship and assistance of their Indian friends.

The Indians helped the first settlers, who in turn have blazed the trails for the generations of Americans after them. As we today remember those who have helped and guided us, there is one special group which, I feel, deserves special recognition and consideration. Our senior Americans have blazed the trail for us, they have made it possible for us to enjoy a land of freedom and progress which is second to none.

In view of this, it seems deplorable that many of our older citizens should have to spend this traditional day of togetherness alone and forgotten in institutions and nursing homes.

That is why I am wholeheartedly endorsing the VIP project to pay special tribute to our older Americans, and I encourage all Senators to do the same.

We owe our senior Americans a debt that money and simple words cannot

ACKNOWLEDGMENTS

It's impossible to write a book without a lot of help. In my case, probably more help than either I or anyone close to me ever realized. There are many people who did more than they will ever know to get me going, sometimes without even realizing how they were helping. There were also lots of people who gave their time for interviews, and amazingly, they seemed to enjoy every minute of it. It's a testament to my father how willing and generous people were with their time. In addition to helping me write this book, they also let me live my life one more time with both my mother and father. For that, I will be eternally grateful to the following people:

Caroline Aaron, Dennis Aaron, Millie Addazio, Steve Alexander, Michael Anselmi, Roberto C. Arguero, Miriam G. Arguero, Roberto C. Arguero Jr., Jill Arguero, Nicolas Arguero, Kelly Arguero, Guillermo Arguero, Theresa Arguero, Carlos Arguero, Daniel Arguero, Tom Bast, Gary Berger and family, Raymond Berry, Sally Berry, Bob Bowie, Victoria Brown, Butch Burdette, Dick Butkus, Joe Carlozo, Tim Cashen, Bradley Chambers, Joe Chilleo, Tom Clancy, Keith Conklin, Bill Curry, Carolyn Curry, Skip Darrell, Joe DeNittis, Peachy Dixon, Dottie Donovan, Artie Donovan, Kevin Dunbar, Pete Enfield, Joe Ehrmann, Jimmy Ernest, Cleveland Evans, Jonathan Faber, Clyde Falls, Kalli Federhofer, Scott Garceau, Mike Gibbons, Gerald Haddock, Hon. Diane Haddock, Kathy Harvey, Sheila Harvey, Bud Hatfield, Alex Hawkins, Lou Heidrich, Nelson Heumann, David Huddle, Fred Kail, Rob Kasper, Cardinal William Keeler, Craig Kelley, Mel Kiper, Nova Lanktree, Bruce Latta, Burt Lawson, Ralph Lawson, Ruta Lee, Tom Lekas, James Liatta, Fanny Logan, Jerry Logan, Charlie Lopresto, Webb Lowe, Andrew Luck, Dr. Lew Lyons, Lumiary Group, Bob Mackin, Sylvia Mackey, John Marinacci,

Jack Marsch, Tom Matte, Dr. Les Matthews, Tom Mavrellos, Don McCafferty, T. Wray McCurdy, Robert Merette, Lenny Moore, Roger Mohlhenrich, Jim Mutscheller, Jerry Nassano, Bill Neill, Peter Newton, Karen O'Brien, Michael Olesker, Jimmy Orr, Joe Paglia, Orville Peacock, Ron Petrelli, Jon Platakis, Gordon Priest, Elizabeth Priest, Tom Renda, Brooks Robinson, Connie Robinson, Mitchell Rogatz, Warren Rosenfeld, Richard Sammis, Johnny Sauer, Greg Schwalenberg, Dave Sears, Peter Seiden, Ron Shapiro, Dave Sherer, Francis Smyth, Stephen Spears, Bart Starr, Cherry Starr, Bart Starr Jr., Ken Stratemeyer, Dick Szymanski, Mitzi Takeuchi, Rhett Tallas, Bill Tate, Jack A.S. Tilghman, Mike Tolzien, Scott Tolzien, Mitch Tullai, Bobby Unitas, Christopher Unitas, Christine Unitas, Kenneth Unitas, Leonard Unitas, Ann Unitas, Janice Unitas, Jillian Unitas, J.C. Unitas, Romeo Valianti, Jobie Waldt, Harvey Weeks, Ray Weiss, Joe White, Alex Wolff, Dan Worthington, Patty Young, John Ziemann, and all the wonderful strangers who have told me stories about Dad in the grocery store, or on the street, or wherever.

I'd like to also thank my brothers and sister, Janice, Robert, Christopher, and Kenneth along with their families; we've had a adventurous journey together as the children of our parents, some good and some not so good, but when we need to rally, we all come together as one. We haven't always been close, but I do really truly love each one of you in my own special way.

Finally, in my life the source of that light has been my wife, Christine, the LOVE of my life for 33 years and counting. You continue to show me the way. I hope and pray that our journey never ends. We've been blessed with two beautiful children, our son, John (J.C.) Unitas III and our daughter, Jillian Leigh Unitas. Jillian and J.C., we couldn't be more proud of you both in what you have accomplished in your lives so far. Thank you for allowing me and your mom into your daily lives as you continue your journey. It means so very much to us. I thank you for your help and support during this process; you both continue to teach me the power and beauty of unconditional *love*. This book publishing is like football; it's the ultimate *team sport*.

DISCLAIMER

Although this is a work of non-fiction, it's also a work of memory. This is one perspective on the world I lived in; it's not the only one. I'm sure there are people—some I know and many I don't—who will remember some of the events in this book differently. Nonetheless, I would like to think everything in here is accurate, but if it's not, it's totally on me and no one else is to blame for inaccuracies.

ABOUT THE AUTHORS

John C. Unitas Jr.

The idea for a book about growing up and living in the shadow of the great NFL quarterback, Johnny Unitas, has been percolating in John Jr.'s mind for more than 10 years. Setting the record straight—separating myth from reality—has never been done. Previous books about Johnny Unitas focus on his football career, and so will Junior's, but it will juxtaposition his career to his life outside football with his family and community. The book has less to do with his passing statistics and records or rehashing the 1958 Championship Game again and more with showing the human side of his father, the difficult moments inside the family and outside the constraints of the football field and locker room, while contextualizing his playing career and life around football.

Junior has spent his life surrounded by football. While it was a part of his life, football didn't dominate his childhood. It was simply his father's job. He rarely went to games and only knew there were games to be played because someone came to babysit him and his siblings on Sundays. When he was nine, he went to preseason camp in Westminster, Maryland, as a ball boy and gopher and his dad's roommate, with Raymond Berry and Jimmy Orr in the room next door. During his teens he watched his father lose the most important Super Bowl and two years later win one. He didn't attend either. Once his father retired, he attended games in California that his father announced. Upon returning to Baltimore after college, he reunited with his father, helping his father start Unitas Management Corporation, a two-man operation that marketed Johnny U's Hall of Fame career. He also befriended many of his father's former teammates and opponents: Artie Donovan, Lenny

Moore, Tom Matte, Bart Starr, Dick Butkus, and Raymond Berry. He became an unofficial advisor and agent to players as he helped them with card show opportunities and speaking engagements. He continues in that "role" today, often visiting with Donovan on Fridays before he passed away this past year and attending retired Colt functions, both as a presence for his dad and also in support of former players' needs. He's also gotten to know other popular athletes including Stan Musial, Pete Rose, Mickey Mantle, and Joe DiMaggio, to name a few.

Although John Jr. was born in Pittsburgh in 1956, he moved to Baltimore when he was one and has essentially lived there ever since. Since returning from college in Californiain 1979, he has built a successful life as a businessman and family man and as Johnny Unitas' son. While his father's career as a Baltimore Colt has embedded the name Unitas into the area's psyche, Junior has taken the name beyond the field and community. Currently, he works four different jobs, but two define him most: president of The Johnny Unitas Golden Arm Educational Foundation and president of Unitas Management Corporation. In many ways he's as stubborn as his father; he's also as competitive and as hard-working, too, traits he's used in the business world. Junior is a connector, introducing people in and about Baltimore, football, and business who have ideas and needs. Like his father who made his teammates better, Junior does the same thing, enhancing opportunities, seeing possibilities, shaking hands with strangers, and keeping his father's name alive. Junior has done more than live on his father's coattails; he understands the importance of his father's legacy, a reflection of a different era and temperament, reminding the public of what did exist and still can.

EDWARD L. BROWN

Edward's professional relationship with John Unitas began when Edward taught J.C. Unitas III, ninth-grade English, an experience that prepared him for a future—not one that he foresaw—of writing about Johnny Unitas. J.C. is John Jr.'s son and Johnny's grandson. Edward also taught Junior's daughter, Jillian, photography. J.C. has his grandfather's stubborn streak, willingness to express opinions regardless of their popularity, and competitiveness in everything he does. Edward was also privy to family secrets as J.C. wrote more than a few essays about his grandfather Johnny's love for riding his tractor and working his small farm. In another essay, J.C. wrote about his grandfather working on his passing technique. Later, John Jr. hired Edward to be his photographer at the annual Golden Arm Awards ceremony in Baltimore where the best senior college quarterback is presented with the Johnny Unitas/ Golden Arm trophy.

In preparation for the writing of this book, Edward has spent multiple hours interviewing John Unitas Jr. He has also interviewed roughly 100 other people, ranging from prominent teammates like Raymond Berry, Artie Donovan, Lenny Moore, Tom Matte, and Bill Curry, to other Baltimore icons like Brooks Robinson—all important people in Johnny's professional and private lives. He has also spent time with Junior's family, including his siblings, wife, and children. Pittsburgh childhood friends of Johnny U's have been interviewed, as well as Baltimore neighbors and business associates. Some of the most interesting stories come from strangers to Unitas who were touched by his life both on and off the field. Included is new information gleaned from first-time conversations with Unitas' sister, for example. In addition, Edward has read more than 50 books pertaining to John Unitas, the NFL, and the era he grew up in, played football in, and retired to.

Edward has taught high school English and creative writing for more than 25 years, read sports-related books for more than 40, and been a sports fanatic for more than 50. Before he started teaching, he was a journalist for three years, working for the Raleigh News and Observer in the sports department. He then moved to Okeechobee, Florida, where he was a general assignment reporter in addition to doing what he loved most—writing about sports, mainly the local high school athletic teams. Author of four completed but not fully revised novels—three of them involving sports in important ways—Edward worked with Tom Vennum, a senior ethnomusicologist emeritus at the Smithsonian Institute, edited two books, including Little Brother of War (published by Johns Hopkins University Press), an examination of Native American lacrosse and the definitive history of early lacrosse. He has also worked for the past 21 years at the Bread Loaf Writers' Conference in Vermont.

When not writing and reading, Edward plays squash, rides bikes, and roots for the Baltimore Orioles. Since his starting role as a defensive back in high school, Edward has followed football less and less. He prefers the sport as it was played in the late 1960s and 1970s.

QUOTES ABOUT JOHNNY U

WHAT THE WORLD SAYS ABOUT
JOHNNY U, THE GOLDEN ARM

Dick Butkus, College and Pro Football Hall of Famer and linebacker of the Chicago Bears:

"The greatest quarterback I ever played against and an honor to share the same heritage as a fellow Lithuanian."

Joe Namath, Pro Football Hall of Famer and quarterback of the New York Jets in Super Bowl III:

"He was my boyhood hero. I wore his jersey number, 19, in high school. Johnny U. was special, real special."

Lee Corso, ESPN College Game Day analysis:

"John was a great football player, but as good a player as he was, he was a better friend. I would never have gotten the University of Louisville head coaching job if it weren't for John's help. A true friend."

Mel Kiper, ESPN NFL draft analysis:

"Every quarterback I've evaluated since 1978, Johnny Unitas was the standard by which every other QB was judged. Johnny Unitas is the only one I've given a 10."

Sid Luckman, College and Pro Football Hall of Famer and quarterback of the Chicago Bears:

"Johnny Unitas is the greatest to ever play the game. Better than me; better than Sammy Baugh; better than anyone."

Brooks Robinson, Baseball Hall of Fame and Baltimore Oriole:
"I wish I could have played third base like he quarterbacked."

Weeb Ewbank, Pro Football Hall of Fame coach and Johnny's coach with the Baltimore Colts:
"I'm glad I was on his side. What a gifted, determined athlete. He never took football or life for granted. Johnny worked at making himself the best he could be and truly earned the respect that every coach, player, and fan in America holds for him."

Jack Kemp, quarterback in the AFL and NFL and former Presidential candidate:
"His life story, like his football career, is one out of Horatio Alger. What he represents to football and to America, epitomizing the 'kid from the other side of the tracks,' sounds the part of fiction, but everything about Johnny U is real and authentic. Just so genuine."

Dave Anderson, New York Times *sports columnist:*
"His story sounds like make-believe, but Johnny Unitas is fact, not fiction. I can't imagine now a quarterback could be more courageous, brilliant under fire, and consumed with football in such a no-nonsense way."

Tom Clancy, best-selling author:
"Johnny Unitas would have been a brilliant military commander. He had an ability to conceptualize how the opposition would next deploy its coverages. Then he'd hit them at the point of their vulnerability. His skills were God-given. No other quarterback ever had the talent of Unitas. He stands alone."

Frank DeFord, novelist and national magazine sports writer:
"Johnny Unitas invented the modern position of quarterback, and that, in effect, all quarterbacks of the last half-century are his heirs. As a Baltimore native, I know how much he meant to our city, giving us a pride and a glamour we never had before he led the Colts. Johnny Unitas mattered to his sport and his city as much as any athlete, ever."

346

INDEX